Polysemy and Compositionality

Hituzi Linguistics in English

No.1	Lexical Borrowing and its Impact on English	Makimi Kimura-Kano
No.2	From a Subordinate Clause to an Independent Clause	
		Yuko Higashiizumi
No.3	ModalP and Subjunctive Present	Tadao Nomura
No.4	A Historical Study of Referent Honorifics in Japanese	
		Takashi Nagata
No.5	Communicating Skills of Intention	Tsutomu Sakamoto
No.6	A Pragmatic Approach to the Generation and Gender Gap in Japanese Politeness Strategies	Toshihiko Suzuki
No.7	Japanese Women's Listening Behavior in Face-to-face Conversation	
		Sachie Miyazaki
No.8	An Enterprise in the Cognitive Science of Language	
		Tetsuya Sano et al.
No.9	Syntactic Structure and Silence	Hisao Tokizaki
No.10	The Development of the Nominal Plural Forms in Early Middle English	
		Ryuichi Hotta
No.11	Chunking and Instruction	Takayuki Nakamori
No.12	Detecting and Sharing Perspectives Using Causals in Japanese	
		Ryoko Uno
No.13	Discourse Representation of Temporal Relations in the So-Called Head-Internal Relatives	Kuniyoshi Ishikawa
No.14	Features and Roles of Filled Pauses in Speech Communication	
		Michiko Watanabe
No.15	Japanese Loanword Phonology	Masahiko Mutsukawa
No.16	Derivational Linearization at the Syntax-Prosody Interface	
		Kayono Shiobara
No.17	Polysemy and Compositionality	Tatsuya Isono
No.18	fMRI Study of Japanese Phrasal Segmentation	Hideki Oshima
No.19	Typological Studies on Languages in Thailand and Japan	
		Tadao Miyamoto et al.

Hituzi Linguistics in English No. 17

Polysemy and Compositionality
Deriving Variable Behaviors of Motion Verbs and Prepositions

Tatsuya Isono

Hituzi Syobo Publishing

Copyright © Tatsuya Isono 2013
First published 2013

Author: Tatsuya Isono

All rights reserved. Except for the quotation of short passages for the purposes of criticism and review, no part of this publication may be reproduced, stored in a retrieval system, or transmitted in any form or by any means, electronic, mechanical, photocopying, recording or otherwise, without the written prior permission of the publisher.
In case of photocopying and electronic copying and retrieval from network personally, permission will be given on receipts of payment and making inquiries. For details please contact us through e-mail. Our e-mail address is given below.

Hituzi Syobo Publishing
Yamato bldg. 2F, 2-1-2 Sengoku Bunkyo-ku Tokyo, Japan
112-0011

phone +81-3-5319-4916 fax +81-3-5319-4917
e-mail: toiawase@hituzi.co.jp
http://www.hituzi.co.jp/
postal transfer 00120-8-142852

ISBN978-4-89476-545-0
Printed in Japan

Acknowledgements

This book is based on my dissertation submitted in 2008. I am indebted to the people who supported me during the completion of this book. First of all, my greatest and sincere gratitude goes to Takane Ito, my supervisor. Since my first year at the Graduate School of the University of Tokyo, she has continued to pose significant questions and give me insightful suggestions that have broadened my analytical viewpoint of the linguistic issues under consideration. For me her words have always gone on the way ahead of me, and she has patiently waited for me to understand their significance. Without her help, my preceding papers would not have been completed, still less this book.

My interest in linguistics began in my undergraduate student days, when I met Heizo Nakajima at Tokyo Metropolitan University. In his classes I first encountered Generative Grammar, the principle of which made a strong impression on me. Additionally, his intense energy towards research in this discipline, his logical explanations of the themes he dealt with taught me to have a logical and broad view on matters I considered, for which I am tremendously grateful to him.

I have consistently attended the study meetings of the Lexicon Study Circle for about twelve years. I would like to express my deepest thanks to the participants of these meetings, especially Yoko Sugioka, Yuriko Hatori, Reiko Shimamura, Ikuko Hasebe and Noboru Kamiya for their constructive suggestions. After getting an instructor position at Kurashiki Sakuyo University and moving to Okayama, I have joined also the meetings of the Kansai Lexicon Project. I am heartily grateful to Taro Kageyama, Yoko Yumoto, Hideki Kishimoto, Seiji Ueno and the other members for accepting me as a member of KLP and giving me opportunities to talk about earlier versions of this book. Every time I presented my papers at these meetings, they took enough time to have productive discussions. In the meetings of both LSC and KLP I have received much information about my field of interest and related fields, and it has enhanced my motivation to continue my research.

In not only writing but also preparing for this book, I have been supported by the members of the judging committee of this thesis, namely Christopher

Tancredi, Naoyuki Ono, Eijiro Tsuboi and Tsuneaki Kato. Their perceptive comments and suggestions gave me clues to improve my analyses. In addition, they advised me to be particular about generalization of the principles I propose, showed me a lot of relevant English and Japanese data and gave me advice concerning the organization of each chapter. I deeply appreciate their help, suggestions and time.

From my graduate student days to the present, Takane Ito and her students, myself included, have consistently held a study meeting named Ito-gumi "Ito's class" almost once a month. In this meeting we have discussed various linguistic issues and almost all the chapters in this book have been presented. Especially discussions with Hiroshi Sakamoto, Ryosuke Takahashi, Mitomo Kanemoto, Reiko Okabe, Ichiro Kanamaru and Kanken Li have always given me insightful and helpful suggestions and led me to the completion of this book. I would like to thank these friends earnestly.

In Okayama, where I worked for eight years, I have also received warm support from many people. I am sincerely grateful to my colleagues at Kurashiki Sakuyo University, namely Hiromasa Akiyama, Hiroshi Goto, Tadashi Adachi and Chieko Yamada. We are all dedicated to research in different disciplines, however, talking with these friends has given me a broad knowledge of academic matters and encouraged me to conduct research. I would also like to thank Bryan Meadows, Philip Postle James and again Christopher Tancredi cordially. They have patiently judged acceptability of an infinite number of English sentences, suggested helpful and relevant examples and, furthermore, helped me improve this book stylistically. Thanks also go to Isao Matsumoto and editorial staff, especially Eri Ebisawa, at Hituzi Syobo for their patience and cooperation. Part of this research has been supported by the Japan Society for the Promotion of Science Grants-in-Aid for Scientific Research (C), Grant No. 18520395 and No. 21520519.

My final gratitude goes to my family. My late mother Fumiko and late father Mitsuyoshi who brought me up to choose research in academic issues in my life, and my wife Yukiko who has permitted me to spend most of my time in pursuing the research concerning this book.

Contents

Acknowledgements v
List of Abbreviations xi

Chapter 1 Introduction 1

Chapter 2 Theoretical Framework 7

2.1 Argument Structure 7
2.2 Event Structure 8
2.3 Qualia Structure 10
2.4 Lexical Representations and Mapping to Syntax 12
2.5 Generative Operations in Semantics 14
    2.5.1 Type Coercion 14
    2.5.2 Co-composition 16
    2.5.3 Selective Binding 17
2.6 Other Approaches 18
2.7 Aspectual Classes of Verbs and Generative Lexicon 20
2.8 Summary 23

Chapter 3 Issues and Proposals 25

3.1 Issues to be Discussed in This Book 25
3.2 Proposals 27
3.3 Diagnostics for Headedness and Transition:
    Durative *For*-phrases and Frame *In*-phrases 28

3.4　Functions in Qualia Structure, Argument Positions in Syntax and Linking　30
3.5　Summary　31

Chapter 4　Event of Movement or Change: Location Verbs and Verbs of Change of State　33

4.1　Event of Movement or Change　34
4.2　Theoretical Consequences　40
   4.2.1　Addition of a Second Goal Phrase to Motion Verbs　40
   4.2.2　Causative-Inchoative Alternation　44
   4.2.3　*Spray/load* Verbs and the Subevent of Movement　48
   4.2.4　Induced Action Alternation　54
4.3　Summary　58

Chapter 5　Polysemy, Headedness and Qualia Structure: Intransitive Locative Alternation and Verbs of Emission　61

5.1　Characteristics of Intransitive Locative Alternation Sentences　63
5.2　Conditions for Locative Alternation and Representation of Emission Verbs: Locative Alternation and Locative Inversion　65
   5.2.1　The Location-type　67
   5.2.2　The *With*-type　71
5.3　Meaning Variation of Verbs and Event Structure: Lexical Representation of Locative Alternation Verbs　74
5.4　Further Elaboration　78
   5.4.1　The Lexical Representation and The Generative Lexicon　78
   5.4.2　The Qualia Structure and Omission of *With*-phrases　80
5.5　Summary　83

Chapter 6　Event Structure and Co-composition: Prepositions and Inversion　85

6.1　Prepositions, Inversion and Co-composition　86
   6.1.1　The Prepositions *To* and *Into*　87

6.1.2	Lexical Representation of Locative Inversion Verbs	88
6.1.3	Proposal	91
6.1.3.1	Lexical Representation of *To*	91
6.1.3.2	Co-composition, Headedness and the Event Structure	95
6.1.4	Locative Inversion Revisited	99
6.1.5	Summary	103
6.2	Nature of Co-composition Operation	103
6.2.1	Event Fusion	105
6.2.2	Addition of Events	109
6.2.3	Residual Issues: Possibility of Extending the Co-composition Operation	112
6.2.3.1	Verbs of Emission with Directional Phrases	112
6.2.3.2	*In* and *On* as Directional Phrases	120
6.2.3.3	Caused Motion Construction and Resultative Construction	122
6.3	Summary	125

Chapter 7 Adjuncts and Semantic Representation: The Japanese Particle *Made* 127

7.1	Adjunct *In*-phrase and its Semantic Representation	129
7.2	The Japanese Particle *Made*	132
7.2.1	Kageyama and Yumoto (1997) and Kageyama (2003a)	133
7.2.2	Matsumoto (1997)	134
7.2.3	Analysis and Proposal	135
7.2.3.1	Characteristics of *Made*	136
7.2.3.2	The Lexical Representation of *Made*	138
7.2.3.3	*Made* and Various types of Verbs	144
7.3	Japanese *Naka-o* Construction	149
7.3.1	*Naka-o* Construction and Proposals by Kageyama (2002, 2003b)	150
7.3.2	Analysis	152
7.4	Another Approach	159
7.5	Summary	159

Chapter 8 Conclusion	163
Bibliography	169
Index	179

List of Abbreviations

ACC = accusative
AGENTIVE = agentive role
ARG = argument
CONST = constitutive role
D-ARG = default argument
D-E = default event
E = event
FORMAL = formal role
GEN = genitive
LA = locative alternation
LCS = lexical conceptual structure
LI = locative inversion
LOC = locative
NOM = nominative
NP = noun phrase
OBJ = object
PAST = past tense
PERF = perfective (aspect)
PP = prepositional phrase
PRES = present tense
Q = qualia
S-ARG = shadow argument
S-E = shadow event
SUBJ = subject
TELIC = telic role
TOP = topic
V = verb
VP = verb phrase

Chapter 1

Introduction

The aim of this book is to reveal the mechanism which yields polysemy of words from the perspective of compositionality. To attain our goal, we mainly investigate characteristics of expressions concerning spatial relation, namely motion verbs and spatial prepositions, and, utilizing the Generative Lexicon framework, propose their lexical representations. Following the localist approach advocated by Gruber (1976) and Jackendoff (1990), we assume that symbolism of concepts abstracted from meanings of expressions concerning spatial relation is generalized to other semantic fields such as ascription of properties, possession and scheduling of activities. In this respect, the research conducted in this book will contribute to understandings of the semantics of verbs and VPs in general.

Motion verbs show variable behaviors, or polysemy, co-occurring with other words or being used in phrases. Co-occurring with PPs, motion verbs express unbounded events in some cases and bounded events in others. For example, although verbs of manner of motion such as *run*, *swim*, *walk* and the like express unbounded events on their own, these verbs express bounded events when they co-occur with some goal phrases such as *to the station*, *into the tunnel* and *home*: Compare *John ran for / *in ten minutes* with *John ran to the station in / *for ten minutes*. In addition to typical verbs of motion, some classes of verbs are used as motion verbs when accompanied by PPs: for instance, verbs of emission are used as motion verbs when they are used with directional PPs (compare *The cart rumbled down the street* with *The thunder rumbled in the sky*). As for the former example, Levin and Rappaport Hovav (1992) claimed that in the interpretation of this example the PP functions as if it were a predicate of this sentence and the verb just expresses the manner of the motion of the cart: that is, the verb expresses the rumbling sound accompanied by the motion. In this way verbs of motion, and verbs which express motion-verb sense, show variable behaviors in the forms of verbal expressions consisting of a verb and a PP. This suggests that PPs play a crucial role in polysemy of verbs. Taking this into consideration, we need to examine not only the meanings of these verbs but also those of prepositions co-occurring with them and the relations between the verbs and the prepositions in order to understand polysemy of motion verbs. Therefore, in this book, we focus on 1) verbs which are used in motion-verb sense, 2) prepositions which are used with verbs expressing motion, 3) motion verbs' phrases such as verbal expressions consisting of a verb and a PP and 4) VPs including an adjunct PP.

As for the research into lexical meanings, the lexical conceptual structure (henceforth, LCS) approach has been developed by Rappaport Hovav and Levin (1995 and 1998) and Kageyama (1996) among others. As we will briefly survey in section 2.6, we do not employ this approach since in this approach one LCS is given for one lexical meaning. One lexical item denotes variable meanings by itself and in combination with other lexical items: thus, polysemous words are supposed to hold more than one LCS. Furthermore, a word sometimes expresses novel meanings in new contexts. Owing to the polysemy of words, it is possible that the number of LCSs available to a lexical item becomes infinite. Since each LCS of lexical items is supposed to be stored in the lexicon, if the number of the set of LCSs is infinite, the entire information cannot be stored in the lexicon. This is not desirable in view of language acquisition either: it is impossible to learn such huge or unlimited information. Instead, the Generative Lexicon approach assumes that a word has one lexical representation and that the lexical representation gives rise to the word's polysemy through operations acting on words' lexical representations or phrases' semantic representations. Thus, in this approach the problem the LCS approach faces does not arise.

As we have just mentioned above, verbs show variable behaviors, or polysemy, in combination with other words such as PPs and argument NPs. We consider the operations such as co-composition and composition, which function on words' lexical representations and phrases' semantic representations, to have to do with verbs' polysemy. The semantic representations of phrases or sentences are formed compositionally from lexical representations, and these issues have been studied by formal semanticists. In their approach, words are regarded as functors or arguments, and the role of each word is static in calculation for building up meanings of phrases. Again, in order to compositionally form semantic representations of phrases containing a polysemous word, as many lexical representations of a word's meanings have to be given for the word as the information stored in the lexicon. We do not adopt the formal semantics, or Fregean, approach for the same reason we keep away from the LCS approach.

Throughout this book we utilize the Generative Lexicon theory. Pustejovsky (1995) proposed this framework in order to grasp polysemy of words and to examine the interaction of word meaning and compositionality. We assume that lexical representation of lexical items consists of structures proposed in this framework and that lexical representations of words are combined with one another into semantic representation of phrases or sentences by the generative devices which are also proposed in this framework.

The Generative Lexicon framework is a promising one to capture polysemy of words. Lexical representation proposed in Generative Lexicon contains three different types of structure, namely event structure, qualia structure and argument structure, which closely interact with one another. Owing to these three structures, lexical representation in Generative Lexicon possesses the ability to denote various aspects of meanings of words and phrases. Furthermore, generative devices, especially the co-composition operation, which operates on event structure and qualia structure and combines lexical representation into semantic representation of phrases or sentences, account for verbs' polysemy and variable syntactic behaviors.

Accordingly the event structure, the qualia structure and the co-composition operation play crucial roles in determining the meanings and behaviors of motion verbs and co-occurring prepositions, and hence constitute the heart of our discussion. Four roles in qualia structure proposed in Pustejovsky (1995) represent various meanings of a word, some of which include meanings associated with world knowledge linked to an event or an entity the word denotes. Moreover, arguments contained in a role of the qualia structure which is associated with a head subevent are claimed to appear in syntax, and so interaction of qualia structure, event structure and headedness is related to syntactic behaviors of verbs such as the causative-inchoative alternation. In addition, change in telicity of verbs or of verbal expressions is accounted for by the co-composition operation involving the two structures. The co-composition operation combines some roles in qualia structure of a verb and a preposition and gives rise to variable behaviors of a class of verbs, for example, a motion-verb usage of emission verbs.

Thus the Generative Lexicon framework provides an adequate framework to represent meanings of words and phrases; however, precise properties of the structures and operations related to semantic representation remain unclear. Specifically, the following are not clear: 1) how the co-composition operation acts on lexical representations, especially of motion verbs and prepositions; 2) how the event structure and the qualia structure are concerned with this operation; 3) how semantic representations of phrases or sentences are composed by this operation. We need to research these issues and comprehend the entire characteristics of these structures and operations, especially of co-composition. To do this, from chapter 4 to chapter 7 we examine linguistic phenomena relevant to these structures and operations. Among the linguistic phenomena we are going to examine, issues regarding subevents in event structure, headedness, qualia structure and relations between verbs and prepositions are included. Through the examination of these issues, we examine precise mechanisms of the Generative Lexicon and elaborate this theory; this book will contribute to the establishment of the Generative Lexicon theory, with which we can retain the idea of minimum lexicon while providing a compositional account for the polysemy of words.

The organization of this book is as follows. In chapter 2 we overview the Generative Lexicon framework and discuss the reasons why we adopt the framework in this book. We also survey other approaches to lexical semantics and event analysis. In chapter 3, after we discuss some issues unclear in Pustejovsky (1995), we present six proposals we make in this book. We also consider two linguistic tests: one is the test utilizing durative adverbials (*for*-phrases) to identify a headed subevent; the other is the test making use of frame adverbials (*in*-phrases) to confirm whether an event structure under discussion contains transition from a process subevent to a state subevent. Before the summary of chapter 3 we introduce functions in qualia structure and linking of arguments in semantic representations to syntactic positions. In chapters 4–7 we will try to verify our proposals by making close investigations of various kinds of data concerning verbs of motion, verbs of change of state and verbs of emission. In chapter 4 we first consider a change of state verb, namely *grow*, which shows the causative-inchoative alternation. We maintain, contra Pustejovsky (1995), that we need to assume a third type of subevent, namely an event which denotes movement or change. Next, we show that the subevent of movement or change explains conditions under which the addition of double goal phrases to motion verbs and the induced action alternation are allowed. Chapter 5 will explore how headedness is determined in event structure. We will deal with emission verbs because verbs of this class, which function as motion verbs when they are used with directional PPs, show variable syntactic behaviors. We argue that the lexical representation we propose, together with the correct understanding of event-headedness, will lead to an explanation of the various syntactic behaviors of this class of verbs. In chapter 6 we consider the co-composition operation, arguing that the structures contained in lexical representations and the notion of action chain are relevant to co-composition, and discuss how this operation works and what conditions should be imposed on this operation. In chapter 7 we study the relation between the event structure of motion verbs and English adverbial prepositional phrases and Japanese adverbial *made* phrases. We will propose that an "event" in the event structure of a verb's lexical representation is inserted into an argument position in the argument structure of an adjunct phrase which co-occurs with the verb, and will also suggest that qualia structure contributes to the interpretation of sentences which contain an adjunct phrase. Chapter 8 summarizes and concludes our discussions.

Chapter 2

Theoretical Framework

This book makes use of the Generative Lexicon theory (henceforth, GL) advocated by Pustejovsky (1995) as its theoretical framework. Through the discussion from chapter 4 to chapter 7 we will elaborate this theory, so the GL framework that we develop in this book will be sometimes different from the original version of GL proposed in Pustejovsky (1995) (henceforth, P (1995)).

In this chapter we survey the system of GL proposed by P (1995). Firstly, we take a brief look at three structures encoding lexical meanings and generative devices, such as co-composition, type coercion and selective binding; secondly, we see the process of mapping from lexical and semantic representation to syntax; thirdly, we briefly compare GL with other approaches such as LCS approach and Davidsonian approach; lastly, we see how GL represents four aspectual classes of verbs proposed in Vendler (1967) and Dowty (1979). Through this survey, we argue GL is a promising theory for grasping polysemy and various usages of words.[1]

2.1 Argument Structure

P (1995: 62–67) assumes that the arguments of a lexical item are represented in the argument structure of the item and introduces four types of arguments. The four types are illustrated in P (1995: 63–64) as is shown in (1), and an example of each type he gives is in (2).

(1) a. True Arguments: Syntactically realized parameters of the lexical item.
    b. Default Arguments: Parameters which participate in the logical

expressions in the qualia, but which are not necessarily expressed syntactically.

c. Shadow Arguments: Parameters which are semantically incorporated into the lexical item. They can be expressed only by operations of subtyping or discourse specification.

d. True Adjuncts: Parameters which modify the logical expression, but are part of the situational interpretation, and are not tied to any particular lexical item's semantic representation. These include adjunct expressions of temporal or spatial modification.

(2) a. <u>John</u> arrived late. (a true argument)
b. John built the house <u>out of bricks</u>. (a default argument)
c. Mary buttered her toast <u>with an expensive butter</u>.
(a shadow argument)
d. Mary drove down to New York <u>on Tuesday</u>. (a true adjunct)

In GL it is assumed that arguments of a lexical item are represented in argument structure, where the argument types in (1) except for true adjuncts are directly encoded. For example, the argument structure for the verb *build* is the one in (3).

(3) *build*

$$\text{argument structure} = \begin{bmatrix} \text{ARG1} = \text{animate\_individual} \\ \text{ARG2} = \text{artifact} \\ \text{D-ARG1} = \text{material} \end{bmatrix}$$

Arguments are projected into syntax through the interaction of argument structure, event structure and qualia structure. We will survey how these arguments are licensed or expressed in syntax in section 2.4.

2.2 Event Structure

P (1995: 67–75) assumes that events are classified into three sorts: processes, states and transitions, and he also assumes subevents which make up a complex event. In an event structure the relation between an event and its proper subevents is represented. He considers an event structure with subevents to be represented as an event tree structure such as the one in (4a), whose definition is in (4b), and proposes to encode temporal relations between subevents, which are shown in (5).[2]

(4) a.

```
        e<α
       /    \
      e1     e2
```

b. [$_{e3}$ e1 <$_α$ e2] = $_{def}$ <$_α$ ({e1, e2}, e3)

(5) a. exhaustive ordered part of: <$_α$
b. exhaustive overlap part of: o$_α$
c. exhaustive ordered overlap part of: < o$_α$

In (5), < is a strict partial order and o is overlap. In (4a) the temporal relation between event 1 and event 2 is the "exhaustive ordered part of": event 1 precedes event 2, each event is a logical part of e3 and there is no other event that is part of e3. In the event structure with o$_α$, the temporal relation of events is "exhaustive overlap part of" and two subevents occurs simultaneously; in the event structure with < o$_α$, event 1 starts before event 2 and the two events overlap.

Furthermore, P (1995) assumes event headedness, which provides a way of foregrounding and backgrounding subevents: According to P (1995: 72) "the head is defined as the most prominent subevent in the event structure for a predicate, which contributes to the 'focus' of the interpretation." Headedness is a property of all types of event structure, and it specifies which subevent is focused on by a lexical item.

Positing headedness is motivated by modification of subevents by prepositional and adverbial phrases. When these phrases are adjoined to predicates denoting transitions, they can modify not only the whole event but also the individual subevents. P (1995) argues that heads license certain types of modification. Such examples are shown in (6)–(7) (cited from P (1995: 74–75)).

(6) a. John ran home <u>for an hour</u>.
b. My terminal died <u>for two days</u>.
(7) a. John built the house <u>carelessly</u>.
b. Mary <u>quietly</u> drew a picture.

The schematic event tree structure for *die* is the one in (8), where the head subevent is marked with "*."

(8) *die*

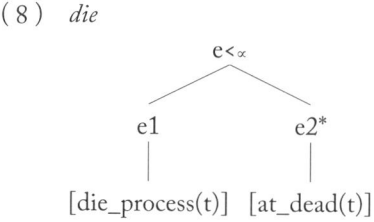

It is generally assumed that process events and state events license a *for*-phrase, but modification by a *for*-phrase in (6) is grammatical although the whole event expressed by *run home* and *die* is a transition. In the available interpretation of (6) the *for*-phrase modifies the final state expressed by the predicate; the interpretation of (6a) is that John spent an hour at home and that of (6b) is that the terminal was dead for two days; thus the state subevents are the head in their event structures.

In (7) the manner adverbs modify the initial head subevent in the event structure of the predicates: *carelessly* modifies the act of building and *quietly* that of drawing: accordingly, their process subevents comprise the head. The event structure of *build*, which incorporates a head subevent and temporal relation between subevents is the one in (9).

(9) event structure = $\begin{bmatrix} E1 = e1\text{: process} \\ E2 = e2\text{: state} \\ e1 <_\alpha e2 \\ \text{head: } e1 \end{bmatrix}$

Interacting with argument structure and qualia structure, event structure representing a head subevent provides us with a way for capturing syntactic behaviors of verbs such as the causative-inchoative alternation, as we will see in section 2.4.

2.3 Qualia Structure

P (1995: 76) proposes qualia structure in order to "capture polymorphic behavior as well as sense creation phenomena." The qualia structure is composed of four basic roles. The four roles and what they represent are as follows:

(10) The Qualia Structure (P (1995: 85–86))
   1. Constitutive: The relation between an object and its constituents, or proper parts: material, weight parts and component elements.
   2. Formal: That which distinguishes the object within a larger domain: orientation, magnitude, shape, dimensionality, color, position.
   3. Telic: Purpose and function of the object: purpose that an agent has in performing an act, built-in function or aim which specifies certain activities.
   4. Agentive: Factors involved in the origin or "bringing about" of an object: creator, artifact, natural kind, causal chain.

These roles are proposed in P (1995) to represent meanings of nouns. For example, the qualia structure for the noun *novel* is the one in (11).

(11) *novel* (cf. P (1995: 78))
$$\text{qualia structure} = \begin{bmatrix} \text{CONSTITUTIVE} = \textbf{narrative}(x) \\ \text{FORMAL} = \textbf{book}(x) \\ \text{TELIC} = \textbf{read}(y, x) \\ \text{AGENTIVE} = \textbf{write}(z, x) \end{bmatrix}$$

Each role in (11) contains a function which captures aspects of meanings shown in (10). P (1995) considers the qualia values to be expressions with well-defined types and relational structures, which accounts for the interpretations of examples such as (12) (we will discuss the interpretation of a sentence similar to (12b) in section 2.5.1.).

(12) a. Mary enjoyed the novel.
     b. Mary began a novel.

The four roles are also utilized in qualia structure of verbs and adjectives. According to P (1995: 79–80), the formal role for verbs specifies "state of affairs which exists" and the agentive role specifies "the bringing into being of the resulting state" or active process events. P (1995:80) suggests the event structure and the qualia structure of the verb *break* as in (13).

(13) *break*
event structure = $\begin{bmatrix} E1 = e1\text{: process} \\ E2 = e2\text{: state} \\ e1 <_\alpha e2 \end{bmatrix}$
qualia structure = $\begin{bmatrix} \text{AGENTIVE} = \textbf{break\_act}(e1, x, y) \\ \text{FORMAL} = \textbf{broken}(e2, y) \end{bmatrix}$

As is shown in (13), the qualia structure of a verb does not necessarily contain all the four roles: it depends on the characteristics of a verb's meanings which roles are contained in the verb's qualia structure. In the qualia structure in (13), the agentive role expresses a causing subevent and the formal role a resultant subevent. In this respect, the concept of qualia structure, agentive roles and formal roles, accords with that of the causal chain analysis proposed by Croft (1991) and Langacker (1991) among others.

2.4 Lexical Representations and Mapping to Syntax

In this section we survey mapping from semantic structure to syntactic structure. P (1995: 101–104) claims that arguments in a quale in qualia structure map to syntactic argument positions and that the quale value associated with a headed subevent is projected to syntax when more than one quale is given. When a verb expresses a complex event, transition, there are two possibilities of mapping:

(14) a. Q_i: R(e1*, x, y) ⟶ x:SUBJ, y: OBJ
　　b. Q_j: P(e2, y) ⟶ shadowed
(15) a. Q_i: R(e1, x, y) ⟶ shadowed
　　b. Q_j: P(e2*, y) ⟶ y: SUBJ

As an example, consider the mapping of the configurations of the verb *break*. The lexical representation for *break* is in (16).

(16) *break*
event structure = $\begin{bmatrix} E1 = e1\text{: process} \\ E2 = e2\text{: state} \\ e1 <_\alpha e2 \\ \text{head: underspecified} \end{bmatrix}$

$$\text{argument structure} = \begin{bmatrix} \text{ARG1} = x \\ \text{ARG2} = y \end{bmatrix}$$

$$\text{qualia structure} = \begin{bmatrix} \text{AGENTIVE} = \textbf{break\_act}(e1, x, y) \\ \text{FORMAL} = \textbf{broken}(e2, y) \end{bmatrix}$$

The head subevent is underspecified in the event structure of *break* (that is, either subevent has a potential of being the head). Headedness determines which quale in qualia structure is projected to syntax. When the process event, e1, is the head, the arguments in the quale associated with e1 appear in syntax: both x and y appear in syntax and the verb functions as a causative. When the state event, e2, is the head, the argument in the formal role is projected to syntax: y is expressed in syntax and *break* functions as an inchoative. The event structure tree with the qualia associated with subevents is shown in (17).

(17)   *break*   (cf. P (1995: 102))

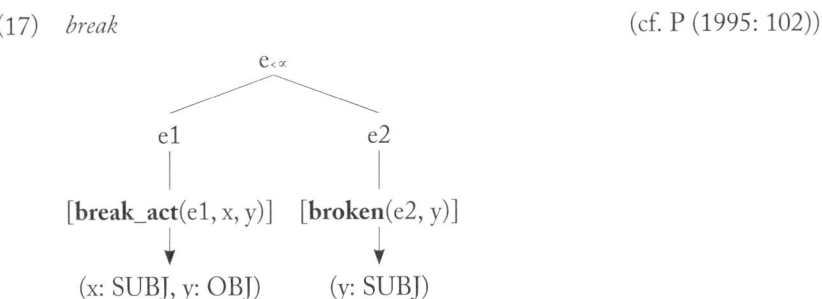

P (1995: 103) maintains that a headed quale of a lexical expression must be fully interpreted in the syntactic structure, and calls the full interpretation "saturation." The qualia saturation and the related notion of "covering" are defined as follows:

(18)   Qualia Saturation
          A qualia structure is saturated only if all arguments in the qualia are *covered*.
(19)   Covering
          An argument x is covered only if:
             (i)   x is linked to a position in s-structure; or
             (ii) x is logically dependent on a covered argument y; or
             (iii) x is existentially closed by virtue of its type.

We can consider that x in (19i) and x in (19ii) correspond to true arguments and default arguments, respectively. As an example of default arguments, consider the lexical representation for *build*:

(20) *build*

$$\text{event structure} = \begin{bmatrix} E1 = e1\text{: process} \\ E2 = e2\text{: state} \\ e1 <_\alpha e2 \\ \text{head: } e1 \end{bmatrix}$$

$$\text{argument structure} = \begin{bmatrix} ARG1 = x\text{: animate\_ind} \\ ARG2 = y\text{: artifact} \\ \qquad\qquad [\text{CONSTITUTIVE: } z] \\ D\text{-}ARG3 = z\text{: material} \end{bmatrix}$$

$$\text{qualia structure} = \begin{bmatrix} \text{AGENTIVE} = \mathbf{build\_act}(e1, x, z) \\ \text{FORMAL} = \mathbf{exist}(e2, y) \end{bmatrix}$$

In the event structure in (20) the head event is e1, and so the arguments x and z in the agentive role associated with e1 should be projected to syntax; however, instead of z, y is expressed since z is logically dependent on y in the constitutive role of argument 2. Here the argument z is covered in terms of (19ii). An argument x in (19iii) may approximately correspond to shadow arguments. Shadow arguments are semantic contents basically incorporated into verbs and do not appear in syntax. They can appear only under specific conditions like *margarine* in *Mary buttered her toast with margarine*.

2.5 Generative Operations in Semantics

P (1995) proposes three operations in order to capture polysemy and variable behaviors of words. The three operations, namely type coercion, selective binding and co-composition, make the three structures encoding lexical meanings (introduced thus far) interact with one another and provide compositional interpretations of words.

2.5.1 Type Coercion

The type coercion operation is introduced to account for systematic ambiguity of lexical items by P (1995: 106–122). Consider the sentences in (21).

(21) a. John began a book. (P (1995: 115))
b. John began to read a book. (ibid.)

Although the verb *begin* basically takes an event noun as its complement, the sentence in (21a), in which *begin* takes an NP denoting an entity, is judged acceptable in the reading in (21b). The lexical representations for *begin* and *book* are in (22).

(22) a. *begin*
event structure = $\begin{bmatrix} E1 = e1\text{: process} \\ E2 = e2\text{: event} \\ e1 <o_\alpha e2 \end{bmatrix}$

argument structure = $\begin{bmatrix} ARG1 = x\text{: human} \\ ARG2 = y\text{: event} \end{bmatrix}$

qualia structure = $\begin{bmatrix} FORMAL = \mathbf{P}(e2, x) \\ AGENTIVE = \mathbf{begin\_act}(e1, x, e2) \end{bmatrix}$

b. *book*
argument structure = $\begin{bmatrix} ARG1 = x\text{: information} \\ ARG2 = y\text{: physical\_object} \end{bmatrix}$

qualia structure = $\begin{bmatrix} FORMAL = \mathbf{physical\_object}(y \cdot x) \\ CONST = \mathbf{paper}(y) \cdot \mathbf{information}(x) \\ TELIC = \mathbf{read}(e, w, x) \\ AGENTIVE = \mathbf{write}(e, v, x) \end{bmatrix}$

The type of the NP (here, *book*) is coerced to an event function because the NP does not satisfy the type required by *begin*. Event functions available in the qualia structure of *book* are the ones in the telic role or in the agentive role. One of them is inserted into argument 2 and the formal role in the lexical representation of *begin*. If the function and the arguments in the telic role of *book* is inserted, the derived semantic representation of *begin a book* will be the one in (23).

(23) begin a book
event structure = $\begin{bmatrix} E1 = e1\text{: process} \\ E2 = e2\text{: event} \\ e1 <o_\alpha e2 \end{bmatrix}$

$$\text{argument structure} = \begin{bmatrix} \text{ARG1} = \text{x: human} \\ \text{ARG2} = \text{y: event} \end{bmatrix}$$
$$\text{qualia structure} = \begin{bmatrix} \text{FORMAL} = \textbf{read}(e2, x, z) \\ \text{AGENTIVE} = \textbf{begin\_act}(e1, x, y) \end{bmatrix}$$

Thus interpretation (21b) is obtained.

2.5.2 Co-composition

In this subsection we see the co-composition operation, by which more than one lexical meaning is conflated to make a new meaning of a phrase. This operation derives creation verbs like *bake a cake* from change-of-state verbs like *bake* in *bake potatoes*. In this book we mainly discuss the co-composition operation which works on verbs and PPs co-occurring with them. For example, the lexical representation of *run* in (24a) and that of *into* in (24b) are "combined through co-composition" and the derived sense of the phrase *run into* in (25) is provided.

(24) a. *run*

$$\text{event structure} = \begin{bmatrix} \text{E1} = e1\text{: process} \\ \text{E2} = e2\text{: process} \\ e1 \circ_\alpha e2 \\ \text{head: } e1 \end{bmatrix}$$

argument structure = [ARG1 = x]

$$\text{qualia structure} = \begin{bmatrix} \text{AGENTIVE} = \textbf{act}(e1, x) \\ \textbf{move}(e2, x) \end{bmatrix}$$

b. *into* (P 1995: 126)

$$\text{event structure} = \begin{bmatrix} \text{E1} = e1\text{: process} \\ \text{E2} = e2\text{: state} \\ e1 <_\alpha e2 \\ \text{head: } e2 \end{bmatrix}$$

$$\text{argument structure} = \begin{bmatrix} \text{ARG1} = x \\ \text{ARG2} = y \end{bmatrix}$$

$$\text{qualia structure} = \begin{bmatrix} \text{AGENTIVE} = \textbf{move}(e1, x) \\ \text{FORMAL} = \textbf{at}(e2, x, y) \end{bmatrix}$$

(25)　*run into*　　　　　　　　　　　　　　　　　　　　　　(cf. P 1995: 126)
　　　　event structure = $\begin{bmatrix} E1 = e1: \text{process} \\ E2 = e2: \text{process} \\ E3 = e3: \text{state} \\ e1 \circ_\alpha e2 \quad e2 <_\alpha e3 \\ \text{head: } e3 \end{bmatrix}$
　　　　argument structure = $\begin{bmatrix} ARG1 = x \\ ARG2 = y \end{bmatrix}$
　　　　qualia structure = $\begin{bmatrix} \text{AGENTIVE} = \textbf{act}(e1, x) \; \textbf{move}(e2, x) \\ \text{FORMAL} = \textbf{at}(e3, x, y) \end{bmatrix}$

The co-composition operation operates on qualia structures of more than one lexical item, combines qualia in each qualia structure and gives rise to the qualia structure, in this case, of a verbal expression consisting of a verb and a PP. When qualia are combined, the PP's subevent is added to the verb's event structure, and this can change the telicity of the verb:

(26) a.　John ran *in an hour/for an hour.
　　　b.　John ran into the station in an hour/*for an hour.

In sections 6.1.3.2 and 6.2 we will discuss how the head subevent is determined and how verbs' telicity is changed through co-composition.

2.5.3　Selective Binding

The selective binding operation accounts for polysemy of adjectives, examples of which are shown in (27).

(27) a.　We will need a <u>fast</u> boat to get back in time.　　　(P (1995: 127))
　　　b.　John is a <u>fast</u> typist.　　　　　　　　　　　　　　　　(ibid.)

P (1995: 127–131) argues that the selective binding operation treats an adjective as a function and applies it to a particular quale of a head N co-occurring with the adjective. For example, consider the lexical representation of the noun *typist*:

(28)　*typist*
　　　　argument structure = [ARG1 = x: human]

$$\text{qualia structure} = \begin{bmatrix} \text{FORMAL} = x \\ \text{TELIC} = \textbf{type}(e, x) \end{bmatrix}$$

As a function, the adjective *fast* applies to the telic quale of *typist*. Since this operation does not change the type of the NP *fast typist*, the sentence in (27b) is well-formed.

2.6 Other Approaches

In this section, we survey other approaches to lexical meanings or events than GL. One is the LCS approach, which has been developed by Rappaport Hovav and Levin (1998) and Kageyama (1996) among others. This approach employs the means of predicate decomposition: meanings of verbs are decomposed into several primitive elements such as ACT, BECOME, BE-AT, CAUSE and the like. Utilizing these primitives, LCS can capture verbs' telicity, or Aktionsart, and represent the four classes of verbs or verbal expressions which were proposed by Vendler (1967) and Dowty (1979). The LCSs for the four classes proposed by Kageyama (1996) are shown in (29).

(29) a. stative verbs: [$_{\text{STATE}}$ y BE AT-z]
 b. activity verbs: [$_{\text{EVENT}}$ x ACT ON-y]
 c. achievement verbs: [$_{\text{EVENT}}$ BECOME [$_{\text{STATE}}$ y BE AT-z]]
 d. accomplishment verbs: [$_{\text{EVENT}}$ x ACT ON-y] CAUSE
 [$_{\text{EVENT}}$ BECOME [$_{\text{STATE}}$ y BE AT-z]]

The primitives also represent semantic or thematic relations of arguments which are taken by verbs, and argument positions in LCSs are linked to positions in argument structure: subjects of BE are themes and linked to the internal argument position in argument structure, those of ACT are agents and linked to the external argument position, objects of ON are patients and linked to the internal argument position.

The LCS approach has explored what aspects of verbs' meanings are relevant to their syntactic behaviors. Through the research, numbers of similarities and dissimilarities among verb classes such as the ones shown in Levin (1993) have been revealed, the causative-inchoative alternation is captured at the LCS level, and change in telicity of verbs or verbal expressions is accounted for by template augmentation, which operates upon LCS.

Although the LCS approach has made these significant findings, yet there still remain some shortcomings. The operation similar to co-composition in GL is proposed also in the LCS approach. LCS can represent the conceptual structure of verbal expressions consisting of motion verbs and PPs and of resultative construction sentences. Thus, the approach accounts for change in telicity of both cases. However, in other cases relations between primitive elements and their arguments remain static: therefore, for one lexical meaning one LCS has to be provided. For example, in an LCS approach two types of LCS are proposed for locative alternation verbs such as *spray* and *load*. The locative alternation sentences and their LCSs are shown in (30)–(31) (the examples and their LCSs are cited from Kageyama (1997: 61)).

(30) a. He loaded hay on the truck.
   b. [x CAUSE [BECOME [y BE-ON z]]]
(31) a. He loaded the truck with hay.
   b. [x CAUSE [BECOME [z_i BE [WITH [y BE ON z_i]]]]]

In this respect, we must assume as many LCSs as meanings of one lexical item.

Furthermore, LCS cannot deal with polysemy of lexical items such as we have just surveyed in section 2.5.1 and section 2.5.3. Since LCS has been developed especially to grasp and represent meanings of verbs, other devices or mechanisms are required in order to represent meanings of nouns and adjectives.

As for the notion of "event," it was introduced into modern Linguistic theory by Davidson (1967) and worked out by Parsons (1990) and Kearns (2000) among others. The assumptions about events by Parsons (1990: 6) are illustrated in (32).

(32) a. Caesar died.
   b. For some event e,
      e is a dying, *and*
      the object of e is Caesar, *and*
      e culminates before now.
   c. ($\exists$e) [Dying(e) & Object(e, Caesar) & Culminate(e, before now)]

According to Parsons (1990), the sentence in (32a) expresses what is stated in (32b), which is represented in the formalism of symbolic logic as is in (32c). In

(32c) the existential quantifier dominates the three formulas in which the event variable is contained.

P (1995: 68) points out that in the event structure in (32c) internal aspects of the event are inaccessible and argues "that finer-grained distinctions are necessary for event descriptions in order to capture some of the phenomena associated with aspect and Aktionsarten." Thus, along with argument structure and qualia structure, he proposes the event structure which represents the relation between an event and its proper subevents in order to capture aspect of predicates and their projection to syntax.

2.7 Aspectual Classes of Verbs and Generative Lexicon

In this section we see how lexical representations of aspectual verb classes proposed in Vendler (1967) and Dowty (1979) are represented in the GL framework. Vendler (1967) classifies verbs (and verb phrases) into four distinct classes by their restrictions on time adverbials, tenses and logical entailments. The four classes and their examples are shown below (The examples are cited from Vendler (1967) and Dowty (1979).):

(33) a. stative verbs: *be, resemble, possess, own, have, know, love, believe*
　　b. activity verbs: *dance, jog, swim, play, bark, laugh, weep, push a cart*
　　c. achievement verbs: *die, arrive, win, happen, occur, notice, recognize, spot*
　　d. accomplishment verbs: *build, kill, paint a picture, draw a circle, make a chair*

Pustejovsky (1992) claims that achievement verbs and accomplishment verbs belong to one class named "a transition event" and Pustejovsky (1992: 55–61) and P (1995: 68) argue that events denoted by verbs are subclassified into three types: states, process and transition. The transition event is schematically shown in (34).

(34)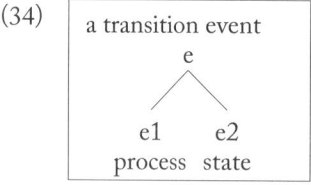

Let us consider the lexical representations for the four aspectual verb classes. The lexical representation of a state verb, *float*, is shown in (35).

(35) *float* (a state verb) (P (1995: 125))
event structure = $\begin{bmatrix} \text{E1 = e1: \textbf{state}} \\ \text{head: e1} \end{bmatrix}$
argument structure = [ARG1 = x: **physical_object**]
qualia structure = [AGENTIVE = **float**(e1, x)]

The event structure in (35) holds only one event, namely a state event. In the argument structure only one argument is contained and the argument is restricted to a physical object. In the qualia structure the function **float** is involved and this function takes as its arguments e1 linked to event 1 in the event structure and x linked to argument 1 in the argument structure.

As an example of activity verbs the lexical representation of *drive* is shown in (36).

(36) *drive* (an activity verb) (P (1995: 114))
event structure = $\begin{bmatrix} \text{E1 = e1: \textbf{process}} \\ \text{E2 = e2: \textbf{process}} \\ \text{e1 <o}_\propto \text{ e2} \\ \text{head: e1} \end{bmatrix}$
argument structure = $\begin{bmatrix} \text{ARG1 = x: \textbf{human}} \\ \text{ARG2 = y: \textbf{vehicle}} \end{bmatrix}$
qualia structure = $\begin{bmatrix} \text{AGENTIVE = \textbf{drive\_act}(e1, x, y)} \\ \text{FORMAL = \textbf{move}(e2, y)} \end{bmatrix}$

The argument structure in (36) contains two arguments: argument 1 is restricted to a human being or human beings, and argument 2 a vehicle or vehicles. The event structure consists of two process subevents: event 1 is linked to the **drive_act** function in the agentive role in the qualia structure and event 2 is linked to the **move** function in the formal role. Thus, event 1 and event 2 are associated with driving activities and movements of a vehicle or vehicles, respectively, and the two events overlap with each other. The qualia structure suggests that the driving activity causes the movement of a vehicle to occur.

The event structure of every activity verb does not contain two subevents.

According to P (1995: 80–81), *sleep*'s event structure holds only a process event linked to **sleep**(e1, x, y) in the formal role of the qualia structure. P (1995) assumes a subevent representing movement for *drive* and *walk* but seems not to assume the one for *run* (cf., P (1995: 103)); in this respect, it is not clear how to determine (or license) subevents which constitute the event structure of one lexical item.

The lexical representation of an achievement verb *arrive* is in (37).

(37)   *arrive* (an achievement verb)   (P (1995: 160))

$$\text{event structure} = \begin{bmatrix} E1 = e1: \textbf{process} \\ E2 = e2: \textbf{state} \\ e1 <_\alpha e2 \\ \text{head: } e2 \end{bmatrix}$$

$$\text{argument structure} = \begin{bmatrix} ARG1 = x: \textbf{individual} \\ D\text{-}ARG2 = y: \textbf{location} \end{bmatrix}$$

$$\text{qualia structure} = \begin{bmatrix} AGENTIVE = \textbf{arrive\_act}(e1, x) \\ FORMAL = \textbf{at}(e2, x, y) \end{bmatrix}$$

The event structure contains two subevents and the state subevent, event 2, is the head. P (1995) contends that this event structure is the event type of achievement verbs. In the argument structure argument 1 denotes some entity arriving and the default argument, argument 2, denotes some location the entity arrives at. The function **arrive_act** in the agentive role represents some activity preceding an arrival and is associated with event 1; the function **at** represents the state after the arrival and is associated with event 2.

P (1995: 160) says that the head subevent of *arrive* is event 2 and that it is lexically determined. However, some verbs' head subevents are underspecified: as we saw in section 2.4, *break*'s head event is underspecified, and when its event 2 becomes the head, the verb behaves as an achievement.

The verb *build* is classified as an accomplishment verb, and in section 2.4 we have already seen its lexical representation, which is repeated as (38).

(38) *build* (an accomplishment verb)

$$\text{event structure} = \begin{bmatrix} E1 = e1\text{: process} \\ E2 = e2\text{: state} \\ e1 <_\propto e2 \\ \text{head: } e1 \end{bmatrix}$$

$$\text{argument structure} = \begin{bmatrix} ARG1 = x\text{:} & \begin{bmatrix} \textbf{animate\_individual} \\ \text{FORMAL} = \textbf{physical\_object} \end{bmatrix} \\ ARG2 = y\text{:} & \begin{bmatrix} \textbf{artifact} \\ \text{CONST} = z \\ \text{FORMAL} = \textbf{physical\_object} \end{bmatrix} \\ D\text{-}ARG3 = z\text{:} & \begin{bmatrix} \textbf{material} \\ \text{FORMAL} = \textbf{mass} \end{bmatrix} \end{bmatrix}$$

$$\text{qualia structure} = \begin{bmatrix} \text{AGENTIVE} = \textbf{build\_act}(e1, x, z) \\ \text{FORMAL} = \textbf{exist}(e2, y) \end{bmatrix}$$

In section 2.4 we have surveyed *build*'s argument structure, so here we only see its event structure and qualia structure. The event structure of *build* consists of a process subevent and a resultant state subevent, and the temporal relation is "exhaustive ordered." The head event is lexically determined: event 1 serves as the head, and this type of event structure, P (1995: 71, 81–82) claims, is the one for accomplishment verbs. The process subevent is associated with **build_act**(e1, x, z) in the agentive role, which represents the developing process of construction, and the state subevent is linked to **exist**(e2, y) denoting the resulting state of construction.

In chapter 4 we propose to differentiate a process event concerning action from another process event concerning movement or change. We also modify some of the lexical representations we have seen in this section (e.g., *build* and *arrive*).

2.8 Summary

As we have surveyed in this chapter, P (1995) proposes the three structures and the three generative operations functioning on some of these structures. As a result, GL can represent various meanings of lexical items and explain their variable behaviors. We consider the theory of Generative Lexicon to be a promising one.

At the same time, however, GL holds some problems to be solved or issues to be clarified. These problems and issues arise from the complexity of the GL system. In the next chapter we discuss those matters and present our main proposals to this book.

Endnotes
1. We utilize our own notation when we cite representations proposed by P (1995) if there is no significant difference between his way and ours.
2. P (1995: 69) calls the representation concerning an event and its proper subevents "extended event structure." In this book we call it event structure.

Chapter 3

Issues and Proposals

In this chapter we see issues which Pustejovsky (1995) does not fully discuss and introduce the six major proposals we make in this book. As we saw in the previous chapter, in order to capture polysemy of words, Pustejovsky (1995) proposes GL, which contains a lexical representation with three lexical-semantic structures and three generative devices. Through interaction of these structures and devices, GL is able to account for polysemy of words and phrases and explain their variable behaviors. However, GL still has several issues which are not fully discussed and remain unclear, and these issues are crucial for understanding polysemy and behaviors of words and phrases and, at the same time, are closely related to one another. We bring up four issues in section 3.1. In section 3.2 we present six proposals to solve the issues discussed in section 1. As we stated above, the four issues are closely related, and in addition, in GL the three structures and generative devices, especially co-composition operations, interact with one another. Therefore, the issues in section 3.1 and our proposals shown in section 3.2 are not related on a one-to-one basis. That is, some proposals concern more than one issue. In section 3.3 we show two linguistic tests utilizing durative *for*-phrases and frame *in*-phrases by which we confirm event structure of verbs and head subevents.

3.1   Issues to be Discussed in This Book

We need to examine four issues concerning GL as proposed by Pustejovsky (1995) in order to understand and represent polysemy of words and phrases. The four issues to be discussed are as follows:

(1) a. The number of event types of subevents: In Pustejovsky (1995) it is claimed that the event structure of a lexical item contains two subevents at most, namely, a process subevent and a state subevent. Basically, the former is associated with the **act** function in the qualia structure and the latter the **at** function. Are there any other types of subevent in event structures?
b. Headedness: How is a head event decided?
c. The rule of the co-composition operation: What are conditions for co-composition of events to operate?
d. Functions of the qualia structure: What functions does the qualia structure have that are peculiar to GL?

Since all these issues are related to the essential parts of GL, namely the structures in a lexical representation or the generative devices, to resolve them is vital for an elaboration of GL.

The issue in (1a) concerns the constitution of event structure and the lexical aspects of meanings which verbs (and prepositions) express. The notion of headedness in (1b) is also related to the constitution of event structure; furthermore, this notion is important in that a quale associated with a head subevent expresses verbs' foregrounding, i.e., semantically focused, meanings and determines their syntactic behaviors. As for (1c), the co-composition operation gives rise to variable behaviors of verbs and causes change in their telicity. Similar operations have also been proposed by Rappaport Hovav and Levin (1998) and Kageyama and Yumoto (1997) among others. However, it has not been made clear how and under what conditions this operation works in GL. Concerning (1d), qualia structure represents various aspects of meanings words express. Furthermore, this structure represents words' meanings in terms of paradigmatic relations: for example, the nouns *dictionary* and *novel* are distinguished by their formal roles; the formal role of *dictionary* contains the function **word_list** and that of *novel* **narrative**.[1] In addition, following Pustejovsky (1995) and Ono (2005) we assume that information contained in qualia structure sometimes reflects speakers' experiences and world knowledge and that this yields polysemy of words. Qualia structure also takes an important part in the co-composition operation. So we need to investigate the precise functions of qualia structure.

Through investigation of the issues above, we make six proposals in this book.

In the next section we survey the proposals.

3.2 Proposals

Proposals which we pose in this book are summarized in (2).

(2) a. **Event of movement or change**
We propose a third type of subevent in the event structure, namely, a process subevent which represents movement or change. Adopting this subevent, we consider that a lexical item can denote an event consisting of three subevents at most.
b. **Underspecification of headedness**
We argue that in the event structure of verbs showing variable behaviors a head subevent is underspecified and, furthermore, that in such an event structure basically any subevent can be the head.
c. **Co-composition operation and its conditions**
We propose the co-composition operation concerning motion verbs and co-occurring prepositional phrases and conditions on the operation.
d. **Generative ability of the qualia structure**
We consider that the qualia structure gives rise to polysemy of words by containing information which sometimes reflects experiences and world knowledge of speakers.
e. **Composition of semantic representations of verbs and adjunct PPs: Event Insertion**
When subevents of a verb are substituted for an argument in a lexical representation of a PP by a composition operation, the PP functions as an adjunct.
f. **Co-composition, composition and headedness: the Inheritance of Headedness**
We propose the relationship between operations such as co-composition and composition and headedness.

These proposals correspond to the issues we saw in the last section. An "event of movement or change" in (2a) we will discuss in chapter 4 is related to the issue in (1a). The notion of "underspecification of headedness" in (2b) which we will discuss in chapter 5 is a partial answer to the issue in (1b). The proposal in (2b) deals with headedness of lexical representations of verbs; in this sense this is the characteristic of headedness at a word level. The "co-composition operation and its conditions" in (2c) is a direct answer to the issue in (1c); in addition, since the co-composition operation involves event structure, a head event and qualia structure, (2c) is also related to the other issues in (1). "Generative ability of the qualia structure" in (2d) is examined to make the issue in (1d) clear. This will explain polysemy of words and phrases and their variable syntactic behaviors. The proposal "Composition of semantic representations of verbs and adjunct PPs: Event Insertion" in (2e) is discussed to understand the overall relation between motion verbs and prepositional phrases. Some prepositions are combined with co-occurring motion verbs, and by co-composition telicity of verbs are sometimes changed. On the other hand, some prepositions do not undergo co-composition, and remain as adjunct phrases and form VPs with co-occurring verbs. By proposing (2e) in addition to (2c), we can capture all the relationships between motion verbs and co-occurring prepositional phrases. After comprehension of the co-composition operation in (2c) and composition of verbs and adjunct PPs in (2e), ways of determination of head subevents are proposed as is shown in (2f). The proposal in (2f) is an answer to the issue in (1b) at the phrase level. We will deal with (2c), (2d) and (2f) in chapter 6 and (2e) and some part of (2f) in chapter 7.

3.3 Diagnostics for Headedness and Transition: Durative *For*-phrases and Frame *In*-phrases

In order to verify the event structure of a certain lexical item (or a predicate), we mainly utilize two types of expressions as linguistic tests. We survey these tests in this section.

First, let us discuss how we can identify which subevent is a head in a complex event structure. Pustejovsky (1995: 74–75) maintains that heads license modification by a durative adverbial such as *for an hour*. The durative adverbial can basically modify a process event and a state event, which is shown in (17). This PP has been considered not to be compatible with bounded events such as the ones in (18): the events expressed by *arrive* and *run to the post office* are bounded.

(17) a. Kenji read the book on musicology for three hours.

  b. Sakura stayed in the U.S. for six weeks.
(18) a. *The train arrived for ten minutes.
  b. ??Hiroshi ran to the post office for five minutes.

However, close investigation reveals that (18b) can hold the interpretation that Hiroshi continued to run toward the post office for five minutes and did not get there if this example is put under a forceful interpretation.[2] In this interpretation of (18b), the event expressed by the sentence is unbounded, namely, a process event which is expressed by *run*, and we consider that this event of *run* is the head in the event structure of the verb, and that this event can be modified by the *for*-phrase.

  As additional examples, the examples in (19) can be construed without forceful interpretation. In (19a) *for two hours* modifies a state subevent: that is, the interpretation is that the terminal was dead for two hours, which, we consider, shows that the head of *die* is the state subevent. In the same way, the interpretation of (19b) is that Mary was out of town for two weeks, where the head event is also the state subevent (The examples in (19) are taken from Pustejovsky (1995: 74–75)).

(19) a. My terminal died for two hours.
  b. Mary left town for two weeks.

We make use of this durative *for*-phrase when we check which subevent is a head in an event structure of a verb.

  Next, we consider a frame adverbial phrase like *in an hour* to be compatible with expressions which contain culmination in their event structure. The culmination of events is the beginning or the end of an event or the transition from one event to another event, such as from a process event to a state event. Thus, the frame *in*-phrase can appear in sentences like the ones in (20).

(20) a. The cherry blossoms will bloom in two days.
  b. Hiroshi ran to the post office in ten minutes.
   i. 'Hiroshi began to run ten minutes later.'
   ii. 'Hiroshi ran, and ten minutes later he reached the post office.'

(20a) has the interpretation that the cherry blossoms will get into the state of blooming two days later. This reading and the interpretation in (i) of (20b) are cases in which the beginnings of events, the beginning of the blooming state of the cherry blossoms and that of the running process of Hiroshi, are focused by the frame *in*-phrases.

On the other hand, in the reading in (ii) of (20b) the same frame *in*-phrase focuses on the transition between two events, namely a process event of Hiroshi's running and a state event of Hiroshi's being at the post office. In this book the latter interpretation is utilized in order to verify whether the event structure of some semantic representation contains a transition of events in it. Put in other words, if there is a transition between events in the event structure of a verb or a verbal expression, the verb can co-occur with an *in*-phrase.

3.4 Functions in Qualia Structure, Argument Positions in Syntax and Linking

In this section we suggest the way arguments are linked from lexical representation to syntax. As we saw in section 2.3, Pustejovsky (1995) argues that arguments in a quale map to syntactic argument positions such as subject or object positions. In this book, we assume that arguments in a quale map to an external or internal argument position (or a specifier position or complement position) in syntax.

Examples of Pustejovsky (1995)'s linking system are repeated below:

(21) a. $Q_i: R(e1^*, x, y) \rightarrow$ x:SUBJ, y: OBJ
   b. $Q_j: P(e2, y) \rightarrow$ shadowed
(22) a. $Q_i: R(e1, x, y) \rightarrow$ shadowed
   b. $Q_j: P(e2^*, y) \rightarrow$ y: SUBJ

These are the cases of complex events consisting of a process subevent and a state subevent. Although the linking given in (22) derives an unaccusative use of verbs, this linking system cannot deal with syntactic behaviors of unaccusative verbs. Among generative syntactitians, it has been considered that the syntactic characteristics of some resultative sentences, e.g. *The river froze solid.* and those of locative inversion sentences such as *On the horizon appeared a large ship.* are accounted for by regarding the NPs *the river* and *a large ship* as being projected into the internal argument position or the complement of a head V. If argument y in (22) is directly projected into a subject position, syntactic characteristics of unaccusative verbs have to be explained in other ways.

In this book, following research in LCS, we assume that functions in qualia determine the syntactic positions of their arguments. The relations between the functions we utilize (or propose) and the syntactic positions of their arguments are given in (23).

(23) a. **act**(e, x) ⟶ x: an external position
b. **act-on**(e, x, y) ⟶ x: an external position, y: an internal position
c. **at**(e, x, y) ⟶ x: an internal position, y: an oblique or internal position
d. **move**(e, x) ⟶ x: an internal position
e. **cause-move**(e, x, y) ⟶ x: an external position, y: an internal position

The function **act** denotes a volitional or nonvolitional activity of some entity; the function **act-on** represents some entity's volitional or nonvolitional activity which affects another entity or other entities. The function **at** denotes some entity's existence at some location and, in abstract senses, some entity's or event's existence at some temporal point (See also the next paragraph). The functions **move** and **cause-move**, which we propose in chapter 4, represent movement or change; the former denotes autonomous movement or change and the latter non-autonomous movement or change (See section 4.2.2 for detailed discussions).

Moreover, we should note two matters concerning our notation we make use of in order to capture generality of functions and their linking. We utilize such simplified functions as shown in (23) instead of lexically specified functions such as **break_act** which Pustejovsky (1995) utilizes. In addition we make use of the **at** function and lexically specific arguments such as BROKEN to denote resultant states. By doing so, similarity between spatial relations and other semantic fields is explicitly represented. Arguments denoted in capital letters are shadow arguments and do not appear in syntax.

3.5 Summary

In this chapter we saw issues which are left unclear in Pustejovsky (1995) and briefly discussed six proposals we will make in this book. These issues are closely related to event structure, qualia structure, the co-composition operation and the composition operation. In order to solve these issues we need to examine linguistic phenomena relevant to the two structures and the operations. Through the examination of their characteristics, their functions and relations will be revealed, which, we are sure, leads to achievement of our aim, namely revealing how compositionality concerns polysemy of words and phrases. From the next chapter through chapter 7 we study various linguistic phenomena to find out answers to the vital issues.

Endnotes

1 The representations of *novel* and *dictionary* are proposed in Ono (2005) and the formal roles suggested here are cited from Ono (2005: 32).
2 Readers are referred to chapter 6 in this book, Alsina (1999) and Isono (2001) among others for the relevant interpretation here.

Chapter 4

Event of Movement or Change: Location Verbs and Verbs of Change of State

From this chapter to chapter 7, we will study various linguistic phenomena relevant to understanding the properties of lexical representation and operations proposed in the Generative Lexicon framework and we justify the proposals we surveyed in the last chapter. In this chapter and the next we will focus on two structures contained in lexical representation, namely event structure and qualia structure, and the notion of headedness, which is closely related to the two structures. After comprehending representation at the word level, in chapters 6 and 7 we will see representation at the phrase level and operations concerning formation of such representation.

First, in this chapter the event structure for movement or change is proposed.[1] The subevent of movement or change represents change in the action chain advocated by Croft (1991) and Langacker (1991) among others, which consists of action, change and resultant state. In contrast to Pustejovsky (1995), who argues that accomplishment verbs and achievement verbs all consist of a process subevent and a state subevent, this chapter adduces empirical evidence that the event structure of some of these verbs consists of three subevents. By adopting an event type representing movement or change we shed light on necessary conditions for the causative-inchoative alternation of verbs. Furthermore, the subevent of movement or change theoretically explains the difference between the verb *spray* and *load*, which have been considered to belong to the same verb class, the possibility of addition of double goal phrases to motion verbs and the possibility of induced action alternation.

4.1 Event of Movement or Change

Pustejovsky (1995) assumes that in the event structure of *break*, which undergoes the causative-inchoative alternation, a head subevent is basically underspecified but that in the event structure of verbs which are used only as transitive verbs, for example *build*, event 1 is always the head.

(1) a. *break*
event structure = $\begin{bmatrix} E1 = e1\text{: process} \\ E2 = e2\text{: state} \\ e1 <_\alpha e2 \\ \text{head: underspecified} \end{bmatrix}$

b. *build*
event structure = $\begin{bmatrix} E1 = e1\text{: process} \\ E2 = e2\text{: state} \\ e1 <_\alpha e2 \\ \text{head: e1} \end{bmatrix}$

According to Pustejovsky (1995), the verb *break* is used as a transitive when the process event is a head, and this verb is an intransitive (or unaccusative) when the state event is a head.

However, this proposal faces a problem when we consider the interpretation of a sentence containing the verb *grow*. The verb *grow*, like *break*, is a verb of change of state and also undergoes the causative-inchoative alternation, as is shown in (2). So, in Pustejovsky's analysis, the lexical representation of *grow* should be the one in (3).

(2) a. The farm grew the little plants.
  b. The little plant grew.
(3) *grow*
event structure = $\begin{bmatrix} E1 = e1\text{: process} \\ E2 = e2\text{: state} \\ e1 <_\alpha e2 \\ \text{head: underspecified} \end{bmatrix}$

$$\text{argument structure} = \begin{bmatrix} \text{ARG1} = x \\ \text{ARG2} = y \end{bmatrix}$$
$$\text{qualia structure} = \begin{bmatrix} \text{AGENTIVE} = \mathbf{act}(e1, x, y) \\ \text{FORMAL} = \mathbf{at}(e2, y, \text{GROWN}) \end{bmatrix}$$

On this account, *grow* functions as a transitive and the two arguments, namely *the farm* and *the little plants*, appear in syntax as in (2a) when the process subevent e1 is a head. This verb works as an intransitive and the single argument *the little plant* appears as in (2b) when the state subevent e2 is a head. Now, we should notice that the intransitive *grow*, whose head is supposed to be a state subevent, co-occurs with a durative *for*-phrase, and that the interpretation of (4a) is that the little plant continued to grow for a week.

(4) a. The little plant grew for a week.
  b. The little plant grew in two weeks.

Although in this reading *for a week* seems to modify a process subevent which denotes the event of the little plant's growing, the subevent representing the change of state of the plant is not contained in the event structure in (3) (Furthermore, we should note that *grow* can be used with an *in*-phrase as in (4b), which we will discuss below (8)).

In addition, if we consider that causative events form an 'action chain' and the verb *grow* expresses a causative event, in (3) the process subevent represents an action event and the state subevent a resulting state event, but no subevent represents a change event: a subevent which denotes change should be contained in the event structure in (3).

Let us see other examples in (5), which are not correctly accounted for by the representation proposed in Pustejovsky (1995). The lexical representation of relevant verbs would be the one in (6).

(5) a. In a hurry they gradually built the building.
  "They were in a hurry, but the building of the house proceeded gradually."
  b. In a hurry Ken carried the bag to his room slowly.
  c. In a hurry they pulled the log along the stairs slowly.

(6)

$$\text{event structure} = \begin{bmatrix} \text{E1} = \text{e1: process} \\ \text{E2} = \text{e2: state} \\ \text{e1} <_\alpha \text{e2} \\ \text{head: e1} \end{bmatrix}$$

$$\text{argument structure} = \begin{bmatrix} \text{ARG1} = x \\ \text{ARG2} = y \\ \text{ARG3} = z \end{bmatrix}$$

$$\text{qualia structure} = \begin{bmatrix} \text{AGENTIVE} = \textbf{act-on}(e1, x, y) \\ \text{FORMAL} = \textbf{at}(e2, y, z) \end{bmatrix}$$

If we consider (6) to be the lexical representation of the verb *build*, the activity 'they set up a building' is expressed by the subevent e1, which is associated with **act-on** (e1, x, y) in the qualia structure, and the resultant state 'a building exists' is expressed by the subevent e2, which is associated with **at** (e2, y, z) in the qualia structure.

We should note here that the adverbials *in a hurry* and *gradually* are used in (5a). We assume that when the semantic representation of a verb contains a subevent which an adverb can modify, the adverb can co-occur with the verb. As for an example such as *Tom spoke slowly*, the verb *speak* contains a process subevent **act** (e1, x), which represents Tom's conducting the action of speaking in its lexical representation. The adverb *slowly* modifies this subevent and can co-occur with the verb *speak*. The representation in (6) does not adequately represent subevents which the adverbial phrases in (5) can modify: the adverbials *in a hurry* and *gradually* in (5a) specify the situation in which the people build a building in a hurry and the building gradually takes form accordingly. However, no subevent in (6) represents an event whose modification by *gradually* will yield such an interpretation.

In the same way, if we suppose that the representation in (6) represents the meaning of the verb *carry*, Ken's intention and action of conveying the bag in (5b) is represented by the subevent e1 associated with **act-on** (e1, x, y) and the bag's existence in Ken's room is represented by the subevent e2, which is associated with **at** (e2, y, z). In (5b) the adverbial *in a hurry* specifies the situation in which Ken's action on the bag was conducted in a hurry, and the adverb *slowly* specifies Ken and the bag's slow movement to his room. However, no subevent in (6) represents Ken and the bag's movement. A similar explanation applies to the example in (5c): *in a hurry* modifies the manner of the people's action and *slowly* that of the log's movement, and there is no subevent representing the log's movement in (6).

We propose that the semantic representation for the verbs *grow*, *carry*, *build* and *pull* should contain a subevent of movement or change. The type of this subevent is a process, and we assume that this subevent is associated with a **move** or **cause-move** function in the qualia structure. The **move** and **cause-move** functions are assumed as in (7), and we propose the lexical representation of *grow* as the one in (8). These functions differentiate an autonomous movement or change from a non-autonomous one, as Levin & Rappaport (1995), Kageyama (1996) and Maruta (1998) among others discuss. (As for the function **cause-move**, see the discussion which begins below (22) in section 4.2.2.)

(7) The functions which are associated with the subevent of movement or change
   a. **move** (e, x): the referent of x autonomously changes or moves.
   b. **cause-move** (e, x, y): the referent of x changes or moves that of y.

(8) *grow*
$$\text{event structure} = \begin{bmatrix} E1 = e1\text{: process} \\ E2 = e2\text{: process} \\ E3 = e3\text{: state} \\ e1o_\propto e2 \quad e2 <_\propto e3 \\ \text{head: underspecified} \end{bmatrix}$$

$$\text{argument structure} = \begin{bmatrix} ARG1 = x \\ ARG2 = y \\ ARG3 = GROWN \end{bmatrix}$$

$$\text{qualia structure} = \begin{bmatrix} AGENTIVE = \textbf{act-on}(e1, x, y) \\ \textbf{move}(e2, y) \\ FORMAL = \textbf{at}(e3, y, GROWN) \end{bmatrix}$$

(e.g., (2a): x = the farm, y = the little plants)

In (8) the farm's acting on the plants is represented by the process subevent e1, the plants' growing by e2 and the resultant state of the grown plants by e3. The event structure represents that the temporal relation between the subevent e1 and e2 is overlapping, and the subevent e3 follows e2 without any intervening subevent. As we briefly mentioned, Pustejovsky (1995) assumes the subevent of motion for some motion verbs such as *drive* and *walk*; however, probably not for *run* and verbs of change of state. We consider verbs of motion and verbs of change of state to basically contain the subevent of movement or change and are able to make use of adverbials in (5) as a diagnostic of this subevent's existence.

Concerning the function for the subevent of movement or change, it is possible to differentiate the function for change from the one for movement: for example, we may use the function **change** in order to represent the subevent of change. In this book, however, we employ **move** for both types of subevent mainly for two reasons: 1) Some verbs can express both movement and change (e.g., *John went to the lake.* vs. *The milk went sour.*) If we use the functions **move** and **change**, we need to assume two lexical representations for the verb *go*. 2) Following the localist approach, we consider the characteristics of spatial relation to be generalized to other relations such as properties or temporal relation. Naturally, we need to study those relations one by one, and while doing so, we might find it necessary to assume functions other than **move**. That is our next step after the research in the present one.

Assuming the lexical representation in (8) for *grow*, we can correctly deal with the examples in (2) and (4). For the transitive *grow* in (2a), the head is subevent e1. The role **act-on** (e1, x, y) in the qualia structure is semantically focused, and the two arguments *the farm* and *the little plants* appear in syntax. For the intransitive *grow*, we assume that the head is subevent e2. Therefore, the role **move** (e2, y) is focused and the argument *the little plant* is projected into syntax. The focus on e2, the subevent of change, yields the interpretation of (4a) in which the plant continued to grow for a week. Furthermore, the representation in (8) contains a transition from e2 to e3, which allows the frame adverbial *in two weeks* to be used in (4b).

Assuming the subevent of movement or change also accounts for the examples in (5), which are problems to Pustejovsky (1995)'s representation. We repeat only (5a, b) below:

(5) a.　In a hurry they gradually built the building.
　　b.　In a hurry Ken carried the bag to his room slowly.

Let us see (5b) first. We assume the lexical representation of *carry* should be the one in (9).

(9) *carry*
   event structure = $\begin{bmatrix} \text{E1} = \text{e1: process} \\ \text{E2} = \text{e2: process} \\ \text{E3} = \text{e3: state} \\ \text{e1o}_\alpha\text{e2} \quad \text{e2}<_\alpha\text{e3} \\ \text{head: e1} \end{bmatrix}$
   argument structure = $\begin{bmatrix} \text{ARG1} = \text{Ken} \\ \text{ARG2} = \text{bag} \\ \text{ARG3} = \text{room} \end{bmatrix}$
   qualia structure = $\begin{bmatrix} \text{AGENTIVE} = \textbf{act-on}(\text{e1, Ken, bag}) \\ \qquad\qquad\quad \textbf{cause-move}(\text{e2, Ken, bag}) \\ \text{FORMAL} = \textbf{at}(\text{e3, Ken\&bag, room}) \end{bmatrix}$

In (9), Ken's acting on the bag is represented by e1, Ken's action of moving the bag is represented by e2 and the existence of Ken and the bag in his room are expressed by e3. The adverbial *in a hurry* modifies the subevent of Ken's acting related to **act-on** (e1, Ken, bag) and the adverb *slowly* does the subevent of Ken and the bag's movement related to **cause-move** (e2, Ken, bag), and thus these adverbials are permitted to co-occur with *carry*.

The verb *build* in (5a) is a verb of creation, which expresses a kind of change of state, and in this respect the lexical representation of *build* is similar to that of *grow*, a change-of-state verb: the representation of *build* contains the subevent of people's action and that of change, namely the formation of the building, and *in a hurry* modifies the former subevent and *gradually* modifies the latter subevent. The important difference between *build* and *grow* is that the head subevent of *build* is always the process subevent e1, which is related to an agentive role **act-on** (e1, they, material). This subevent represents acting on the material of the building, and since this subevent is always the head, the two arguments are projected into syntax and the verb *build* always functions as a transitive.[2]

In this section, we argued that the event structure of *grow*, *build* and *carry* contains a third type of event, which denotes movement or change and is distinct from the activity subevent and the state subevent. Assuming this third type of subevent, we can correctly account for the examples in (4) and (5), which Pustejovsky's (1995) representation cannot correctly deal with.

4.2 Theoretical Consequences

In the last section we proposed the subevent of movement or change. Assuming the notion of a causal chain, the event structure can contain at most three subevents, namely two process subevents and one state subevent. In the event structure, the contained subevents are arranged in a temporal order. From the assumed types of subevents, the possible event arrangements of the event structure should be the ones in (10).

(10)   The Possible Event Types of the Event Structure
    a.   a process event - a process event - a state event
    b.   a process event - a process event
    c.   a process event - a sate event
    d.   a process event
    e.   a state event

A verb and a verbal expression which consists of a verb and a PP need to conform to one of these event types. We consider the event arrangement in (10a) to be the most complex one which a verb or a VP can express. The first process event corresponds to action in a causal chain, the second one to movement or change in a causal chain and the state event to the final resultant state.

By assuming the events of movement or change and keeping (10) in mind, we can now deal with some linguistic phenomena. In the following subsections, the possibility of the addition of double goal phrases to motion verbs, the locative alternation (or the *spray/load* alternation), the causative-inchoative alternation and the possibility of an induced action alternation are discussed one by one.

4.2.1   Addition of a Second Goal Phrase to Motion Verbs

In this subsection we see that a lexical representation containing a subevent of movement or change explains the well-formedness of sentences where double goal phrases are used with motion verbs. The examples we consider in this subsection are in (11) below.

(11) a.   John ran into the room to the blackboard.   (Gruber (1976: 113))
     b. *He {arrived at/reached} New York to the Statue of Liberty.

In (11a) the second goal phrase *to the blackboard* is added after the first goal phrase *into the room*. The interpretation of (11a) we consider in this subsection is that John ran into the room, continued to run and got to the blackboard.

On the other hand, the verbs *arrive* and *reach* in (11b) does not permit a second goal phrase to be added. At first glance the examples in (11b) seem unacceptable because these verbs express arrival at some goal in contrast to *run*. The events expressed by these verbs are completed when someone gets to New York, and so, additional movement to the Statue of Liberty cannot be expressed. However, when we see (12), we notice that this is not the case: the examples in (11b) should not be ruled out only by the specification of a goal by the verbs, since the verb *approach* in (12) also implies a goal.

(12)   The airplane approached Tokyo to Narita.

The sentence *The airplane approached Tokyo* entails that the airplane got to an area near Tokyo. In spite of its implication of getting to a goal, this verb permits a second goal phrase to be added as we can see in (12), which makes a contrast with (11b) containing *arrive* and *reach*.

We argue that the example in (12) is acceptable because the verb *approach* expresses movement to a goal as well as accession to some location and that the examples in (11b) are unacceptable because *arrive* and *reach* do not imply movement to a goal. In fact, *arrive* does not co-occur with a *through*-phrase which implies a path of movement in (13a), while the phrase *approach NP through* in (13b) emphasizes movement toward the city, and does not imply getting at the city.

(13) a.   ??He arrived at Kurashiki city through the long tunnel.
     b.   He approached Kurashiki city through the long tunnel.

Thus, we contend that a *to*-phrase, which implies movement, can co-occur with verbs which express movement such as *approach* but cannot be used with verbs which do not express movement, namely *arrive* and *reach*.

Now, keeping this in mind, let us see the lexical representation of *arrive*, *approach* and *to*[3]:

(14) *arrive*
event structure = $\begin{bmatrix} E1 = e1: \text{process} \\ E2 = e2: \text{state} \\ e1 <_\alpha e2 \\ \text{head: } e1 \end{bmatrix}$
argument structure = $\begin{bmatrix} ARG1 = x \\ ARG2 = y \end{bmatrix}$
qualia structure = $\begin{bmatrix} \text{AGENTIVE} = \textbf{move}(e1, x) \\ \qquad\qquad\qquad [\text{CONST} = p_0 <_\alpha p_1] \\ \text{FORMAL} = \textbf{at}(e2, x, y) \end{bmatrix}$

(15) *approach*
event structure = $\begin{bmatrix} E1 = e1: \text{process} \\ E2 = e2: \text{process} \\ E3 = e3: \text{state} \\ e1 o_\alpha e2 \quad e2 <_\alpha e3 \\ \text{head: } e1 \end{bmatrix}$
argument structure = $\begin{bmatrix} ARG1 = x \\ ARG2 = y \end{bmatrix}$
qualia structure = $\begin{bmatrix} \text{AGENTIVE} = \textbf{act}(e1, x) \quad \textbf{move}(e2, x) \\ \text{FORMAL} = \textbf{at}(e3, x, \text{NEAR } y) \end{bmatrix}$

(16) *to*
event structure = $\begin{bmatrix} E1 = e1: \text{process} \\ E2 = e2: \text{state} \\ e1 <_\alpha e2 \\ \text{head: underspecified} \end{bmatrix}$
argument structure = $\begin{bmatrix} ARG1 = x \\ ARG2 = y \end{bmatrix}$
qualia structure = $\begin{bmatrix} \text{AGENTIVE} = \textbf{move}(e1, x) \\ \text{FORMAL} = \textbf{at}(e2, x, y) \end{bmatrix}$

First, let us consider the representation for *arrive* in (14). Relevant examples are given in (17).

(17) a. John arrived at the station in ten minutes.
   b. *John arrived at the station for ten minutes.
   c. John was arriving at the station.

(= "John was about to arrive at the station.")

As is shown in (17a), the frame PP *in ten minutes* can co-occur with *arrive*: this verb's event structure contains a transition from one subevent to another subevent. In (17b) the durative adverbial phrase *for ten minutes* cannot co-occur with this verb: this suggests that neither a process subevent nor a state subevent is the head (if there is any). Pustejovsky (2000) argues that there should be a distinction between binary predicates and scalar predicates and proposes the Binary opposition and the Polar opposition for opposition structure. The Binary opposition is for predicates which do not focus on the scale, or gradability, of change or state which they denote: the adjective *dead* is one of this type of predicates and the distinction of *employed / unemployed* is this type of opposition. The Polar opposition is the one expressed by predicates which focus on the scale of change or state: one example is the verb *melt*, which expresses a change of state of some solid substance to a liquid. Now we consider *arrive* represents a movement characterized as the Binary opposition: the verb expresses a sequence of events such that an entity is not some location, the entity appears at a certain location and it stays at the location. In this whole events, no intermediate path is not included. The notation $[p_0 <_\alpha p_1]$ in (14) denotes this type of movement, or a shift of situations.

The movement or change expressed by *to*, *carry* and the like is of the Polar opposition, which contains an in-between path or state in a movement or change. This suggests that an event characterized as the Polar opposition is durative while the one characterized as the Binary opposition is instantaneous. Thus, the subevent e1 in (14) is instantaneous and does not accord with the durative *for*-phrase semantically, which makes (17b) ungrammatical.[4] Furthermore, the example in (17c), which contains the progressive form of *arrive*, is given a future tense reading, not a progressive reading. This suggests that an "ordinary" process subevent, which licenses a progressive reading, is not contained in the event structure. Thus, we propose the lexical representation for *arrive* in (14).

The event structure in (14) contains two subevents. Taking (17a) as an example, event 1 represents the instantaneous event which expresses the shift from John being at some location other than the station to his being at the station; event 2 represents John being at the station. The lexical representation for *arrive* contains a subevent of movement which is characterized as the Binary opposition. This subevent does not accord with a subevent of movement contained in the event structure of the preposition *to*.

The lexical representation of *approach* in (15), as that of *to*, contains the subevent of movement, which is related to **move** (e2, x) in the qualia structure.

Now we maintain that the preposition *to* can co-occur with the verb *approach* because the lexical representations of these two words contain the subevent of movement. We consider the co-occurrence of *approach* and *through* to be licensed by the co-composition operation: when a verb's event structure and a preposition's contain the subevent of movement, the co-composition operation combines the two words' lexical representations into the semantic representation of a derived verbal expression such as *approach NP through* in (13b). The representation of *arrive* does not contain the same type of subevent of movement as *to*, the co-composition operations does not operate and so *arrive* cannot co-occur with *to*. (As for the co-composition operation, see the discussions in section 4.2.3.)

We argued that the lexical representation including a subevent of movement or change can correctly explain the possibility of co-occurrence of motion verbs and prepositional goal phrases. A system of representation which does not assume the subevent of movement or change cannot represent the lexical representation of *arrive* and *reach* in (11b) and of *approach* in (12) appropriately, and cannot account for the difference of acceptability between (11b) and (12).

4.2.2 Causative-Inchoative Alternation

In this subsection we consider the relation between the causative-inchoative alternation of verbs and the events of movement or change. As we can see in (18) and (19), the verb of change of state *bake* can be used as both a transitive verb and an intransitive verb. On the other hand, the verb *cut*, which also belongs to the class of verbs of change of state, is used only as a transitive verb.

(18) a. Ken baked potatoes in the oven.
  b. Potatoes baked in the oven.
(19) a. John cut the cake with a small knife.
  b. *The cake cut with a small knife.

Many researchers have conducted research on semantic conditions of the causative-inchoative alternation of verbs. In this subsection we review the analysis in Ono (2005), address a question about his analysis and propose our own analysis. Ono (2005) assumes a process subevent, e1, representing an action and a state subevent, e2, which represents a resultant state, and claims that participants taking part in each subevent are relevant to verbs' behaviors concerning the causative-inchoative alternation. These participants are represented as arguments in the argument structure and the qualia structure in a lexical representation.

According to his explanation, regarding the verb *bake* in (18), which shows the causative-inchoative alternation, Ken and potatoes are taking part in e1, and only potatoes is involved in e2. See the lexical representation for *bake* in (20).

(20) *bake*
$$\text{event structure} = \begin{bmatrix} E1 = e1: \text{process} \\ E2 = e2: \text{state} \\ e1 <_\alpha e2 \\ \text{head: underspecified} \end{bmatrix}$$
$$\text{argument structure} = \begin{bmatrix} \text{ARG1} = \text{Ken} \\ \text{ARG2} = \text{potatoes} \end{bmatrix}$$
$$\text{qualia structure} = \begin{bmatrix} \text{AGENTIVE} = \textbf{act-on}(e1, \text{Ken}, \text{potatoes}) \\ \text{FORMAL} = \textbf{at}(e2, \text{potatoes}, \text{BAKED}) \end{bmatrix}$$

Both arguments for the lexical representation of the verb *cut* (namely, *John* and *cake*) are taking part in e1 and e2 because an action of cutting requires a person using an instrument until the end of cutting. We show the relation between each subevent expressed by *bake* and *cut* and the involved arguments proposed by Ono (2005) in (21) below:

(21)
	e1	e2
bake	Ken, potatoes	potatoes
cut	John, cake	John, cake

According to Ono (2005), the resultant state event e2 of the verb *bake* involves potatoes but not Ken, and thus, the event expressed by *bake* is an autonomous event. So, when e2 becomes a head event, only the argument *potatoes* is needed and the verb functions as an intransitive. On the other hand, the event expressed by the verb *cut* needs an agent from the beginning of the event to the end, and so, e2 involves the referents of both arguments *John* and *cake*: therefore, this event is not an autonomous event, and even if e2 were to become a head, the two arguments would still be needed. Thus, the verb *cut* cannot function as an intransitive.

Ono (2005) argues that the same explanation goes for other verbs of change of state showing the causative-inchoative alternation, for example *open*, *break* and the like, and verbs not showing the alternation like *build*.

Although the analysis proposed by Ono (2005) is impressive, his account raises one question relating to the event structure and the qualia structure in (20) and (21). It is not clear why the formal role associated with the resultant state subevent contains an agent argument. Let us look at the relevant part of the lexical representation of *cut* in (22).

(22) *cut*
qualia structure = $\begin{bmatrix} \text{AGENTIVE} = \textbf{act-on}(e1, \text{John, cake}) \\ \text{FORMAL} = \textbf{at}(e2, \text{John \& cake, CUT}) \end{bmatrix}$

According to Ono's explanation, the verb *cut*, which does not show the causative-inchoative alternation, is supposed to contain an agent argument John in the resultant state subevent e2. However, it is not clear whether the resultant state subevent includes an agent as one of its arguments, because the quale in the formal role in (22) represents the state of an entity which was cut, and for John to cut the cake does not require John to be cut as well. We need to further consider which argument is involved or taking part in which subevent in (22).

We consider the notion of an autonomous event, which many researchers as well as Ono (2005) discuss, to be relevant to the causative-inchoative alternation. Furthermore, we maintain that the distinction between an autonomous event and a non-autonomous event should be made by the participants which are involved in the subevent of movement or change, not by the participants in the resultant state subevent. For example, in the example *Potatoes baked in the oven* in (18b), the verb *bake* expresses an autonomous event because potatoes undergo change in the oven after Ken puts them there and Ken, the agent, is irrelevant to the potatoes' change of state once the oven begins to work. In this respect, this verb focuses on the change of state of potatoes, not Ken's activity. On the other hand, in the example **The cake cut with a small knife* in (19b), the event expressed by the verb *cut* is not an autonomous event because this verb does not focus on the change of state of a cake but on John's action accompanying use of an instrument.

In (7) we assumed that an autonomous event is denoted by the **move** function and a non-autonomous one by the **cause-move** function. Thus, we argue that a whole event is autonomous if a referent undergoing change of state or movement appears as a single argument in a subevent of movement or change which is included in the entire event.

We consider the relation between each subevent and involved arguments to be the one in (23), where we add the subevent of movement or change.

(23)
	e1	e2	e3
bake	Ken, potatoes	potatoes	potatoes
cut	John, cake	John, cake	cake

In e2 of *bake* only a referent undergoing change of state, that is, potatoes, appears as an argument, the whole event expressed by *bake* is autonomous, and this verb shows the causative-inchoative alternation. Based on the relation shown in (23), we propose the lexical representation of *cut* as the one in (24).

(24) *cut*

event structure = $\begin{bmatrix} E1 = e1: \text{process} \\ E2 = e2: \text{process} \\ E3 = e3: \text{state} \\ e1o_\propto e2 \quad e2<_\propto e3 \\ \text{head: } e1 \end{bmatrix}$

argument structure = $\begin{bmatrix} \text{ARG1 = Ken} \\ \text{ARG2 = cake} \\ \text{S-ARG3 = knife} \end{bmatrix}$

qualia structure = $\begin{bmatrix} \text{AGENTIVE} = \textbf{act-on}(e1, \text{John, cake}) \\ \quad\quad\quad\quad\quad \textbf{cause-move}(e2, \text{John, cake}) \\ \quad\quad\quad\quad\quad [\text{FORMAL} = \textbf{with}(e, \text{John, knife})] \\ \text{FORMAL} = \textbf{at}(e3, \text{cake, CUT}) \end{bmatrix}$

In (24), the agentive role itself contains the formal role because during John's acting on the cake and his causing it to be changed John holds a knife. As we saw in section 2.3, a formal role distinguishes an object or an event within a larger domain: that is, an object's formal role denotes the object's property such as its shape or color, and an event's formal role denotes a situation in which the event happens. Regarding the verb *cut*, John's acting on the cake and causing it to be changed accompany his holding a knife, and so *cut*'s agentive role holds the formal role **with** (e, John, knife). Subevent 2 and its associated agentive quale, **cause-move** (e2, John, cake), denote that John takes part in the cake's change, and due to this subevent *cut* is used only as a transitive verb. The subevent e3 and the formal role associated with e3, namely **at** (e3, cake, CUT) represent the resultant state properly.

In this subsection we saw that by assuming the subevent of movement or change we could modify the analysis by Ono (2005) and explain the causative-inchoative alternation appropriately.

4.2.3   *Spray/load* Verbs and the Subevent of Movement

In this subsection we focus on *spray/load* verbs and show that our system of event structure, which contains the subevent of movement or change, represents lexical representations of this class of verbs appropriately and that these representations also account for the linguistic behavior of verbs belonging to this class of verbs, especially the possibility of verbs' participation in the causative-inchoative alternation and co-occurrence with *to*-phrases.

The verb *spray* appears in locative alternation sentences, as is shown in (25). The sentence in (25a) has generally been considered to denote the event of paint moving to the wall.

(25) a. Jack sprayed paint onto the wall.   the location-type
     b. Jack sprayed the wall with paint.   the *with*-type

This verb can co-occur not only with an *onto*-phrase and an *on*-phrase but also with a *to*-phrase or a *toward*-phrase and, moreover, the PPs can be omitted.

(26) a. Jack sprayed paint to the wall.
     b. Pat sprayed the paint toward the window.   (Goldberg (1995: 175))
     c. Tom sprayed paint.

Example (26b) shows that the verb *spray* in this construction does not necessarily imply that the paint reaches the window, and this shows that the complex event expressed by *spray* consists of a process subevent of jetting the paint out and a process subevent of the paint's movement. Tenny (2001) makes a similar suggestion. She argues that *send*, which belongs to the verb class expressing change of location of some entity, can take a *to*-phrase because this verb has the subevent of movement in its event structure.

(27) She sent the letter to America by airmail.

She also suggests that the event structure of *spray* contains a process subevent of movement. We maintain that the lexical representation of *spray* consists of a process subevent of an activity and a process subevent of movement but does not contain a result subevent, and furthermore, we maintain that the telic role of *spray*, the role which expresses the purpose of activities denoted by the verb, contains **with** (e3, z, y): this quale denotes that the referent of z has the referent of y. The representation of *spray* we propose is given in (28).

(28) *spray*

$$\text{event structure} = \begin{bmatrix} \text{E1 = process} \\ \text{E2 = process} \\ \text{e1} <_\alpha \text{e2} \\ \text{head: underspecified} \end{bmatrix}$$

$$\text{qualia structure} = \begin{bmatrix} \text{AGENTIVE} = \begin{bmatrix} \textbf{act-on}(\text{e1, x, y}) \\ \textbf{move}(\text{e2, y}) \end{bmatrix} \\ \text{TELIC} = [\textbf{with}(\text{e, z, y})] \end{bmatrix}$$

(z: location)

The verbal expression *spray NP onto NP* in (25a) is derived by the co-composition operation which we mentioned in section 3.2.[5] The preposition *onto* has the following lexical representation.

(29) *onto*

$$\text{event structure} = \begin{bmatrix} \text{E1 = e1: process} \\ \text{E2 = e2: state} \\ \text{e1} <_\alpha \text{e2} \\ \text{head: e2} \end{bmatrix}$$

$$\text{argument structure} = \begin{bmatrix} \text{ARG1 = y} \\ \text{ARG2 = z} \end{bmatrix}$$

$$\text{qualia structure} = \begin{bmatrix} \text{AGENTIVE} = \textbf{move}(\text{e1, y}) \\ \text{FORMAL} = \textbf{at}(\text{e2, y, z}) \end{bmatrix}$$

Because the qualia associated with the process subevent e2 of *spray* and the process subevent e1 of *onto* are both **move** (e, y), *spray* and *onto* are combined and forms the verbal expression *spray NP onto NP*.[6]

In contrast to *spray*, the verb *load*, though it shows the locative alternation, co-occurs with neither *to*-phrases nor *toward*-phrases:

(30) a. Bill loaded cartons onto the truck.
    b. Bill loaded the truck with cartons.
    c. *Bill loaded cartons to/toward the truck.

This difference between *spray* and *load* can be ascribed to whether the event structure of these verbs contains a subevent of movement or not. The adverbial phrase *all the way* makes clear the distinction of these two verbs:

(31) a. Jack sprayed the paint all the way.
    b. *Bill loaded the carton all the way.

Since the adverbial *all the way* modifies a path of movement, co-occurrence with this phrase shows the existence of the subevent of movement: *spray* in (31a) contains the subevent in question but *load* does not.[7] The representation of *load* is in (32):

(32) *load*
event structure = $\begin{bmatrix} E1 = e1: \text{process} \\ E2 = e2: \text{state} \\ E3 = e3: \text{state} \\ e_1 <_\alpha e_2 \quad e_2 o_\alpha e_3 \\ \text{head: e1} \end{bmatrix}$

qualia structure = $\begin{bmatrix} \text{AGENTIVE} = \textbf{act-on}(e1, x, y) \\ \text{FORMAL} = \textbf{at}(e2, y, z) \\ \text{TELIC} = \textbf{with}(e3, z, y) \end{bmatrix}$
(z: location)

We assume that the head event in the event structure of *load* is lexically determined, namely, event 1.

However, seeing (29) and (30a), we immediately notice a problem of our assumption about the mechanism of co-composition. In discussing the case of *spray NP onto NP*, we assumed that the event structure of *spray* and that of *onto* are combined by co-composition because the qualia corresponding to event 2 of *spray* and the one corresponding to event 1 of *onto* are the same, **move** (e, y). However, as for the case of *load NP onto NP*, although the event structure of *load* lacks the process subevent of movement, it seems to be combined with that of *onto* as in (30a).

Here we should note that the lexical representation of *load* in itself contains the resultant state subevent, while that of *spray* does not (Compare (32) with (28)). Furthermore, in the lexical representation of *onto* the resultant state subevent is the head, and the resultant state subevent of *load* and that of *onto* are temporally overlapping. So, we assume that the event structures of *load* and *onto* are combined owing to *onto*'s headedness and the temporal overlapping of the relevant two subevents.[8]

The prepositions *onto* and *to* are different in that in the event structure of *onto* the head event is the state subevent but in that of *to* the head is underspecified.[9] The representation of *to* is repeated below:

(33) *to*
event structure = $\begin{bmatrix} E1 = e1: \text{process} \\ E2 = e2: \text{state} \\ e1 <_\alpha e2 \\ \text{head: underspecified} \end{bmatrix}$
argument structure = $\begin{bmatrix} ARG1 = x \\ ARG2 = y \end{bmatrix}$
qualia structure = $\begin{bmatrix} AGENTIVE = \textbf{move}(e1, x) \\ FORMAL = \textbf{at}(e2, x, y) \end{bmatrix}$

In the event structure in (33), we find a process subevent and a resultant state subevent, and headedness is underspecified. In other words, in (33) neither of the two subevents is basically prominent, which is different from the event structure of *onto*, where, as we saw in (29), the resultant state subevent is the head. When *to* co-occurs with a verb, the verb's event structure must contain the subevent of movement or change, and if so, the representation of *to* and that of the verb are composed by the co-composition operation. The preposition *to* cannot co-occur with the verb *load* since the event structure of this verb does not contain the subevent of movement.

Thus, we tentatively assume the condition for the co-composition operation as the one below.

(34) The Condition for the Co-composition Operation[10]
   If the event structure of a verb contains a subevent of movement or change and arguments associated with this subevent are the same as arguments which are associated with the subevent of movement or change of a prepositional phrase, the event structures of the verb and the prepositional phrase must be combined.

Thus, the example in (25a), repeated as (35) below, is the case where the co-composition operation works.

(35) Jack sprayed paint onto the wall.

As we saw, the event structure of *spray* in (28) contains the subevent of movement e2 and the argument associated with e2 is paint, and the event structure of *onto* in (29) also has the subevent of movement e1 and the argument associated with e1 is paint. So, the event structures of *spray* and *onto* are combined and the semantic representation of (35) is derived.

As for the causative-inchoative alternation, *spray* has an intransitive form of the location-type but *load* does not.

(36) a. Jack sprayed paint onto the wall.
   b. Bill loaded boxes onto the truck.
(37) a. Paint sprayed onto the wall.
   b. *Boxes loaded on the wagon. (Maruta (2000: 254))

Based on the lexical representations of *spray* in (28) and *load* in (32), we can schematically show the relation between each subevent contained in the event structures of both verbs and associated arguments as in (38).

(38)
	act	move	state
spray	Jack, paint	paint	paint
load	Bill, boxes		boxes

As we contended in section 4.2.2, the subevent relevant for the causative-inchoative alternation is the subevent of movement or change. The event structure of *load* does not contain this type of subevent and this lack of the relevant subevent prevents this verb from functioning as an intransitive.

We argue that containing the subevent of movement or change in the event structure is a necessary condition both for the causative-inchoative alternation and for co-occurrence with a *to*-phrase.[13] Table 1 shows whether the verbs which exhibit the transitive locative alternation have the inchoative use and whether they co-occur with the preposition *to*. This table seems to support our suggestion. This table only shows whether the dictionary contains the intransitive use and examples where each verb co-occurs with *to*. So we need to do more careful research on usage of these verbs. (The verbs in Table 1 are listed in Kageyama (2001: 105), and "?" indicates that the verb in question is not included in the dictionary.)[12]

In this subsection we have considered the *spray/load* verbs, based on our proposal of the event of movement or change. Furthermore, we have shown that our proposal accounts for the causative-inchoative alternation of these verbs and the possibility of their co-occurrence with a *to*-phrase.

Table 1. Inchoative use and co-occurrence with *to* of verbs

verb	inchoative use	co-occurrence with *to*	verb	inchoative use	co-occurrence with *to*
grease	not found	not found	spray	ok	ok
brush	not found	not found	sprinkle	ok	ok
dab	not found	not found	squirt	ok	ok
daub	not found	not found	bestrew	?	?
plaster	ok	ok	scatter	ok	ok
rub	not found	not found	sow	not found	not found
smear	not found	not found	strew	not found	not found
smudge	ok?	?	pack	not found	not found
spread	ok	ok	cram	not found	not found
streak	?	?	crowd	ok	not found
heap	ok	ok	jam	ok	ok
pile	ok	ok	stuff	not found	not found
stack	ok	ok	wad	not found	not found
inject	not found	not found	load	not found	not found
spatter	ok	ok	pack	not found	not found
splash	ok	ok	stock	not found	not found
splatter	ok	ok			

4.2.4 Induced Action Alternation

In this subsection we show the relation between the subevent of movement or change and the possibility of induced action alternation. Some examples of this alternation are shown in (39) and (40).

(39) a. The soldiers marched to the forest.
  b. The general marched the soldiers to the forest.
(40) a. The rats ran through the maze.
  b. The psychologist ran the rats through the maze.

Verbs of manner of motion such as *march* and *run* are unergative by nature and cannot basically take an internal argument, as is shown in (41).

(41) a. *The general marched the soldiers.
  b. *The psychologist ran the rats.

However, some verbs of this class function as if they were transitive when prepositional phrases expressing a path or goal co-occur with them. Compare (41) with (39b) and (40b). Many researchers such as Levin and Rappaport Hovav (1995), Kageyama (1996) and Maruta (1998) among others have pointed out the following characteristics of the induced action sentences. Firstly, they contain a goal or path prepositional phrase. Secondly, they have several interpretations: in one the referent of an external argument induces that of an internal argument to move, and in another interpretation an external argument's referent induces itself and an internal argument's referent to move together. Thus, (39b) has interpretations like the following: the general made the soldiers march to the forest and he just watched them walk; he made them march to the forest and he himself marched with them.

We assume the lexical representation of the verb *march* as the one in (42).

(42) *march*
  event structure = $\begin{bmatrix} E1 = e1: \text{process} \\ E2 = e2: \text{process} \\ e1o_\propto e2 \\ \text{head: } e1 \end{bmatrix}$
  argument structure = [ARG1= x]

$$\text{qualia structure} = \begin{bmatrix} \text{AGENTIVE} = \mathbf{act}\,(e1, x) \\ \mathbf{move}(e2, x) \end{bmatrix}$$

The representation in (42) represents that argument x does the action of marching, and by doing so, x moves. Thus, only argument x appears in syntax and *march* acts as an intransitive verb.

Then, why can the NPs appear after the verbs in (39b) and (40b)? We suggest that this is because the event structure and the qualia structure (and the argument structure) of the prepositional phrases are combined with those of the verbs in the semantic representation of these examples. We repeat the lexical representation of *to* below:

(43) *to*
$$\text{event structure} = \begin{bmatrix} E1 = e1\text{: process} \\ E2 = e2\text{: state} \\ e1 <_\alpha e2 \\ \text{head: underspecified} \end{bmatrix}$$
$$\text{argument structure} = \begin{bmatrix} \text{ARG1} = y \\ \text{ARG2} = z \end{bmatrix}$$
$$\text{qualia structure} = \begin{bmatrix} \text{AGENTIVE} = \mathbf{move}(e1, y) \\ \text{FORMAL} = \mathbf{at}(e2, y, z) \end{bmatrix}$$

In the argument structure in (43) there are two arguments: y represents a moving entity and z represents a goal. The qualia structure represents the referent of argument y undergoing change of location and its existence at the location expressed by argument z.

When verbs of manner of motion like *march* and *walk* co-occur with prepositional phrases such as *to*, the event structures of the verb and the PP are combined through co-composition in the semantic representation. The semantic representation of the verbal expression *march to* in (39a), which is repeated as (44a), is the one in (44b).

(44) a.   The soldiers marched to the forest.

b. *march to*

$$\text{event structure} = \begin{bmatrix} E1 = e1\text{: process} \\ E2 = e2\text{: process} \\ E3 = e3\text{: state} \\ e1o_\alpha e2 \quad e2<_\alpha e3 \\ \text{head: } e1 \end{bmatrix}$$

$$\text{argument structure} = \begin{bmatrix} \text{ARG1} = x\text{: soldiers} \\ \text{ARG2} = y\text{: forest} \end{bmatrix}$$

$$\text{qualia structure} = \begin{bmatrix} \text{AGENTIVE} = \begin{bmatrix} \textbf{act}(e1, \text{soldiers}) \\ \textbf{move}(e2, \text{soldiers}) \end{bmatrix} \\ \text{FORMAL} = [\textbf{at}(e3, \text{soldiers}, \text{forest})] \end{bmatrix}$$

The co-composition operation, satisfying the condition in (34) we have proposed in subsection 4.2.3, works here. The relevant event structures and associated qualia are schematically shown in (45).

(45) *march* event1: **act**(e1, x) o_α (event2: **move**(e2, x)
 to event1: **move**(e1, x)) <_αevent2: **at**(e2, x, y)
 ↓
 march to event1: **act**(e1, x) o_α event2: **move**(e2, x) <_αevent3: **at**(e3, x, y)

In the rectangle in (45), the functions of the relevant subevents are the same type, **move**, the xs of both the verb *march* and the preposition *to* refer to the same referent (namely, soldiers), which undergoes movement, and these two subevents temporally overlap.

We argue that induced action sentences such as (39b) and (40b) are formed when the referents of the arguments of the verb and the preposition are different. The relevant event structures and associated qualia of (39b) are shown in (46).

(46) *march* event1: **act**(e1, x) o_α (event2: **move**(e2, x)
 to event1: **move**(e1, z)) <_αevent2: **at**(e2, z, y)
 ↓
 march to event1: **act**(e1, x) o_αevent2: **move**(e2, z(&x))
 <_αevent3: **at**(e3, z(&x), y)

In *march*'s representation in (46) the entity which has an intention to move and, at the same time, moves is x, while in *to*'s representation the moving entity is z: the moving entities expressed by *march* and *to* are different. These structures do not meet the condition for co-composition we saw in (34), and in this point, this co-composition operation is an exceptional one. We suggest that the semantic representation of (39b) is the one in (47).

(47) *march NP to NP*

event structure = $\begin{bmatrix} E1 = e1\text{: process} \\ E2 = e2\text{: process} \\ E3 = e3\text{: state} \\ e1o_\alpha e2 \quad e2<_\alpha e3 \\ \text{head: e1} \end{bmatrix}$

argument structure = $\begin{bmatrix} ARG1 = x\text{: general} \\ ARG2 = z\text{: soldiers} \\ ARG3 = y\text{: forest} \end{bmatrix}$

qualia structure = $\begin{bmatrix} \text{AGENTIVE} = \begin{bmatrix} \mathbf{act}(e1, \text{general}) \\ \mathbf{move}(e2, \text{soldiers (\& general)}) \end{bmatrix} \\ \text{FORMAL} = [\mathbf{at}(e3, \text{soldiers (\& general), forest})] \end{bmatrix}$

In (47) it is represented that the general has an intention to move but that soldiers move by marching. In the agentive role associated with subevent e2 in (47) remains the argument, general, which is originally contained in the representation of *march*. So, (47) denotes the interpretations of (39b) that the general made an order and kept watching the soldiers march or that the general made an order and marched together with the soldiers.

As we mentioned above, this kind of co-composition operation is an exceptional one, because the condition we saw in (34) is not met in this case: the referents of the arguments in the subevents of movement of both *march* and *to* are different. We consider that this exceptional operation may be permitted because the internal argument position of the verb is available.

In this subsection we have seen that by assuming the subevent of movement we can explain the relation between the semantic representation of induced action sentences such as (39b) and (40b) and that of verbs appearing in those sentences. As we mentioned above, we consider the semantic representation of these sentences to be formed by an exceptional operation of co-composition, and resolution of the precise mechanism working in this case is left for further research.

4.3 Summary

In this chapter we proposed the event structure for movement or change, which represents change in an action chain consisting of action, change and resultant state. From this proposal we suggested the possible event types of the event structure in (10). We showed that the adoption of the event of movement or change suggests necessary conditions for the causative-inchoative alternation of verbs. Furthermore, utilizing the event of movement or change, we theoretically explained the possibility of addition of double goal phrases to motion verbs and the possibility of induced action alternation.

In this chapter we have revealed the constitution of event structure. In the next chapter we will study a notion relevant to this structure, namely headedness, and the constitution of qualia structure and the interaction of headedness, event structure and qualia structure.

Endnotes

1 As we mentioned in section 3.2.1, Pustejovsky (1995) assumes the movement subevent for some verbs.
2 Pustejovsky (1995: 81–83) argues that the head subevent of *build* is event 1 and that this verb's transitivity derives from its headedness.
3 We will discuss the lexical representation of *to* in chapter 6 in detail.
4 For a precise discussion as to the Binary / Polar opposition and the lexical representation, see Isono 2010a.
5 We discuss the co-composition operation in detail in section 6.2.
6 In order to explain the *with*-type of *spray* in (25b) we need to work out the representation of *spray* in (28). The discussions and the representations of verbs of emission we propose in chapter 5 will give us a clue to do it.
7 Tenny (2001), using the same phrase, argues that *put* does not have the event of movement, based on the fact that this verb does not co-occur with this phrase.
8 We consider this case to be an exception to the condition we propose in (34).
9 See the discussion in section 6.1.4. There we will argue the head subevent of the preposition *into*, which undergoes the locative inversion, is the state subevent and that that of *to* is underspecified. We will see the preposition *onto* also undergoes locative inversion, which shows that the state subevent is the head in its representation.
10 One more condition should be added here. Namely, the subevent of movement or change of a verb and that of a preposition are temporally overlapping. The final version of this condition appears in section 6.2.

11 Tenny (2001) also makes the same claim in her discussion.
12 KDEC is made use of for Table 1. The verb *smudge* in Table 1 poses a problem to our current discussion.

Chapter 5

Polysemy, Headedness and Qualia Structure: Intransitive Locative Alternation and Verbs of Emission

In the last chapter we discussed the event structure of a lexical item and proposed a subevent of movement or change. In this chapter we explore the characteristics of headedness and the qualia structure. After the discussion in this chapter, together with the findings in the last chapter we will have comprehended the properties of lexical representation as a whole in the Generative Lexicon framework.

As we saw in section 2.3, the qualia structure denotes various aspects of words' meanings, so we regard this structure as playing a crucial role in yielding words' polysemy. In addition, since a quale associated with a head subevent is linked to syntax, the qualia structure and headedness take part in determining verbs' syntactic behaviors. As far as we know, the notion of headedness proposed by Pustejovsky (1995) has not been discussed much in the literature so far, and the mechanism yielding polysemy or variable behaviors of a particular lexical item has not been made clear.

In order to shed light on the notion of headedness and the relation between headedness and the qualia structure and verbs' polysemy and, moreover, to attain overall comprehension of the properties of lexical representation, this chapter deals with verbs of emission, which exhibit various patterns of behavior, including motion verb usage. Examples of variable behaviors of this class of verbs are shown in (1)–(6).

(1) a. Bees buzzed in the bottle. location-type
    b. The bottle buzzed with bees. *with*-type (Salkoff (1983: 301))
(2) a. The stars flashed in the sky.
    b. The sky flashed with stars. (Salkoff (1983: 319))

(3) a. Gnats are buzzing.
  b. The traffic lights were flashing.
(4) a. On the crown sparkled a lot of jewels.
  b. On one hand FLASHES a 14-carat round diamond; on the other hand SPARKLES an 8-carat stone flanked by the diamond-studded initials WN. (L & R (1995: 225))
(5) The stagehand flashed the light.
(6) a. A bee buzzed irritatingly around my head.
  b. She buzzed in for a chat.

Elaborating on lexical representations that can account for the behavior of these verbs, we will discuss the relation among headedness, subevents and the qualia structure, and also suggest the generative characteristics of the qualia structure. The subclasses of emission verbs which are dealt with in this chapter are shown in (7).

(7) a. Verbs of Light Emission: beam, blaze, flame, flash, flicker, gleam, glimmer...
  b. Verbs of Sound Emission: babble, bang, beat, beep, bellow, buzz, chatter, clack, clatter, ding, groan, growl, jangle...
  (Levin (1993: 234–236))

Emission verbs, which undergo intransitive locative alternation as is shown in (1)–(2), behave sometimes as unergative verbs and at other times as unaccusative verbs. The verbs of this class are used in the progressive form, which suggests that these are activity verbs, that is, unergative verbs (See (3).). On the other hand, as is shown in (4), these verbs, accompanying locational prepositional phrases, appear in locative inversion sentences. Verbs appearing in locative inversion sentences are generally classified as unaccusative (But see Levin & Rappaport Hovav (1995)). In addition, verbs in this class take an internal argument and behave as transitive verbs, and, when co-occurring with a directional PP, behave as verbs of motion, as is shown in (5) and (6) respectively.

We propose that the verbs in (1a) and (2a) express existence of some entity and that the ones in (1b) and (2b) express existence of some states. Furthermore, we argue that in the lexical representation of emission verbs, various subevents can become the head. In considering the lexical representation of emission verbs and the semantic representation of sentences in which these verbs appear, we explore general properties of qualia structure, the notion of headedness and event structure. We claim that assignment of headedness to a subevent depends on the nature or meaning of a lexical item: the head subevent in the event structure of some verbs is lexically determined, while the head subevent of other verbs is underspecified. We argue that underspecification of head subevents accounts for characteristics of emission verbs. We also suggest that qualia structure plays a generative role in semantic representation in that this structure should provide information about how the semantic representation is composed. The findings in this chapter will also be crucial to our analysis of the motion-verb usage of emission verbs from the perspective of co-composition in the next chapter.

In this chapter, in section 5.1 we examine the characteristics of intransitive locative alternation, which most emission verbs undergo. Based on those characteristics, we specify conditions on verbs which undergo intransitive locative alternation and propose the lexical representation of emission verbs in section 5.2. In section 5.3 we show that the lexical representation of emission verbs proposed in section 5.2 also applies to the semantic representation of the sentences where emission verbs appear. In section 5.4 we consider further the elaboration of the lexical representation of emission verbs and the functions of the qualia structure. We see the relation between omission of *with*-phrases in locative alternation sentences and the qualia structure of verbs appearing in these sentences. In section 5.5 we summarize this chapter.[1]

5.1 Characteristics of Intransitive Locative Alternation Sentences

Examples of intransitive locative alternation are given below in (8)–(10).

(8) a. Bees buzzed in the bottle.   (=(1))   location-type
    b. The bottle buzzed with bees.   *with*-type
(9) a. The stars flashed in the sky.   (=(2))
    b. The sky flashed with stars.   (Salkoff (1983: 319))
(10) a. Jewels sparkled on the crown.
    b. The crown sparkled with jewels.
(11) a. Jack sprayed paint onto the wall.
    b. Jack sprayed the wall with paint.

As for the transitive LA exemplified in (11), extensive research has been conducted by Rappaport and Levin (1988) and Pinker (1989) among others, and there is a general consensus among lexical semanticists that verbs appearing in this type of LA express "causation of movement of some entity" in (11a) and express "change of state of some location" in (11b). On the other hand, the intransitive LA as shown in (8)–(10) has not been studied as much, with exceptions like Salkoff (1983) who gives a precise descriptive analysis of intransitive LA sentences, and Dowty (2000) among others. In this section we survey the characteristics of intransitive LA sentences based on Salkoff (1983).

According to Salkoff (1983), intransitive LA sentences have four main characteristics. Firstly, the *with*-type has a holistic interpretation: (9b) has the interpretation that the whole sky seemed to be covered with stars although (9a) can mean that only a few stars flashed and were in the sky. The *with*-type implies that some location, e.g. the bottle, the sky, etc., is entirely covered with some entity, for example, bees and stars, and so this type is also considered to express a state in which some location is affected (by some entity). The second characteristic, which is related to the first one, is that in the *with*-type the object NP of the preposition *with*, which refers to some entity (or some locatum), is in a plural form or a collective noun (Salkoff (1983: 292–293)). Thirdly, in the location-type the preposition *in* is most frequently utilized, with *on* the second most common. The preposition *into* implying motion is only used in very limited cases and *to* is hardly used at all. From the kinds of prepositions utilized, we can conclude that location-type sentences do not fundamentally express motion to some location. Fourthly, based on the data shown in Salkoff (1985), Dowty (2000: 115–117) suggests that most verbs undergoing LA express primitive activities and that such activities can be recognized instantly or with only a look at some parts of location where those activities are being performed. He classifies LA verbs into five classes, as is shown in (12) below.[2]

(12) a. Physical movements visually readily recognizable and at a 'small scale', usually found occurring repetitively: *crawl, drip, bubble, dance, hop, run, shake, shiver*…
 b. Animal sounds and other perceptually simple sounds: *hum, buzz, twitter, creak, boom*…
 c. Conceptually simple visual perception of some kind of light emission: *beam, blaze, brighten, glow, flash, glimmer, glitter, shimmer*…

d. Smells: *reek*, *smell*…
   e. Predicates indicating degree of occupancy or abundance: *abound*, *teem*, *be rich*…

As for the verbs in (12a), when a fountain is bubbling or a hand is shaking, these are recognized in a moment, and when someone's body shivers or a dance floor shakes, those are perceived if only some parts of the objects, not the whole of them, are seen. That is, in the latter cases, parts of some entity or location make the same move as the whole. Since verbs in (12b)–(12d) denote sound, light and smell, they are perceived instantly. We should note that if there is some sound, light or smell at some location, the sound, light or smell can be easily perceived and recognized and may characterize the location: that is, the existence of the sound etc. characterizes the location. In this respect, the fourth characteristic is closely related to the first one, that is, some location is affected.

Taking into consideration the four characteristics we have just seen, we next consider conditions under which verbs undergo LA and propose the lexical representation of emission verbs.

5.2 Conditions for Locative Alternation and Representation of Emission Verbs: Locative Alternation and Locative Inversion

In this section, based on the observation we summarized in the last section, we argue that LA verbs have two fundamental characteristics:

(13) a. LA verbs express existence and some activity of some entity.
   b. Existence of some entity affects or characterizes some location.

Many LA verbs can appear in locative inversion (henceforth, LI) sentences. Examples of LI sentences are given in (14), where the subject NP and the locational-directional PP are inverted.

(14) a. Into this room ran a number of boys.
   b. On the horizon appeared a large ship.

LI sentences, where verbs of existence or appearance are most commonly used, are considered to express the existence of some entity at some place.

Many LA verbs can appear in LI sentences and vice versa (cf. Levin (1993)). Verb classes which can occur in both constructions are the ones in (15)–(22).[3]

(15) Verbs of Light Emission: *beam, blaze, flame, flash, gleam, glimmer...*
    a. Jewels sparkled on the crown. (Levin (1993: 234))
    b. The crown sparkled with jewels. (ibid.)
    c. On the crown sparkled a lot of jewels.

(16) Verbs of Sound Emission: *babble, beat, beep, boom, buzz...*
    a. The cries of geese and turkeys rang out in the barn.
    b. We went into a barn that rang out with the cries of geese and turkeys...
    c. In the barn rang out the cries of geese and turkeys.

(17) Verbs of Smell Emission: *reek, smell, stink*

(18) Verbs of Substance Emission: *bleed, bubble, dribble, drip, gush, leak, ooze...*

(19) Verbs of Entity-Specific Modes of Being: *bloom, blossom, bristle, sprout...*
    a. Roses flowered in the garden. (Levin (1993: 251))
    b. The garden flowered with roses. (ibid.)
    c. In the garden flowered roses.

(20) Verbs of Modes of Being Involving Motion: *dance, flutter, shake, sway...*
    a. A large flag fluttered over the fort. (Levin (1993: 252))
    b. The stadium fluttered with handkerchiefs. (Salkoff (1983: 303))
    c. Over the fort fluttered a large flag.

(21) Verbs of Sound Existence: *echo, resonate, resound...*

(22) Swarm Verbs: *abound, bustle, crawl, creep, hop, run, swarm...*
    a. Bees are swarming in the garden. (Levin (1993: 253)
    b. The garden is swarming with bees. (ibid.)
    c. In the garden were swarming bees.

Some of the verb classes which can appear neither in LA sentences nor in LI sentences are shown in (23)–(26) below.

(23) Herd Verbs: *accumulate, amass, assemble...*
    a. The cattle are herding in the pasture. (Levin (1993: 254))
    b. *The pasture is herding with cattle. (ibid.)
    c. *In the pasture are herding the cattle.

(24) Bulge Verbs: *bristle, bulge, seethe*
 a. *Groceries are bulging in the bag. (Levin (1993: 255)
 b. The bag is bulging with groceries. (ibid.)
 c. *In the bag are bulging groceries.
(25) Other Alternating Verbs of Change of State: *abate, advance, age, alter, awake…*
(26) Lodge Verbs: *board, camp, dwell, live, lodge, reside…*

The classes in (27)–(33) can be used only in LI sentences.

(27) Exist Verbs: *exist, extend, linger, loom, tower…*
 a. A crowd of people remained in the square. (Levin (1993: 250))
 b. *The square remained with a crowd of people. (ibid.)
 c. ?In the square remained a crowd of people.
(28) Verbs of Spatial Configuration: *balance, bend, bow, crouch, dangle…*
 a. A statue of Jefferson stood on the corner of the two boulevards.
  (Levin (1993: 255))
 b. *The corner of the two boulevards stood with a statue of Jefferson.
 c. On the corner of the two boulevards stood a statue of Jefferson. (ibid.)
(29) Appear Verbs: *appear, arise, break, come, emerge…*
(30) Verbs of Occurrence: *ensue, happen, occur…*
(31) Verbs of Body-Internal Motion: *fidget, flap, kick, sway, totter…*
(32) Verbs of Assuming a Position: *bend, bow, crouch, kneel, slouch…*
(33) Verbs of Inherently Directed Motion: *advance, arrive, enter, go…*

We consider that the verb classes in (27)–(33) do not undergo LA because they do not hold meanings having the characteristics of LA verbs in (13), as we will discuss later concerning (42).

5.2.1 The Location-type

In this subsection we see linguistic phenomena which suggest that LA verbs express some activity and existence of some entity. Nakajima (2001) proposes the semantic representation of LI verbs in (34).[4]

(34) ei = final event (Nakajima (2001: 46))
event structure = $\begin{bmatrix} ... \\ Ei = ei: state \\ head: ei \end{bmatrix}$
argument structure = $\begin{bmatrix} ARG1 = x \\ ARG2 = y \end{bmatrix}$
qualia structure = $\begin{bmatrix} ... \\ FORMAL = \textbf{at}\,(ei, x, y) \\ ... \end{bmatrix}$

In (34) the head subevent is the temporally last one, which is represented as Ei, even if there are several subevents in the verb's event structure, and the head event must be a state. In the argument structure two arguments are represented, and the formal role in the qualia structure represents the existence of argument x in the place denoted by argument y in the final state subevent. Thus, LI verbs denote that some entity exists at some location.

We consider that the lexical representation of the verbs in (15)–(22) has some characteristics in common with the representation in (34), because these verbs can be used in LI sentences as well as LA sentences. We argue that the lexical representation of LA verbs contains **at** (e, x, y) in its formal role as (34) does. This proposal is supported by three kinds of evidence.

The first evidence comes from *there* construction. The verb *sparkle* can be used in *there* construction sentences as is shown in (35).

(35) There sparkled a magnificent diamond on his finger.

Note that an argument PP can follow a post verbal NP as we can see in (36a). On the other hand, in this order neither an adjunct PP in (36b) nor a PP in (36c) which is introduced by the co-composition operation is judged acceptable.

(36) a. There appeared a ship on the horizon. (Levin (1993: 89))
   b. *There ran a little boy in the yard. (Levin (1993: 90))
   c. ??There darted a little boy into the room. (Levin (1993: 89))

These facts suggest that the PP in (35) is an argument phrase of *sparkle*, and its representation contains **at** (e, x, y).

It is also well-known that Japanese has LA sentences (e.g. *Ongaku-ga heyaju-ni nari-hibii-te-iru.* 'Music resounds through the room.' (location-type) vs. *Heya-ju-ga ongaku-de nari-hibii-te-iru.* 'The room resounds with music.' (*with*-type)) Japanese verb classes which undergo LA also resemble English verb classes. Examples of Japanese LA verbs are the following: *nuru* 'paint, smear', *yamazumini-suru* 'heap, pile', *tumeru* 'stuff', *kagayaku* 'sparkle, twinkle, glitter', *hankyo-suru* 'echo' (Compare English LA verbs in (15)–(22) and see Kishimoto (2001) for the list of English and Japanese LA verbs).

Japanese LA sentences in (37) and (38) sound awkward when used as independent ones, while the examples in (39) and (40), where *teiru* is added to the verbs, seem natural.

(37) a. ??Omotya-ga   heya-ni   tiraka-ru.
         toys-NOM   room-LOC   litter-PRES
        'Toys litter the room.'
     b. ??Heya-ga   omotya-de   tiraka-ru.
         room-NOM   toys-with   litter-PRES
        'The room is littered with toys.'
(38) a. ??Hito-ga   miti-ni   afure-ru.
         People-NOM   street-LOC   fill-PRES
        'People fill the street.'
     b. ??Miti-ga   hito-de   afure-ru.
         Street-NOM   people-with fill-PRES
        'The street is full of people.'
(39) a. Omotya-ga   heya-ni   tirakat-teiru.
         toys-NOM   room-LOC   litter-ing. PRES
     b. Heya-ga   omotya-de   tirakat-teiru.
         room-NOM   toys-with   litter-ing. PRES
(40) a. Hito-ga   miti-ni   ahure-teiru.
         People-NOM   street-LOC   fill-ing. PRES
     b. Miti-ga   hito-de   ahure-teiru.
         Street-NOM   people-with fill-ing. PRES

The Japanese suffix *teiru* makes verbs' resultant states salient in their interpretations: for example, (39a) expresses 'the state of toys lying about in the room.' The example (40a) also has a resultant state reading, and we argue that the verbs *tirakaru* and *afureru* contain resultant state subevents expressing the existence of some entity at some location. Thus, we contend that the verbs appearing in Japanese LA sentences contain **at** (e, x, y) in their lexical representation. Japanese LA sentences have the same characteristics as English LA sentences: they express existence of some entity and verb class appearance are common in both, so we consider English LA verbs in the location type to contain resultant state subevents.

The second piece of evidence comes from interpretations of English sentences containing *a lot*. Kageyama (1996) utilizes the phrase *a lot* as a diagnostic of activity verbs: when this phrase co-occurs with activity verbs, it modifies the **act** function in the lexical representation of the verbs and gives interpretations which express the quantity or frequency of activities denoted by those verbs. See (41).

(41) a. The lecturer talked a lot.
 b. She danced a lot.

Now, let us see the interpretations of location-type sentences and sentences without any locational PP, both of which include emission verbs and the phrase *a lot*.

(42) a. Bees buzzed a lot.
 1) Some bees buzzed and were very noisy.
 2) ?Many bees buzzed.
 b. Bees buzzed in my room a lot.
 1) Some bees buzzed and were very noisy.
 2) Many bees buzzed.
(43) a. Diamonds sparkled a lot.
 1) Several diamonds sparkled many times.
 2) ?Many diamonds sparkled.
 b. Diamonds sparkled in the showcase a lot.
 1) Several diamonds sparkled many times.
 2) Many diamonds sparkled.

All the sentences in (42)–(43) have interpretations of a quantity of activities, which are shown as 1 below each example, and hence we can claim that the verbs *buzz* and *sparkle* are activity verbs and contain the **act** function in their lexical representation. What are crucial here are the interpretations in 2, which are permitted when a locational PP co-occurs. In this interpretation, *a lot* does not necessarily modify the quantity of activities expressed by each verb, but can also modify the quantity of entities denoted by the subject NPs, *bees* and *diamonds*. In this way, when emission verbs such as *buzz* and *sparkle* co-occur with a locational PP, these verbs behave as activity verbs giving interpretation 1 and as another type of verb giving interpretation 2. We should notice that interpretation 2 implies that the entities denoted by the verbs exist at the location expressed by the PPs. Thus, the semantic representations of the entire sentences in (42b) and (43b) contain **at** (e, x, y) in them, which means the semantic representations of these examples have both **act** (e, x) and **at** (e, x, y).

5.2.2 The *With*-type

In this subsection we consider the meanings expressed by *with*-type LA sentences and the semantic relation between the *with*-type in (44b) and the location-type in (44a).

(44) a. The stars sparkled in the sky.
 b. The sky sparkled with stars. (Salkoff (1983: 319))
 c. The beach is swarming with bathers.
 cf. The room shimmered with light, a treasure house of precious cloths and beautiful jewels. (BNC, HH5: 3125)

The verb *sparkle* in (44a) is basically considered an activity verb, and as we just saw in the previous subsection, (44a) expresses the stars' existence in the sky. In the interpretation of the location-type (44a), a semantic focus is put on the stars or the light emitted by the stars. In the *with*-type, LA verbs can be used in the progressive form such as (44c), so the verbs in this type are activity verbs. However, we consider the *with*-type to also express the state of some location as Salkoff (1983) and Maruta (2001) have already pointed out. Thus, the *with*-type sentence in (44b) is ambiguous: it has both an activity reading and a state reading. In the state reading, the semantic focus is put on the state of the sky. This interpretation is to be formed based on our world knowledge: that is, the light of the stars affects the sky and causes it to be changed in its character. Furthermore, such world knowledge is reflected in the qualia structure. The location-type focuses on the existence of some entity, and the *with*-type expresses the some location's resultant state caused by the existence of the entity as well as the entity's activity at the location. Thus, as we mentioned at the beginning of the present section, we maintain that when LA verbs co-occur with a locational PP, they express the existence of some entity as well as some activity of it and, at the same time, this existence of the entity affects or characterizes a relevant location, which leads to the interpretation of *with*-type sentences. This is the reason the verbs in (27)–(33) cannot undergo LA. These verbs are used in LI and location-type LA sentences but are not in *with*-type sentences, because they do not express state of locations.

This claim that the *with*-type such as the one in (44b) expresses a state as well as an activity is based on Salkoff's (1983: 299–306) observation that "[t]he majority of the verbs in this study [about 75% of them]can be adjectivalized by a prefix or a suffix, most frequently in the T form [the *with*-form, in the present paper]." Some of the examples shown in Salkoff (1983) are in (45).

(45) a. The sky   blazed / was ablaze   with stars.
     b. The cushion   crawls / is crawly   with vermin.

The verbs used in the *with*-type can be replaced with related adjectives, which means these *with*-types express state events.[5]

Next, *with*-type sentences do not co-occur with frame *in*-phrases.

(46) a. *The forest blazed with autumn foliage in two weeks.
     b. *The garden swarmed with bees in an hour.
     c. The garden swarmed with bees.
         c = (i) The garden was full of a lot of bees.
           ≠ (ii) The garden became filled with bees.

The forcible interpretation of the examples (46a) and (46b) is an event delay reading: thus, that of (46a) is "The forest began to blaze with autumn foliage two weeks later." Furthermore, the interpretation of (46c) is not (ii) but (i), and so this example does not express a change-of-state event. The verb *blaze* in (46a) also can be replaced with an adjective:

(47) The mountainsides are ablaze with autumn foliage.

Thus, *with*-type sentences express state events and state of locations.

Another piece of evidence which supports the claim that the *with*-type expresses a state is the interpretations of Japanese LA sentences such as (37)–(40). See the examples repeated as (48) and (49) below:

(48) a. ??Heya-ga   omotya-de   tiraka-ru.
        room-NOM   toys-with   litter-PRES
   b. Heya-ga   omotya-de   tirakat-teiru.
        room-NOM   toys-with   litter-ing. PRES
        'The room is littered with toys.'

(49) a. *Miti-ga   hito-de   afure-ru.
        Street-NOM   people-with fill-PRES
   b. Miti-ga   hito-de   afhure-teiru.
        Street-NOM   people-with fill-ing. PRES
        'The street is full of people.'

(48b) and (49b) are better in acceptability in contrast to (48a) and (49a) in which the aspectual suffix -*teiru* is not added. In Japanese there is a class of state verbs which need to be used with -*teiru*: for example, *sobie-ru* "soar" and *men-suru* "front, look out". Verbs of this class express the same meaning when they are relativized: *kawa-ni men-suru biru*, *kawa-ni men-sita biru* and *kawa-ni men-siteiru biru* all express the state of a building, namely "a building which fronts a river." The verb *afure-ru* in (49) behaves in the same way as *men-suru*: *hito-de afure-ru kooen*, *hito-de afure-ta kooen* and *hito-de afure-teiru kooen* all express the state of a park which is full of people. Thus, the difference of acceptability of *with*-type sentences in (48) and (49) shows that the verbs tirakaru "be *littered*" and *afureru* "be full" are state verbs.[6]

Summarizing this section, we have contended that intransitive LA verbs must satisfy the following two conditions, which we mentioned at the beginning:

(50) a. LA verbs express existence and some activity of some entity.
   b. The existence of some entity affects or characterizes the place where the entity exists.

5.3 Meaning Variation of Verbs and Event Structure: Lexical Representation of Locative Alternation Verbs

In this section, we consider examples which contain emission verbs and also propose the lexical representation of LA verbs. The relevant examples are listed in (51):

(51) a. The light flashed.
 b. The stagehand flashed the light.
 c. A bee buzzed irritatingly around my head.
 d. She buzzed in for a chat.
 e. On one hand FLASHES a 14-carat round diamond; on the other hand SPARKLES an 8-carat stone flanked by the diamond-studded initials WN. (L & R (1995: 225))

Maruta (1998: 132) proposes the LCS of the verb *flash*, one of the emission verbs, as the one in (52).

(52) [y OPERATE] CAUSE [BECOME [FLASH IN-EXISTENCE]]

The LCS in (52) represents that the referent of y emits a flash and that the flash exists somewhere in the world. According to Maruta's analysis, this LCS represents the meaning of this verb in (51a). Taking into consideration the fact that this verb undergoes LI as in (51e) and LA, we need to modify (52) since it lacks an argument which corresponds to a PP in LI sentences like *on one hand* in (51e).[7] It might be possible to replace the subevent [FLASH IN-EXISTENCE] with [FLASH BE AT-z] in which AT-z denotes a PP. However, this LCS cannot represent the unergative *flash* in (51a) which lacks a PP.

According to Nakajima (2001), the lexical representation of LI verbs such as *flash* in (51e) is the one in (34), which is repeated as (53):

(53) e_i = final event (Nakajima (2001: 46))
 event structure = $\begin{bmatrix} \ldots \\ E_i = e_i\text{: state} \\ \text{head: } e_i \end{bmatrix}$

$$\text{argument structure} = \begin{bmatrix} \text{ARG1} = x \\ \text{ARG2} = y \end{bmatrix}$$

$$\text{qualia structure} = \begin{bmatrix} \ldots \\ \text{FORMAL} = \mathbf{at}(ei, x, y) \\ \ldots \end{bmatrix}$$

LI verbs express some entity existing in some place, and this existence is represented as **at** (e, x, y) in the qualia structure in (53). Argument y in (53) represents a location and **at** (e, x, y) corresponds to the PP, *on one hand*, in (51e).

As we saw in section 5.2.1, the location-type of LA sentences also expresses the existence of some entity with a locational PP, and this PP is considered to be an argument phrase. In *with*-type sentences a locational NP functions as an argument. Thus, in the lexical representation of emission verbs, an argument corresponding to those locational phrases should be represented.

Thus, the semantic representation of the emission verb *sparkle* is the one in (54). (In (54) "D-E" in the event structure represents a default event, which is implied by a lexical item but is not fundamentally linked to syntax.)

(54) a. *sparkle*

$$\text{event structure} = \begin{bmatrix} \text{E1} = e1\text{: process} \\ \text{E2} = e2\text{: state} \\ e1 o_\propto e2 \\ \text{head: underspecified} \end{bmatrix}$$

$$\text{argument structure} = \begin{bmatrix} \text{ARG1} = x \\ \text{ARG2} = y \end{bmatrix}$$

$$\text{qualia structure} = \begin{bmatrix} \text{FORMAL} = \mathbf{at}(e2, \text{SPARKLE\&}x, y) \\ \text{AGENTIVE} = \mathbf{act}(e1, x) \end{bmatrix}$$

b. *sparkle*

$$\text{event structure} = \begin{bmatrix} \text{E1} = e1\text{: process} \\ \text{E2} = e2\text{: state} \\ \text{D-E3} = e3\text{: state} \\ e1 o_\propto e2 \quad e2 o_\propto e3 \\ \text{head: underspecified} \end{bmatrix}$$

$$\text{argument structure} = \begin{bmatrix} \text{ARG1} = x \\ \text{ARG2} = y \end{bmatrix}$$

$$\text{qualia structure} = \begin{bmatrix} \text{FORMAL} = \textbf{with}(e2, y, \text{SPARKLE\&x}) \\ \textbf{at}(e3, \text{SPARKLE\&x}, y) \\ \text{AGENTIVE} = \textbf{act}(e1, y) \end{bmatrix}$$

This representation is the lexical representation of *sparkle* appearing in various kinds of sentences in (55).

(55) a. Jewels sparkled on the crown. (Levin (1993: 234))
    b. The crown sparkled with jewels. (ibid.)
    c. On the crown sparkled a lot of jewels.
    d. Her earrings sparkled as she turned her head.

(54a) is the representation of *sparkle* appearing in the location-type and (54b) is the one for this verb in the *with*-type. These two representations are closely related because in the formal role of (54b) the quale corresponding to event 2 of (54a), **at** (e, SPARKLE & x, y), is embedded and emitted light, SPARKLE, is contained in both.[8]

In representation (54a) the whole event consists of the two subevents. These are temporally overlapping and the head subevent is underspecified. In its qualia structure the activity of some entity x, which emits light (sparkle), is represented in the agentive role and the existence of the entity and the sparkle is represented in the formal role. In this way, in the qualia structure of (54a) it is represented that some entity does some activity and, at the same time, the entity and the emitted light exist at some location y affected by the entity's activity: the SPARKLE characterizes the location. We suggest that the activity is caused by physical characteristics of some inanimate entity which is an argument of this verb. We consider this activity to be a nonvolitional activity without any purpose, and so it does not operate on other entities. To denote this activity, the function **act**, not **act-on**, is utilized.

When the head is event 1 in (54a), the process event is linked to syntax and the verb in this case behaves as an activity verb in (55d). The verbs in (3), which are given as (56) below, are also within this use.

(56) a. Gnats are buzzing.
    b. The traffic lights were flashing.

In this case the quale associated with event 1 does not contain any argument representing a location, and so, a PP expressing a location is not an obligatory phrase in syntax: that is, a PP is an adjunct and can be omitted.

When event 2 is a head, the verb appears as a verb of existence in syntax and the quale associated with this subevent, **at** (e2, SPARKLE & x, y), contains a location y as an argument, and so, a PP is obligatory in syntax. This verb is the one occurring in the location-type, i.e., (55a). Besides, since this semantic representation is consistent with the representation of LI verbs in (53) when the head is put on the state subevent, the verb is also an LI verb as shown in (55c).

Furthermore, *sparkle* denoted by (54a) co-occurs with PPs such as an *into*-phrase or a *to*-phrase, and this verb behaves as a motion verb through the co-composition operation as we will see in section 6.2.3.

(54b) has **at** (e3, SPARKLE & x, y), which represents that an entity x and sparkles exist in a place y in the formal role, and this is the same as the formal role in (54a). Another formal role in (54b) is **with** (e2, y, SPARKLE & x), which expresses the location having an entity and sparkling.[9] We assume that holding **with** (e2, y, SPARKLE & x) as well as **at** (e3, SPARKLE & x, y) in qualia structure gives rise to a holistic interpretation. That is, having both the interpretation that some sparkles are at some location and the interpretation that the location holds some sparkles leads to a holistic interpretation. In the case of (55a, b), the crown is affected by the sparkles.[10]

When the head is event 2 in (54b), the formal role, related to event 2, is linked to syntax, so the *with*-type of LA sentences is derived, and when the head is event 1, the agentive role related to event 1 appears in syntax, so the verb *sparkle* behaves as an activity verb in a *with*-type sentence.

As we have seen in this subsection, we have proposed that the hypothesis that a head subevent can be underspecified in the lexical representation of some verbs, together with representations such as (54), accounts for various behaviors of emission verbs and the change in adicity of this class of verbs. We generalized the characteristics of verbs undergoing LA in (50) in section 5.2, which we repeat as (57) below:

(57) a. LA verbs express existence and some activity of some entity.
    b. The existence of some entity affects or characterizes the place where the entity exists.

These characteristics are represented in the qualia structure in (54), where the formal role contains **at** (e1, SPARKLE & x, y) and **with** (e2, y, SPARKLE & x). The former role represents that some entity and the light emitted by the entity exist at some location, and the latter that the location holds the entity and the light. We maintain that the existence of the two subevents relating to these qualia derives the characteristics of LA verbs in (57).

5.4 Further Elaboration

In this section we consider further elaboration of the lexical representation of emission verbs and functions of the qualia structure.

5.4.1 The Lexical Representation and The Generative Lexicon

We have proposed the lexical representation of *sparkle* as the one in (54), repeated below as (58), from the last section.

(58) a. *sparkle* (= (54a))

$$\text{event structure} = \begin{bmatrix} E1 = e1: \text{process} \\ E2 = e2: \text{state} \\ e1 o_\alpha e2 \\ \text{head: underspecified} \end{bmatrix}$$

$$\text{argument structure} = \begin{bmatrix} ARG1 = x \\ ARG2 = y \end{bmatrix}$$

$$\text{qualia structure} = \begin{bmatrix} \text{FORMAL} = \textbf{at}(e2, \text{SPARKLE\&x}, y) \\ \text{AGENTIVE} = \textbf{act}(e1, x) \end{bmatrix}$$

b. *sparkle* (= (54b))

$$\text{event structure} = \begin{bmatrix} E1 = e1: \text{process} \\ E2 = e2: \text{state} \\ D\text{-}E3 = e3: \text{state} \\ e1 o_\alpha e2 \quad e2 o_\alpha e3 \\ \text{head: underspecified} \end{bmatrix}$$

$$\text{argument structure} = \begin{bmatrix} ARG1 = x \\ ARG2 = y \end{bmatrix}$$

$$\text{qualia structure} = \begin{bmatrix} \text{FORMAL} = \textbf{with}(e2, y, \text{SPARKLE\&x}) \\ \quad\quad\quad\quad \textbf{at}(e3, \text{SPARKLE\&x}, y) \\ \text{AGENTIVE} = \textbf{act}(e1, y) \end{bmatrix}$$

We argued that the representations in (58a) and (58b) are closely related to each other since they share the role **at** (e, SPARKLE & x, y) in their qualia structures. We maintain that if one lexical representation of a lexical item represents some entity acting, its activity producing some light, sound or material, and its activity or the produced thing affecting some location, the representation will be extended to another lexical representation which represents the location being affected by the entity or the thing produced by the entity's activity. The concept of GL is that the lexical representation is not static but generative under some conditions and rules. In the case under discussion this generativity is first reflected on the qualia structure, and the change or extension is next transmitted or related to the argument structure and the event structure.[11] In the case of emission verbs such as (58), the extension of the meaning, or the representation, is permitted by the condition we suggested in (57), which is repeated below:

(57) a. LA verbs express existence of some entity and some activity of it.
 b. The existence of some entity affects or characterizes the place where the entity exists.

If we consider that one lexical item should have a unique lexical representation, we may suggest the representation in (59) as the one for *sparkle*. In (59) when the referent of an entity emitting sparkles (x) is inserted into z's position and event 1 is the head, the entity appears in the external argument position in syntax as in (55a, d); instead of x, if the referent of a location holding sparkles (y) is inserted, the location appears as a subject as in (55b). In these cases the sentences can be used in the progressive. When event 3 or event 4 is the head, the location-type or the *with*-type appears in syntax, respectively.

(59) *sparkle* (the final version)

$$\begin{bmatrix} \text{event structure} = \begin{bmatrix} \text{E1} = \text{e1: process} \\ \text{S-E2} = \text{e2: state} \\ \text{e2} = \text{e3 or e4} \\ \text{e3: state} \\ \text{e4: state} \\ \text{e1o}_\alpha\text{e2} \\ \text{head: underspecified} \end{bmatrix} \\ \text{argument structure} = \begin{bmatrix} \text{ARG1} = x \\ \text{ARG2} = y \end{bmatrix} \\ \text{qualia structure} = \begin{bmatrix} \text{FORMAL} = \textbf{at}(\text{e3, SPARKLE\&x, y}) \\ \textbf{with}(\text{e4, y, SPARKLE\&x}) \\ \text{AGENTIVE} = \textbf{act}(\text{e1, z}) \\ z = x \text{ or } y \end{bmatrix} \end{bmatrix}$$

(x: entity, y: location)

In (59) S-E2 represents that event 2 is a shadow event. We assume that a shadow event refers to semantic content that is optionally expressed in syntax and that the subevent needs a PP to be syntactically expressed: event 3 related to **at** (e3, SPARKLE & x, y) in the formal role appears in syntax as a locational PP, and event 4 related to **with** (e4, y, SPARKLE & x) appears as a *with*-phrase.[12]

5.4.2 The Qualia Structure and Omission of *With*-phrases

Some *with*-phrases in LA sentences can be omitted. The representation we proposed, together with lexical representation of NPs, will explain why some *with*-phrases can be omitted but others cannot.

While many *with*-phrases co-occurring with emission verbs can be omitted as in (60), those appearing with *Swarm* Verbs are obligatorily required as in (61).[13]

(60) Verbs of Emission
 a. The crown sparkled (with jewels).
 b. The sky glimmered (with stars).
 c. The bottle buzzed (with flies).
 d. The fountain is bubbling (with clear water).

(61) *Swarm* Verbs
   a. The lake abounds *(with fish).
   b. The garden swarmed *(with bees).

Swarm Verbs are repeated as (62).

(62) Swarm Verbs: *abound, bustle, crawl, creep, hop, run, swarm*... (= (22))

First, let us consider semantic representations of sentences in which *with*-phrases can be omitted, taking (60a) as an example. The representation for the verb *sparkle* is in (59), and the lexical representation for the noun *crown* is given in (63).[14]

(63) *crown*
   argument structure = $\begin{bmatrix} \text{ARG1} = \text{x: human} \\ \text{ARG2} = \text{y: physical\_object} \\ \text{ARG3} = \text{z: jewel} \end{bmatrix}$
   qualia structure = $\begin{bmatrix} \text{FORMAL} = \textbf{physical\_object}(y) \\ \text{CONST} = \textbf{with}(e, y, z) \\ \text{TELIC} = \textbf{wear}(e, x, y) \\ \text{AGENTIVE} = \textbf{make}(e, w, y) \end{bmatrix}$
   (y: crown, z: jewel)

The constitutive role in (63) represents a crown holding jewels, while in the representation of the verb *sparkle* in (59), the qualia structure holds **at** (e3, SPARKLE & x, y) and **with** (e4, y, SPARKLE & x) (In this case, x = jewel, y = crown). In forming the semantic representation of *the crown sparkle with NP*, the quale **with** (e4, y, SPARKLE & x) of *sparkle* is projected to syntax and a *with*-phrase appears. Now, in a rough outline, x in **with** (e4, y, SPARKLE & x), namely jewel, is provided by the constitutive role of *crown* which includes "jewel," a potential emitter, and so the noun *jewel* can be dispensed with and the *with*-phrase can be omitted.

Next, let us turn to example (61b) where the *with*-phrase is required. Taking the representation of the verb *sparkle* in (58) and (59) into consideration, we give the lexical representations of the verb *swarm* and the noun *garden* in (64):

(64) a. *swarm*

$$\text{event structure} = \begin{bmatrix} E1 = e1\text{: process} \\ E2 = e2\text{: state} \\ \quad e2 = e3 \text{ or } e4 \\ \quad e3\text{: state} \\ \quad e4\text{: state} \\ e1 \circ_\alpha e2 \\ \text{head: underspecified} \end{bmatrix}$$

$$\text{argument structure} = \begin{bmatrix} \text{ARG1} = x\text{: insect/human/moving entity} \\ \text{ARG2} = y\text{: place} \end{bmatrix}$$

$$\text{qualia structure} = \begin{bmatrix} \textbf{FORMAL} = \textbf{at}(e3, \text{GROUP OF } x, y) \\ \quad\quad\quad\quad\quad \textbf{with}(e4, y, \text{GROUP OF } x) \\ \textbf{AGENTIVE} = \textbf{act}(e1, z) \\ \quad\quad\quad z = x \text{ or } y \end{bmatrix}$$

b. *garden*

$$\text{argument structure} = \begin{bmatrix} \text{ARG1} = x\text{: human} \\ \text{ARG2} = y\text{: place} \\ \text{ARG3} = z\text{: plant} \end{bmatrix}$$

$$\text{qualia structure} = \begin{bmatrix} \textbf{FORMAL} = \textbf{location}(y) \\ \textbf{CONST} = \textbf{with}(e, y, z) \\ \textbf{TELIC} = \textbf{at}(e, x, y) \\ \textbf{AGENTIVE} = \textbf{make}(e, x, y) \end{bmatrix}$$

In the representation of *swarm* in (64a) "GROUP" is contained in its qualia structure, and the constitutive role of *garden* is **with** (e, y, z) and z denotes plants because typically what a garden holds is plants. In forming the semantic representation *the garden swarm with NP*, the quale **with** (e4, y, GROUP OF x) is projected to syntax. For the *with*-phrase to be omitted, x has to be covered by another quale. The constitutive role of *garden* holds plant as its argument and this does not meet the restriction on x of *swarm* (See the argument structure in (64a)). Therefore, *swarm*'s argument x has to be given by some NP, e.g. *bees*, and the *with*-phrase cannot be omitted.[15]

In this way, we can account for the possibility of omission of *with*-phrases in *with*-type sentences by postulating the representations which contain the qualia structure parallel to that in (59) and (64a) together with that of NPs.

In this section, we have proposed to unify the representations of LA verbs into one representation such as the one in (59), and we have shown that the representations we proposed in this chapter can deal with the difference in acceptability of *with*-type sentences not containing a *with*-phrase.

5.5 Summary

In this chapter we have discussed the characteristics of headedness and qualia structure through the examination of emission verbs, which show intransitive locative alternation, and elaborated lexical representations that can account for the various behaviors of these verbs. We have argued that the representation of emission verbs basically should contain the entity which emits light, sound and the like, the location where the entity exists and what it emits in the qualia structure. That is, the qualia structure of emission verbs denotes diverse aspects of meanings. Furthermore, we have maintained that in the lexical representation of emission verbs various subevents can become a head. This claim concerning the notion of headedness and the representation we proposed in this chapter explains the variable behaviors of emission verbs. The proposals we have made in this chapter are relevant to the discussions in the next chapter, where we will discuss the motion-verb usage of emission verbs and argue that the co-composition operation gives rise to this usage, along with the characteristics of emission verbs' lexical representations.

Through the discussions in chapter 4 and this chapter we have understood the overall properties of lexical representation. Our aim of this book is to reveal the mechanism which yields polysemy of words and the roles which compositionality plays in the mechanism. In order to do this, we are trying to comprehend characteristics of motion verbs and spatial prepositions and to offer their semantic representations. Therefore, in the next two chapters we move on to semantic representation compositionally derived from lexical representations. Accordingly, we will deal with not words but phrases, especially verbal expressions consisting of verbs and PPs (Chapter 6) and VPs containing adjunct phrases (Chapter 7) and study operations such as co-composition and composition (Chapter 6 and Chapter 7).

Endnotes

1 The locative alternation we mainly discuss in this chapter is the intransitive type, so we call the intransitive locative alternation just "locative alternation" in this chapter. When we need to distinguish the intransitive type and the transitive type, we add "intransitive" or "transitive." In addition, in this chapter we use the following abbreviations:
   LA = locative alternation   LI = locative inversion
   LA verbs = verbs appearing in locative alternation sentences
   LI verbs = verbs appearing in locative inversion sentences
2 The classification in (12) is cited from Dowty (2000: 115–117).
3 As for the names of verb classes in (15)–(33), we follow Levin (1993).
4 In (34) we employ our notation instead of Nakajima (2001)'s, for expository purposes.
5 Maruta (2001: 651–652) makes a similar statement based on this observation by Salkoff (1983).
6 Takane Ito pointed out the class of verbs and the examples shown here to me (personal communication). This verb class corresponds to "the fourth type of verbs" proposed in Kindaichi (1950).
7 A prepositional phrase in locative inversion sentences is considered to be an argument of an involved verb. For discussion, see Nakajima (2001) and Isono (2001).
8 This analysis applies to other LA verbs, some of which are shown in (15)–(22). For example, the lexical representation of *beep* (verbs of sound emission) contains BEEP and that of *smell* (verbs of smell emission) SMELL and that of *blossom* (verbs of entity-specific modes of being) BLOSSOM. To verbs of modes of being involving motion (*flutter*, *shake*...) and swarm verbs (*abound*, *crawl*...) our analysis also applies with a slight modification.
9 The function **with** corresponds to HAVE proposed by Pinker (1989: 190). As for projection of the arguments in the quale **with** (e, y, x), argument y is projected to an internal argument position, or a complement position, in syntax, and argument x appears as a complement to the preposition *with*.
10 To holistic interpretations, quantity of entities are also relevant as has been pointed out so far by many researchers. Notation to represent holistic interpretations is left for future research.
11 We consider that the qualia structure is crucial to the generativity of the lexical representation.
12 As for a shadow event, we took a cue from the notion of a shadow argument. Pustejovsky (1995: 65) argues that shadow arguments are expressible only under specific conditions within the sentence itself and that the underlined phrases in (i) are shadow arguments:
   (i) a. Mary buttered her toast with margarine / *with butter.
       b. Harry kicked the wall with his gammy leg / *with his leg.
13 In the examples in (i), where state verbs are used, the *with*-phrases can similarly be omitted.
   (i) a. The room echoed (with voices). (Verbs of Sound Existence)
       b. The garden flowered (with roses). (Verbs of Entity-Specific Modes of Being)
14 We show relevant parts of the lexical representations of *crown* in (63) and *garden* in (64), respectively.
15 The explanation given here was suggested to the author by Takane Ito and Naoyuki Ono.

Chapter 6

Event Structure and Co-composition: Prepositions and Inversion

In chapters 4 and 5 we studied the properties of lexical representation and illuminated characteristics of event structure, headedness and qualia structure. In this chapter and the next we examine relations among lexical representations: that is, we study the relationship between lexical representation of verbs and that of co-occurring PPs. In doing so, we will be considering the operations of co-composition and composition. This chapter investigates the semantic representation of verbal expressions consisting of motion verbs and the first and the second type PPs which we discussed in section 3.2.3, namely argument PPs. Through the chapter we discuss event structure, the co-composition operation and its conditions.

GL employs the co-composition operation which composes some events into a complex event. (Similar proposals are presented in Kageyama and Yumoto (1997), Rappaport Hovav and Levin (1998), and Alsina (1999) among others.) In GL the verbal expression *run into*, for instance, is assumed to be derived from *run* and *into* by the co-composition operation.

(1) a. Maria ran for an hour / *in an hour. (Tenny (1994: 77))
       b. Sally ran into the building of the English department *for twenty minutes / in ten minutes.

Section 6.1 is concerned with the co-composition operation proposed by Pustejovsky (1995) and meanings of locative inversion sentences. It proposes the representation of the preposition *to*, and makes clear the nature of the co-composition operation. After that, in section 6.2 conditions of the co-composition operation are proposed and this operation's functions are discussed. Furthermore, the motion-verb usage of emission verbs is analyzed and it is suggested that interrelations among co-composition, underspecificity of head subevents, nonvolitionality and the notion of action chain are relevant to this usage. Through these discussions, the nature of the interaction of the co-composition operation, event structure and qualia structure and the way of determination of the head subevent in the composed event structure will be revealed.

6.1 Prepositions, Inversion and Co-composition

The prepositions *to* and *into* introduce goal phrases and have been considered almost the same in this usage.

(2) a. Maria ran to the next town.
b. She walked into the studio.

However, the difference in acceptability of locative inversion sentences in (3) suggests that these two prepositions differ in some respects.

(3) a. Into this room ran a number of boys.
b. ??To this room ran a number of boys.

In this section we propose a formal analysis of the English prepositions *to* and *into* which provides an explanation for the contrast exemplified in (3).

We will argue that the headedness of the event structure proposed in Pustejovsky (1995) plays an important role in explaining the difference in the distribution of *to* and *into*. In section 6.1.1, we will take a brief look at similarities and differences between *to* and *into* in their behaviors. Section 6.1.2 will examine conditions on locative inversion in terms of the event structure of verbs or verb phrases that appear in this construction. In sections 6.1.3 and 6.1.4 the difference between *to* and *into* will be ascribed to headedness in the event structure of each preposition and the lexical representation of *to*, which is different from that of *into* in headedness, will be proposed. This proposal correctly predicts acceptability of locative inversion sentences, the semantic representations of which are formed by co-composition. Through the discussion we will make clear the event structure and the qualia structure of *to* and *into*, and furthermore, we will reveal the nature of the co-composition operation. Section 6.1.5 concludes our discussion in section 6.1.

6.1.1 The Prepositions *To* and *Into*

In this subsection, we will survey some similarities and differences between the two prepositions. Firstly, as Matsumoto (1997) and Kageyama and Yumoto (1997: 137) argue, both *to* and *into* express a "goal" and can be semantically decomposed as follows:

(4) a. *to*: TO AT
　　 b. *into*: TO IN　　　　　　　　　　　　　(Matsumoto (1997: 133))

Secondly, PPs headed by *to* or *into* delimit events. Delimitedness is a notion proposed in Tenny (1994). Activity verbs such as *run* and *walk* co-occur with durative adverbial phrases like *for an hour* as in (5). However, when a goal *to*-phrase or *into*-phrase is added to these verbs, the durative adverbial phrase is ruled out and, instead, a frame adverbial phrase such as *in an hour* is permitted as is shown in (6) and (7). Thus, both *to*-phrases and *into*-phrases function as delimiters of events.

(5)　Maria ran for an hour / *in an hour.　　　　　(Tenny (1994: 77))
(6)　Maria ran to the next town *for an hour / in an hour.
(7)　Sally ran into the building of the English department *for twenty minutes / in ten minutes.

However, *to* and *into* behave differently when they appear in locative inversion sentences. In (3) (repeated as (8) below) and (9) *into* is fully acceptable, but *to* is not :

(8) a.　Into this room ran a number of boys.　　　　　　　　(=(3))
　　 b. ??To this room ran a number of boys.
(9) a.　Into the room hurried an old lady.
　　 b. ??To the station hurried an old lady.

Moreover, Gruber (1976) notices the difference between *to* and *into* and sets up two prepositional source-goal pairs:

(10) a. *out of - into*
b. *from - to* (Gruber (1976: 53))

Gruber (1976: 111) also presents examples where the acceptability of *to* and *into* is different:

(11) a. *John emerged to the roof.
b. John emerged into the kitchen.
(12) a. *The pod ejected its seeds to the corner.
b. The pod ejected its seeds into the corner.

Thus, *to* and *into* are similar in that they introduce a goal phrase which functions as a delimiter, but they exhibit some differences in distribution as shown in (8), (9), (11) and (12).

6.1.2 Lexical Representation of Locative Inversion Verbs

We noted that there is a difference in acceptability of locative inversion sentences in (8) and (9). In those examples, the *into*-phrases are permitted, whereas the *to*-phrases are excluded. In order to account for this difference of well-formedness, let us examine some restrictions on the lexical representation of verbs that occur in the locative inversion sentence.

The most typical verbs occurring in this construction are verbs of existence and appearance:

(13) a. In the corner was a lamp.
b. On the horizon appeared a large ship.

This class of verbs is one of the main classes of unaccusative verbs, so locative inversion has been considered to be an unaccusative diagnostic. However, another main class of unaccusative verbs, verbs of change of state, cannot be used in this construction.

(14) a. *On the top floor of the skyscraper broke many windows.
(L & R (1995: 224))
b. *On backyard clotheslines dried the weekly washing. (ibid.)

Unergative verbs basically cannot appear in this construction as we can see in (16), except for motion verbs as in (15) (= (8a, 9a)) repeated below.

(15) a. Into this room ran a number of boys.
  b. Into the room hurried an old lady.
(16) a. *In the cafés of Paris talk many artists.
  b. *Into the mirror glanced Jenny.

In the acceptable examples the object NPs in the PPs express the location where the referents of inverted subject NPs exist: in (13a) the lamp was in the corner and in (15a) a number of boys were in the room after running. On the other hand, in the unacceptable examples the object NPs in the PPs do not express the location of the referents of the subject NP, or some PPs such as *in the cafés* in (16a) are adjuncts to the verbs. See (17).[1]

(17) a. *A large ship appeared on the horizon, and a black small boat did so near the shore.
  b. Many novelists talked in the cafés of London, and many musicians did so in the cafés of Paris.

The semantic representation of a VP containing a verb and an adjunct represents existence of the event denoted by the verb, not that of an entity. Concerning (16a), not many artists but the event of many artists' talking existed in the cafés of Paris (although this implies that many artists were in the cafés).

Based on these facts, Nakajima (2001) argues that the verbs or verb phrases which subsume the representation in (18) are permitted in this construction.[2]

(18) e_i = final event (Nakajima (2001: 46))

$$\text{event structure} = \begin{bmatrix} \ldots \\ E_i = e_i: \text{state} \\ \text{head: } e_i \end{bmatrix}$$

$$\text{argument structure} = \begin{bmatrix} ARG1 = x \\ ARG2 = y \end{bmatrix}$$

$$\text{qualia structure} = \begin{bmatrix} \ldots \\ FORMAL = \mathbf{at}(e_i, x, y) \\ \ldots \end{bmatrix}$$

As we noted, the acceptability of locative inversion sentences varies depending on PPs (cf. (8) and (9)). This shows that the semantic representation of the verb phrases, not of verbs, is relevant. Therefore, we take (18) to be a condition on verbal expressions consisting of a verb and a preposition that appear in the locative inversion sentence.

The event structure of verbs of existence consists of a single state, and this state event is the head (cf. (13a)). That of verbs of appearance consists of a process subevent and a state subevent, and the state subevent, that is, the final subevent is the head (cf. (13b)). In the representations of both classes of verbs, the qualia structure linked to the head state subevent represents the existence of something at some place. So these classes of verbs meet condition (18). The unergative verbs with goal phrases (cf. (15)), whose lexical representation is given in (19), also meet condition (18).

(19) *run into* (cf. Pustejovsky (1995: 126))

$$\text{event structure} = \begin{bmatrix} E1 = e1\text{: process} \\ E2 = e2\text{: process} \\ E3 = e3\text{: state} \\ e1 \, o_\alpha e2 \quad e2 <_\alpha e3 \\ \text{head: } e3 \end{bmatrix}$$

$$\text{argument structure} = \begin{bmatrix} \text{ARG1} = x \\ \text{ARG2} = y \end{bmatrix}$$

$$\text{qualia structure} = \begin{bmatrix} \text{AGENTIVE} = \mathbf{act}(e1, x) \quad \mathbf{move}(e2, x) \\ \text{FORMAL} = \mathbf{at}(e3, x, y) \end{bmatrix}$$

In (19) the final state subevent is the head and the referent of the postverbal NP, argument 1, is described to exist at the place denoted by the NP in the preposed PP, argument 2. Take for example (15a), "a number of boys" are in "this room".

On the other hand, the verbs in the ill-formed examples in (14) and (16) do not satisfy (18). Change of state verbs in (14) and unergative verbs in (16) do not denote an object's or a person's existing in a place: the PPs do not express places where an object or a person exists and the formal role **at** (e, x, y) in (18) is not denoted in these verbs' representation.

Since we have seen the lexical representation of verb phrases occurring in locative inversion sentences, let us go on to consider the difference of acceptability between *to* and *into* in this construction.

6.1.3 Proposal

6.1.3.1 Lexical Representation of *To*

As we will see in this subsection, there are remarkable contrasts between sentences containing *to* and those containing *into*. Based on these observations, we will propose the lexical representation of *to*. The lexical representation of *into* proposed by Pustejovsky (1995) and that of *to* we propose in this subsection will account for the difference in acceptability of such locative inversion sentences as in (8)–(9).

Before considering the lexical representations of *into* and *to*, let us first look at the lexical representations of *run* and *come* because these verbs are crucial to identify those of *into* and *to*. Following Pinker (1989) and Kageyama and Yumoto (1997) we consider the event structure of *run* to consist of two subevents as is shown in (20).

(20) *run*
$$\text{event structure} = \begin{bmatrix} E1 = e1: \text{process} \\ E2 = e2: \text{process} \\ e1 \circ_\alpha e2 \\ \text{head: } e1 \end{bmatrix}$$
argument structure = $[\text{ARG1} = x]$
qualia structure = $\begin{bmatrix} \text{AGENTIVE} = \textbf{act}(e1, x) \\ \textbf{move}(e2, x) \end{bmatrix}$

In (20) event 1 is a process subevent, which is associated with an agentive role **act** (e1, x) denoting an activity with a running manner, and event 2 is a subevent of movement we proposed in chapter 4 and is associated with **move** (e2, x) representing a motion along a path. We assume that event 1 is the head in *run*'s event structure. In addition, since example (21) is judged unacceptable, there is no transition from a process subevent to a resultant subevent in the event structure.

(21) *John ran in 5 minutes.

Next, let us consider the verb *come*, whose representation is the one in (22), and relevant examples are given in (23).

(22) *come*
$$\text{event structure} = \begin{bmatrix} E1 = e1: \text{process} \\ E2 = e2: \text{state} \\ e1 <_\alpha e2 \\ \text{head: } e2 \end{bmatrix}$$
$$\text{argument structure} = \begin{bmatrix} ARG1 = x \\ ARG2 = y \end{bmatrix}$$
$$\text{qualia structure} = \begin{bmatrix} \text{AGENTIVE} = \mathbf{move}(e1, x) \\ \text{FORMAL} = \mathbf{at}(e2, x, y) \end{bmatrix}$$

(23) a. Tom came in 5 minutes.
    b. Tom came for an hour.
        ≠ 1) Tom was approaching the speaker for an hour.
        = 2) Tom arrived at the place where the speaker was, and he was there for an hour.

Example (23a) suggests that there is a transition in the event structure, and so the event structure contains a process subevent and a state subevent. The example in (23b) does not have the reading in 1 but has the reading in 2, where the durative *for*-phrase modifies the result subevent. Thus, event 2 in (22) is the head.

Now, we go on to the lexical representations of *into* and *to*. First, let us examine examples containing *into*-phrases and consider the headedness of *into*. Pustejovsky (1995) argues that the lexical representation of *into* should be (24), where the head event is the result state event, event 2. He also claims that by the co-composition operation, the lexical representation of a verb and that of an *into*-phrase are combined into (19). In (19) the final state subevent is the head, which meets the condition on locative inversion in (18).

(24) *into*   (Pustejovsky 1995: 126)
$$\text{event structure} = \begin{bmatrix} E1 = e1: \text{process} \\ E2 = e2: \text{state} \\ e1 <_\alpha e2 \\ \text{head: } e2 \end{bmatrix}$$
$$\text{argument structure} = \begin{bmatrix} ARG1 = x \\ ARG2 = y \end{bmatrix}$$
$$\text{qualia structure} = \begin{bmatrix} \text{AGENTIVE} = \mathbf{move}(e1, x) \\ \text{FORMAL} = \mathbf{at}(e2, x, y) \end{bmatrix}$$

Verbal expressions including an *into*-phrase have been considered ill-formed when these co-occur with durative *for*-phrases, as we saw in (7) repeated below as (25). However, a closer examination tells us that the facts are a bit more complicated. For example, in (26) a durative *for*-phrase is permitted in the interpretation that John ran, arrived at the station and was in it for ten minutes.

(25) Sally ran into the building of the English department *for twenty minutes / in ten minutes. (=(7))
(26) John ran into the station for ten minutes.
(in the interpretation that John ran, got into the station and was there for ten minutes.)

In (26) the *for*-phrase modifies the state subevent introduced by the *into*-phrase, that is, event 3 in (19), so we can say that this final subevent, the state subevent of *into*, is the head event.

Furthermore, *come into* as in example (27a) can occur with a *for*-phrase. The example (27a) has the interpretation that Sally was in the room for an hour but cannot mean that Sally moved for an hour in order to enter the room. (The event structure of *come into* is shown in (27b).)

(27) a. Sally came into this room for an hour.
 b. event structure = $\begin{bmatrix} E1 = e1: \text{process} \\ E2 = e2: \text{state} \\ e1 <_x e2 \\ \text{head: e2} \end{bmatrix}$

From the interpretation of (27a) we can say that the result subevent is the head, as is shown in (27b), and that the process subevents of both *come* and *into* are not heads. In this way, in verbal expressions including an *into*-phrase, the result state of *into* is the head of the whole event.

Next, let us look at the cases which contain *to*-phrases. Although it has been claimed that *run to* cannot co-occur with a durative *for*-phrase as shown in (28b), this verbal expression can be used with a *for*-phrase in a different interpretation such as (29b):

(28) a. Maria ran for an hour.
  b. *Maria ran to the next town for an hour. (=(6))
(29) a. John ran to the station for ten minutes.
  b. John ran to the station for ten minutes, but he walked the rest of the way.

Example (29a) is acceptable in the interpretation of (29b). In (29a) the *for*-phrase modifies the running activity of John, thus the process subevent of *run* is the head and the state subevent of *to* is not. From the contrast in the interpretations of (26) and (29a) we now understand the difference between *into* and *to*: the state subevent of *into* is a head in (26), whereas that of *to* in (29a) is not.

We should note, however, that when the verb *come* is used with *to* as in (30a), the *for*-phrase modifies the result state. That is, its interpretation is the one in (30b), not the one in (30c). So, the result state subevent, not the process subevent, is the head in (30a).

(30) a. The tourists came to a stream for an hour.
  b. The tourists were beside the stream for an hour.
  c. The tourists moved toward the stream for an hour.

Thus, as for *to*, its process subevent is the head in the verbal expression in (29a), while its state subevent functions as a head in the verbal expression in (30a). Based on these observations, we propose that *to*'s head event is underspecified and that its lexical representation is (31).

(31) *to*

$$\text{event structure} = \begin{bmatrix} E1 = e1: \text{process} \\ E2 = e2: \text{state} \\ e1 <_\alpha e2 \\ \text{head: underspecified} \end{bmatrix}$$

$$\text{argument structure} = \begin{bmatrix} ARG1 = x \\ ARG2 = y \end{bmatrix}$$

$$\text{qualia structure} = \begin{bmatrix} \text{AGENTIVE} = \mathbf{move}(e1, x) \\ \text{FORMAL} = \mathbf{at}(e2, x, y) \end{bmatrix}$$

Since the head is underspecified, we consider that the head of a verbal expression containing *to* is determined by the head of a verb. So in (29a) the process subevent of the verb *run* is the head of the verbal expression and in (30a) the state subevent of *come* is. The adequacy for our proposal that the head event of *to* is underspecified is supported by the different interpretations of the sentences modified by durative *for*-phrases in (29a) and (30a).³

Now, we can account for the well-formedness of the locative inversion examples (15a) and (15b), repeated below as (32a) and (33a), respectively:

(32) a. Into this room ran a number of boys.   (=(15a))
     b. ??To this room ran a number of boys.
(33) a. Into the room hurried an old lady.   (=(15b))
     b. ??To the station hurried an old lady.

In the lexical representation of *into* in (24), the head is the state event, as Pustejovsky (1995) proposed. In the semantic representation of *run into* in (19), which is formed through the co-composition operation from the lexical representation of *run* and that of *into*, the final state subevent is the head, which meets the condition on locative inversion in (18), and so, (32a) and (33a) are acceptable. On the contrary, as we have just proposed, the head in the lexical representation of *to* is underspecified and the head of the verbal expression *run to* is the process event in the same way as in (29a), and thus, not meeting the condition in (18), (32b) and (33b) are unacceptable.

In the next subsection, we will discuss in detail how the head event is determined when the co-composition operation is applied.

6.1.3.2 Co-composition, Headedness and the Event Structure

In this subsection we will see how lexical representation of verbs and that of PPs are combined through co-composition and under what conditions the co-composition operation works. We will claim that when a verb's event structure and a PP's hold subevents of movement or change, the two subevents are laid upon each other and the event structure of a verbal expression is co-composed through the co-composition operation (See (38) and the discussion below it.). We will also examine how the head of a derived verbal expression is determined through the co-composition operation.

In the previous subsection we proposed that the head of *to* is underspecified. Now we propose that the head of a verbal expression which contains a *to*-phrase is carried over from a verb by means of the co-composition operation. Thus, when a *to*-phrase forms a verbal expression with *run*, whose head is the process subevent ((34a)), the derived expression *run to* in (34e) has the process event as its head. If a *to*-phrase and *come* make a verbal expression, the result state subevent functions as the head of *come to* since the head of *come* is the result subevent (see (34b) and (34f)). Meanwhile, as we saw in the last subsection, the head of a verbal expression including an *into*-phrase is always the result state subevent, which, we contend, is because the head of an *into*-phrase is the result state subevent and the derived verbal expression takes over its head from the PP. Therefore, even if the verb *run*, whose head is a process subevent (event 1), forms a verbal expression with an *into*-phrase, the head of *run into* is the result subevent, not event 1, ((34g)). Naturally, when this preposition combines with the verb *come*, the result state subevent works as the head of *come into* ((34h)). (In (34) the relevant subevents and qualia are schematized and head subevents are marked with "*". Henceforth, in this kind of figure, the same way of schematization will be employed.)

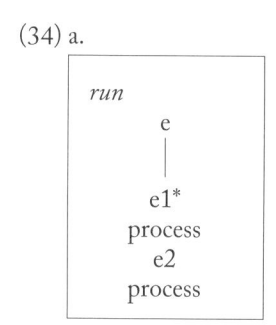

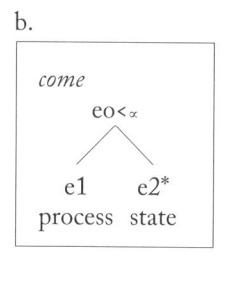

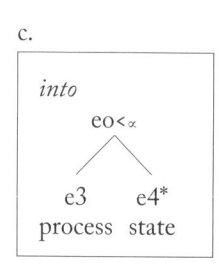

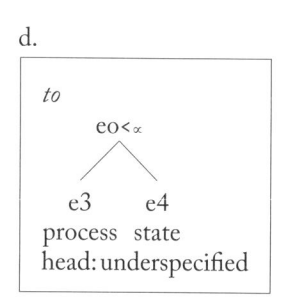

(34) a.

```
run
    e
    │
    e1*
    process
    e2
    process
```

b.

```
come
    eo<α
    ╱  ╲
   e1   e2*
process state
```

c.

```
into
    eo<α
    ╱  ╲
   e3   e4*
process state
```

d.

```
to
    eo<α
    ╱  ╲
   e3   e4
process state
head: underspecified
```

e.

```
run to
    eo<α
   /    \
  e1*    
  process
  e2*
  process
  e3    e4
  process state
```

f.

```
come to
    eo<α
   /    \
  e1    e2*
  process state
  e3    e4
  process state
```

g.

```
run into
    eo<α
   /    \
  e1
  process
  e2*
  process
  e3    e4*
  process state
```

h.

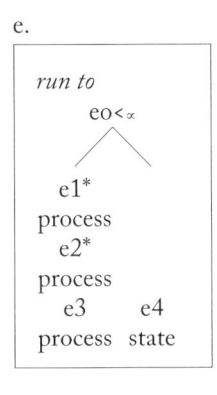

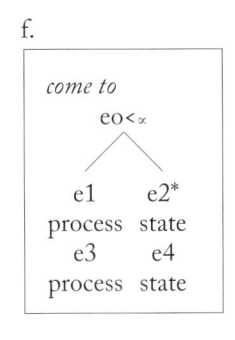

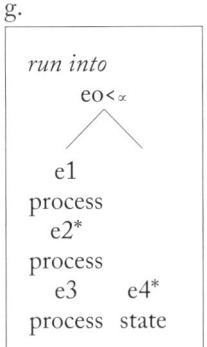

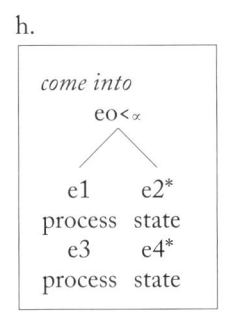

```
come into
    eo<α
   /    \
  e1    e2*
  process state
  e3    e4*
  process state
```

Our proposal on co-composition and headedness can be summarized as in (35):[4]

(35) Co-composition and Headedness: the Inheritance of Headedness (i)
The head of a PP becomes the head of a derived verbal expression when a verb and a PP form a verbal expression. When the head of the PP is underspecified, the head of the derived verbal expression is carried over from the verb contained in the expression.

The head of an *into*-phrase is the result state subevent, so the head of a verbal expression which consists of a verb and an *into*-phrase is the result state subevent. On the other hand, the head of a *to*-phrase is underspecified, and hence the head of the verb functions as the head of the whole verbal expression consisting of a verb and a *to*-phrase.[5]

We can also see the contrast of the interpretations derived from (35) in examples such as the ones in (36).

(36) a. John walked through the long tunnel in five minutes.
= John walked inside the tunnel and reached one of the ends in five minutes.
   b. John walked through the long tunnel for ten minutes.
= John walked inside the tunnel up and down for ten minutes.
≠ John walked inside the tunnel, got out of it and was around there for ten minutes.

We consider the head of *through* to be underspecified, as is shown in (37):

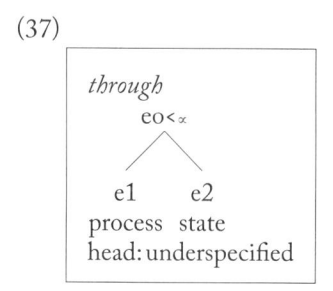

(37)

```
through
    eo<ₓ
   /    \
  e1    e2
process  state
head: underspecified
```

We contend that the interpretation of the example in (36a) arises since the event structure of *through* has a transition and that the interpretation of (36b) arises since the head of *through* is underspecified and *walk*'s head puts a focus on the process subevents.

Furthermore, we propose that the relation between the event structure and co-composition should be stated as in (38):

(38) relation between the event structure and co-composition (extended version is in section 6.2)
If the event structure of a verb contains a process subevent (event 1) and that of a PP consists of a process subevent (event 1) and a state subevent (event 2), the verb and the PP can form a verbal expression by means of the co-composition operation.

(38) says that when a goal PP is added to a verb, the event structure of the PP is laid upon that of the verb (See (34f, h) as examples). Moreover, it suggests that even if the event structure of a verb lacks a state subevent, the formed verbal expression can gain a state subevent which is brought by a PP; examples of this are

(34e, g). In this way, by the co-composition operation, verbs and goal PPs form verbal expressions and give birth to derived meanings of the verbal expressions. Through the co-composition operation, a head event is determined as stated in (35). We consider (38) to be peculiar to Germanic languages. Kageyama and Yumoto (1997) and Kageyama (2003) suggest that Japanese does not have the co-composition operation (or, the composition of LCS in their framework), as we see in section 6.2.2.

6.1.4 Locative Inversion Revisited

Now let us see how our proposal in subsections 6.1.3.1–6.1.3.2 correctly accounts for the acceptability of locative inversion sentences in (32)–(33), which are repeated below as (39)–(40).

(39) a. Into this room ran a number of boys.
  b. ??To this room ran a number of boys.
(40) a. Into the room hurried an old lady.
  b. ??To the station hurried an old lady.

Heads of *to*-phrases are underspecified and hence verbal expressions which include *to*-phrases take over their heads from the verbs contained in the verbal expressions. Thus, in (39b) and (40b) the process subevents function as heads of *ran to* and *hurried to*, since the verbs, *run* and *hurry*, are activity verbs and their process subevents are heads (see (34e)). The lexical representations of (39b) and (40b) do not meet the condition on locative inversion verb phrases in (18), since the condition requires that a final state event be the head. In this way the ill-formedness of (39b) and (40b) is correctly predicted. In (39a) and (40a) the verbal expressions consist of verbs and *into*-phrases and their heads are final state subevents as we saw in (34g) and (35). This satisfies condition (18), and hence the well-formedness of these locative inversion sentences is explained.

In contrast to (39b) and (40b), (41b) is acceptable although the verbal expression includes a goal *to*-phrase.

(41) a. Into that crowded station came a train.
  b. To Ilion came the wedlock-woe. (OED)

The expression *come to* takes over its head from the verb *come*, so its final state subevent is the head, as is shown in (34f). Also in (41a) the final state subevent is the head in the event, which is expressed by *come into*. Thus, both sentences in (41) meet condition (18).

We can extend our proposal in (35) to prepositions which introduce a source, for example, *out of* and *from*. Gruber (1976: 53) classifies the source-goal prepositions into the two pairs we saw in (10). The preposition *from*, which is paired with *to*, cannot appear in locative inversion sentences, whereas *out of* can, as shown in (42).

(10) a. *out of - into*
 b. *from - to*
(42) a. Out of the barn ran a horse. (Hoekstra & Mulder (1990: 31))
 b. *From the room ran a woman. (Nakajima (2001: 65))

Following the classification by Gruber (1976), we propose that the head subevents of *out of* and *from* correspond to those of *into* and *to*, respectively: the head subevent of *out of* is the result subevent as in the case of *into*, and that of *from* is underspecified, as is the case with *to*. Thus, the head of a verbal expression containing *out of* is the result subevent, which meets the condition in (18). Hence (42a) is correctly predicted to be acceptable.

In contrast, the head of the preposition *from* is underspecified, so the head of a verbal expression which consists of a verb and a *from*-phrase is carried over from the verb. In (42b) the head of the verb *run* is the process subevent and this process subevent functions as the head for the derived verbal expression. As a result, (42b) does not satisfy condition (18) and is judged unacceptable.

Our proposal that the head of the preposition *from* is underspecified predicts that this preposition can occur in locative inversion sentences if it is used with a verb whose head is the result state subevent. This prediction is borne out by (43).

(43) From the kitchen appeared a fat woman. (Nakajima (2001: 65))

The verb *appear* is an achievement verb and Pustejovsky (1995: 187) classifies achievement verbs as right-headed. In other words, the result state subevent is the head, as is shown in (44), where we show relevant parts of the representation of *appear* (See also the discussion about *come* below (22).). The head subevent of *appear* is confirmed by the example in (45).[6]

(44) *appear*
event structure = $\begin{bmatrix} \text{E1 = e1: process} \\ \text{E2 = e2: state} \\ \text{e1} <_\alpha \text{e2} \\ \text{head: e2} \end{bmatrix}$

(45) The U.F.O. appeared in the sky for a few minutes.(Kageyama (1996: 109))

The verbal expression in (43) takes over its head from the verb *appear*, and hence the final state subevent is the head in this verbal expression, which satisfies condition (18).

The example in (46a) seems to be a counterexample to our proposal (38) since the event structure of the preposition *in* does not contain a process event.

(46) a. In the room ran a shrieking child. (L & R (1992: 259))
 b. A shrieking child ran inside the room. (*in the room*: a locative PP)
 c. A shrieking child ran into the room. (*in the room*: a directional PP)

The example in (46a) is judged unacceptable in the reading of (46b) (and is marked with '*' in this reading in Levin and Rappaport Havov (1992: 259)), but is acceptable in the interpretation of (46c).

Basically an *in*-phrase expresses a location where an event occurs when it co-occurs with an activity verb. For this case, we will propose in chapter 7 that the subevent of the verb is inserted in the argument position of the lexical representation of the *in*-phrase. We will, furthermore, suggest that this composition operation gives rise to the conceptual structure of a VP involving an adjunct. At present we schematize the lexical representation of *in* as the one in (47a). In (47b) the semantic representation of the VP *run in the room* is schematically shown.[7]

(47) a.
```
     in
      e
      |
     e₁*
    state
  at (e, x, y)
```

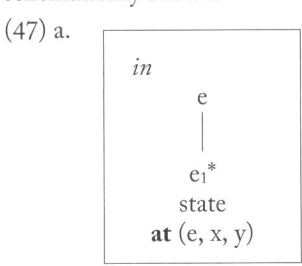

b.
```
  run in the room
        e
        |
       e₁*
      state
  at (e, RUNNING, y)
```

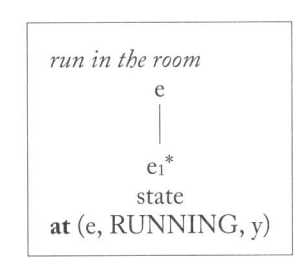

(47b) represents that the running event of a shrieking child exists at a location, namely, the room. The representation in (47b) does not contain **at** (e, x, y), in this example **at** (e, shrieking child, room) and, therefore, (46a) in the interpretation of (46b) does not meet condition (18) and is ruled out.

In order to interpret sentence (46a) as a grammatical one, condition (18) ought to be satisfied. In other words, the result subevent needs to be the head of *run in* through the co-composition operation. Therefore, the preposition *in* must be re-interpreted in such a way that its state subevent is interpreted as expressing a result event. In (48) we schematize the event structure for interpretation (46c): in (48a) the subevents and the qualia associated with the subevents of *run* and *in* are shown, and in (48b) those of the verbal expression *run in* are shown.

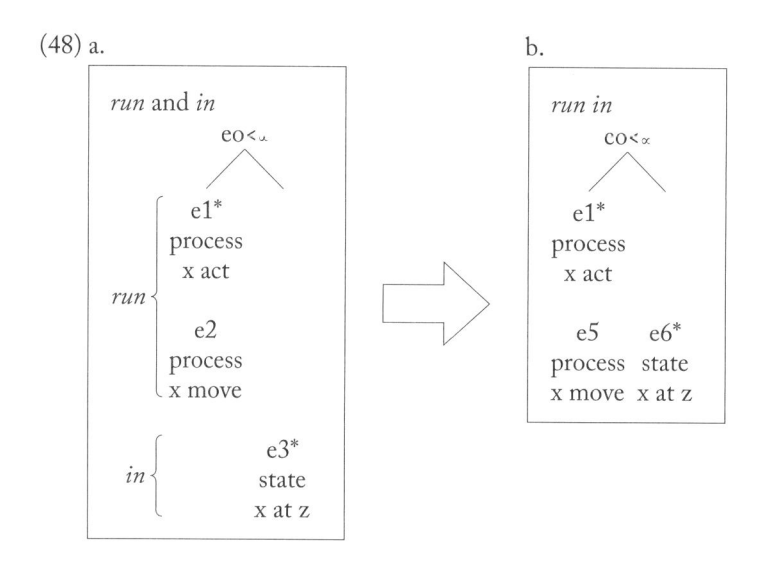

(48) a.

run and *in*

$eo<_\alpha$

run
$e1^*$
process
x act

$e2$
process
x move

in
$e3^*$
state
x at z

b.

run in

$co<\alpha$

$e1^*$
process
x act

$e5$ $e6^*$
process state
x move x at z

The event structure in (48b) is almost the same as that of *run into* in (34g), and satisfies condition (18). In contrast to the event structure of *into*, that of *in* lacks the process event expressing motion of some entity. We consider the event structure in (48b) to be formed by an exceptional co-composition operation in order to interpret the example in (46a) as a well-formed one. We will refer to the co-composition concerning the preposition *in* in section 6.2.3.

The same explanation applies to the preposition *on*. The preposition *onto* is permitted in locative inversion sentences, while a locative *on*-phrase is excluded when it is interpreted as a locational phrase, as shown in (49). The examples in

(49) are taken from Levin (1993: 93):

(49) a. Onto the table jumped a cat.
     b. *On the table jumped a cat.   (*on the table*: a locative PP)

The example in (49b) is acceptable in the directional phrase interpretation. We can account for the behavior of *onto* in the same way as *into*. Furthermore, the explanation for *in* applies to the example of *on*.

In this section, we have seen that our proposal in subsections 6.1.3.1–6.1.3.2 can correctly predict the acceptability of locative inversion sentences.

6.1.5 Summary

In section 6.1 we have been concerned with the prepositions *to* and *into*, locative inversion and the co-composition operation. *To* and *into* used to be treated as prepositions which introduce goal phrases (cf. Matsumoto (1997), Kageyama and Yumoto (1997), among others) and their difference has not been satisfactorily defined in the literature. We have noticed that the acceptability of locative inversion sentences varies depending on the prepositions involved: that is, *into* is permitted in this construction but *to* is not. Based on the interpretations of durative *for*-phrases, we have proposed that the difference between *to* and *into* is ascribable to headedness in the event structure of each preposition: the head of *to* is underspecified, while the head of *into* is the result state subevent. Proposing the relation between co-composition and the event structure, we have shown that our proposal can correctly predict the acceptability of locative inversion sentences. Our proposal also accounts for the behavior of the source prepositions (e.g. *from* and *out of*) and *in*, *on* and *onto*.

6.2 Nature of Co-composition Operation

This section treats the relation among event structure, qualia structure and the co-composition operation which acts on event structures and qualia structures. The operation we consider in this section is shown in (50), which is the extended version of (38):

(50) Co-composition Operation and its Conditions
      a. If the event structure of a preposition contains a subevent of movement

or change, and if the event structure of a verb contains the same type of subevent and the qualia associated with the two subevents are the same type, the two subevents must be combined. In this case, if the event structures of the two lexical items have state subevents, the two subevents are also combined. Or

b. if the event structure of a preposition consists of only a state subevent, and if the event structure of a verb contains the same type of subevent and the qualia associated with the two subevents are the same type, the two subevents must be combined.

The proposal in (50) puts forward conditions on the co-composition operation more explicitly than Pustejovsky (1995). One function of the operation in (50) is to project into syntax the first type of prepositional phrase, namely a prepositional argument: that is, the PPs such as *in Japan* and *into this room* in *This kind of dog exists only in Japan* and *Sally came into this room*. In a sense, this operation corresponds to the argument fusion operation proposed in Jackendoff (1990), but this kind of operation is not suggested explicitly in Pustejovsky (1995). So, we, following Jackendoff (1990), call the operation "event fusion" in this book when operation (50) introduces an argument PP. The other function of the operation in (50) is to compose the semantic representation which contains the second type of prepositional phrase: "addition of an event" to the event structure of verbs. For example, this operation combines the event structure of *run* and that of *to* and, as a result, a resultant state subevent is added to the process subevents denoted by *run*.

Unlike the earlier version in (38), the condition in (50) consists of two parts. The condition in (50a) takes over the essence of (38): as we have seen in (34), when the event structures of both a verb and a preposition contain subevents of movement or change, the co-composition operation combines their lexical representations. In contrast, the condition in (50b) concerns prepositions whose event structure holds only a state subevent: by (50b) the lexical representation of this type of preposition is combined with a verb's only when the verb's event structure contains a state subevent. This condition excludes a case in which otherwise *in* and *walk* are combined (cf. **John walked in the room.* "John entered the room by walking.")[8]

In proposing (50) we assume that the most complex event a VP can express is the one which is shown in (51).[9]

(51)
$$\text{event struture} = \begin{bmatrix} E1 = e1: \text{process} \\ E2 = e2: \text{process} \\ E3 = e3: \text{state} \\ e1 <_\alpha e2 \quad e2 <_\alpha e3 \end{bmatrix}$$

$$\text{qualia structure} = \begin{bmatrix} \text{AGENTIVE} = \textbf{act-on}(e1, x, y) \\ \textbf{move}(e2, y) \\ \text{FORMAL} = \textbf{at}(e3, y, z) \end{bmatrix}$$

This complex event accords with an action chain (or a causal chain) argued by Croft (1991) and Langacker (1991) among others. In an action chain, some force is transmitted from one event to another. That is, some action causes movement or change of some entity, the movement or change leads to some resultant state. The conditions in (50) accord to this concept. The event structure in (51) consists of three subevents: a process subevent of action, a process subevent of movement or change and a state result subevent. In (51) the subevent, event 1, associated with **act-on** (e1, x, y) representing some entity's action is followed by the subevent related to **move** (e2, y), event 2, representing movement or change of an entity, and this type of subevent, in turn, is followed by the subevent which expresses the goal or the resultant state of the movement or change. For example, the representation of *run to* formed by the co-composition operation conforms to (51).

As discussed above, the co-composition operation in (50) derives verb-preposition expressions in which PPs function as the verbs' arguments, which is summarized in (52).

(52) If the event structure of a prepositional phrase is combined with that of a verb by the co-composition operation, the PP is a syntactic argument of the verb.

6.2.1 Event Fusion

First, we take a look at representations "event fusion" operates on. By this operation, an argument PP in a verb's lexical representation appears in syntax. As far as we know, this kind of operation has not been dealt with within GL. Verbs of existence such as *exist* in (53) generally need a PP to express the location of an entity.

(53) This kind of dog exists only in Japan.

The event fusion combines a verb's state subevent and its corresponding quale **at** (e, y, z) with a preposition's state subevent and quale. As a result, argument z appears in a sentence as a complement of the preposition. In (53) the PP does not change the telicity of the verb, so the lexical representation of *exist* contains an argument corresponding to the PP. This PP is an argument, which we discussed in section 3.2.3 (See (4) in section 3.2.3).

The event structures of *exist* and *in* are shown in (54a) and (54b), respectively. (In this section, we show only relevant parts of the lexical representation.)[10, 11]

(54) a. *exist*
event struture = $\begin{bmatrix} E1 = e1: \text{state} \\ \text{head: e1} \end{bmatrix}$
qualia structure = $[\text{FORMAL} = \mathbf{at}(e1, y, z)]$

  b. *in*
event struture = $\begin{bmatrix} E1 = e1: \text{state} \\ \text{head: e1} \end{bmatrix}$
qualia structure = $[\text{FORMAL} = \mathbf{at}(e1, y, z)]$

The event type of *exist* and that of *in* are stative and the quale corresponding to each event contains **at** (e1, y, z). The event type and the type of the corresponding qualia of the two lexical items are the same. So, by (50b) their representations are combined into one event. The representation of *exist in* is schematized in (55).

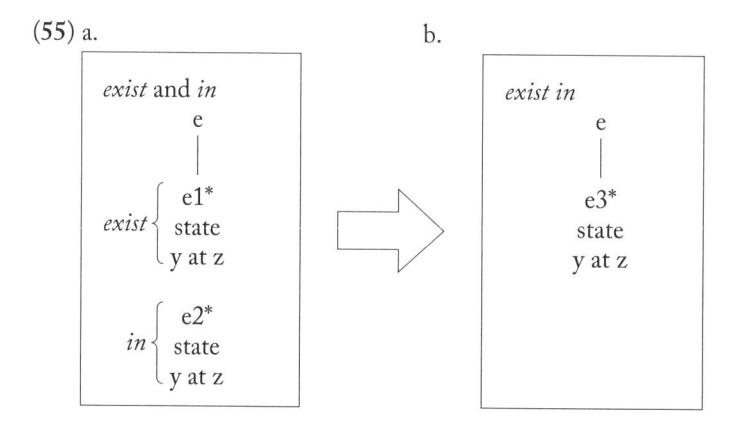

(55) a.   b.

exist and *in*	*exist in*
e	e
$\mid$	$\mid$
exist $\begin{cases} e1^* \\ \text{state} \\ y \text{ at } z \end{cases}$	e3* state y at z
in $\begin{cases} e2^* \\ \text{state} \\ y \text{ at } z \end{cases}$	

In this way, the operation in (50b) operates in order to make a verb's argument appear in syntax.

Next, let us consider examples of verbs of inherently directed motion in (56). The lexical representation of *come*, which we proposed in section 6.1.3, is in (57) and that of *into* is shown in (58); their head is the result state subevent, event 2 (cf. Pustejovsky (1995: 187)). We proposed in section 6.1.3 that the representation of *to* is the one in (59).

(56) a. Sally came into this room for an hour.
     b. Sally came to this room for an hour.

(57) *come*
$$\text{event structure} = \begin{bmatrix} E1 = e1: \text{process} \\ E2 = e2: \text{state} \\ e1 <_\alpha e2 \\ \text{head: } e2 \end{bmatrix}$$
$$\text{argument structure} = \begin{bmatrix} ARG1 = x \\ ARG2 = y \end{bmatrix}$$
$$\text{qualia structure} = \begin{bmatrix} \text{AGENTIVE} = \mathbf{move}(e1, x) \\ \text{FORMAL} = \mathbf{at}(e2, x, y) \end{bmatrix}$$

(58) *into*
$$\text{event structure} = \begin{bmatrix} E1 = e1: \text{process} \\ E2 = e2: \text{state} \\ e1 <_\alpha e2 \\ \text{head: } e2 \end{bmatrix}$$
$$\text{argument structure} = \begin{bmatrix} ARG1 = x \\ ARG2 = y \end{bmatrix}$$
$$\text{qualia structure} = \begin{bmatrix} \text{AGENTIVE} = \mathbf{move}(e1, x) \\ \text{FORMAL} = \mathbf{at}(e2, x, y) \end{bmatrix}$$

(59) *to*
$$\text{event structure} = \begin{bmatrix} E1 = e1: \text{process} \\ E2 = e2: \text{state} \\ e1 <_\alpha e2 \\ \text{head: underspecified} \end{bmatrix}$$
$$\text{argument structure} = \begin{bmatrix} ARG1 = x \\ ARG2 = y \end{bmatrix}$$

$$\text{qualia structure} = \begin{bmatrix} \text{AGENTIVE} = \textbf{move}(e1, x) \\ \text{FORMAL} = \textbf{at}(e2, x, y) \end{bmatrix}$$

The event structure of *come* and those of *to* and *into* are of the same type, process-state. The qualia structure of *come* and that of the prepositions are also the same type, **move** (e1, y) and **at** (e2, y, z). The event structures of *to* and *into* are different in headedness. The head in the event structure of *into* is the state subevent, while the head in that of *to* is underspecified. Still, either lexical representation satisfies (50a) in co-occurrence with *come*. So, the representation of *come* and that of *to* or *into* are combined, as is shown in (60).

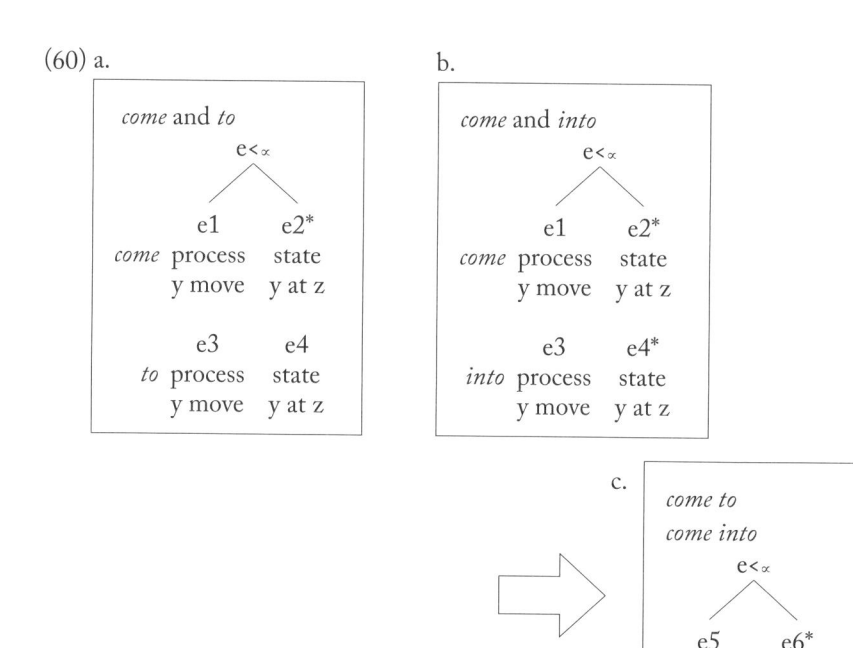

(60) a.

come and *to*

e<α

	e1	e2*
come	process	state
	y move	y at z
	e3	e4
to	process	state
	y move	y at z

b.

come and *into*

e<α

	e1	e2*
come	process	state
	y move	y at z
	e3	e4*
into	process	state
	y move	y at z

c.

come to
come into

e<α

	e5	e6*
	process	state
	y move	y at z

Furthermore, the head in the event structure of *come* is the state subevent. Thus, following the generalization in (35), "Co-composition and Headedness: the Inheritance of Headedness (i)", the head subevent is the state subevent in both event structures of *come to* and *come into*.

The preposition *in* lacks a process subevent in contrast to *to* and *into* (See (54b)). However, since in the representations for *in* and *come* the qualia structure roles corresponding to the state subevent are the same, the event structures of *come* and *in* satisfy (50b), and thus they are combined, as is shown in (61).

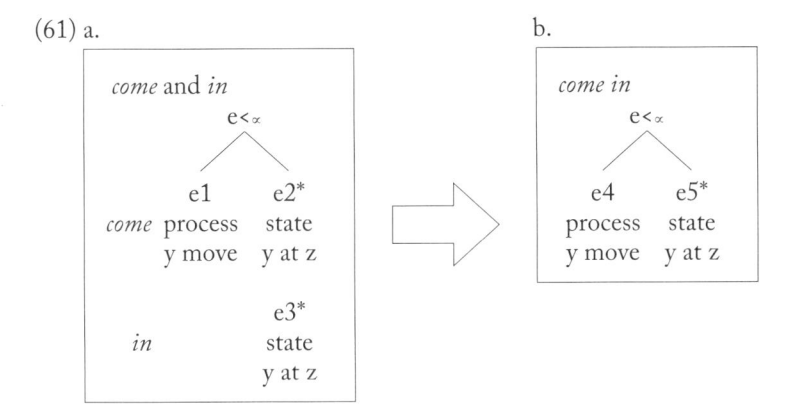

(61) a.

```
┌─────────────────────────┐
│   come and in           │
│        e<α              │
│       /    \            │
│      e1     e2*         │
│ come process  state     │
│      y move  y at z     │
│                         │
│            e3*          │
│  in        state        │
│            y at z       │
└─────────────────────────┘
```

b.

```
┌─────────────────────┐
│   come in           │
│      e<α            │
│     /    \          │
│    e4     e5*       │
│  process  state     │
│  y move   y at z    │
└─────────────────────┘
```

6.2.2 Addition of Events

Now let us consider the cases where the co-composition operation (50) seems to add a subevent to a verb's event structure. We will take the verb *run* as an example.

(62) a. Maria ran for an hour / *in an hour.
  b. John ran to the station *for ten minutes / in ten minutes.
     (in the interpretation that John ran and got to the station)

The event structure of *run* is repeated in (63).

(63) *run*
  event structure = $\begin{bmatrix} E1 = e1: \text{process} \\ E2 = e2: \text{process} \\ e1 \, o_\alpha \, e2 \\ \text{head: } e1 \end{bmatrix}$
  argument structure = $[ARG1 = x]$
  qualia structure = $\begin{bmatrix} \text{AGENTIVE} = \textbf{act}(e1, x) \\ \phantom{\text{AGENTIVE} =} \textbf{move}(e2, x) \end{bmatrix}$

Since *run* lacks a result state subevent, the event structures of *run* and of *in* cannot be combined in the same way as in the case of *come* and *in*. When we see the difference of acceptability between (62a) and (62b), it is obvious that the verbal expression *run to* is telic while *run* is atelic. That is, in the event structure of *run to* there is a transition from a process subevent to a state subevent. To account for this aspectual difference between *run to* and *run*, co-composition operations have been proposed by researchers such as Kageyama and Yumoto (1997), Rappaport Hovav and Levin (1998) and Alsina (1999) among others. We argue that the co-composition operation which co-composes the representation for *run to* in (62b) operates under condition (50a).

Both *run* and *to* have the process subevent whose quale is **move** (e, x), and thus, the verb and the preposition meet condition (50a) and their event structures are combined by co-composition, as is shown in (64c) and (64d).

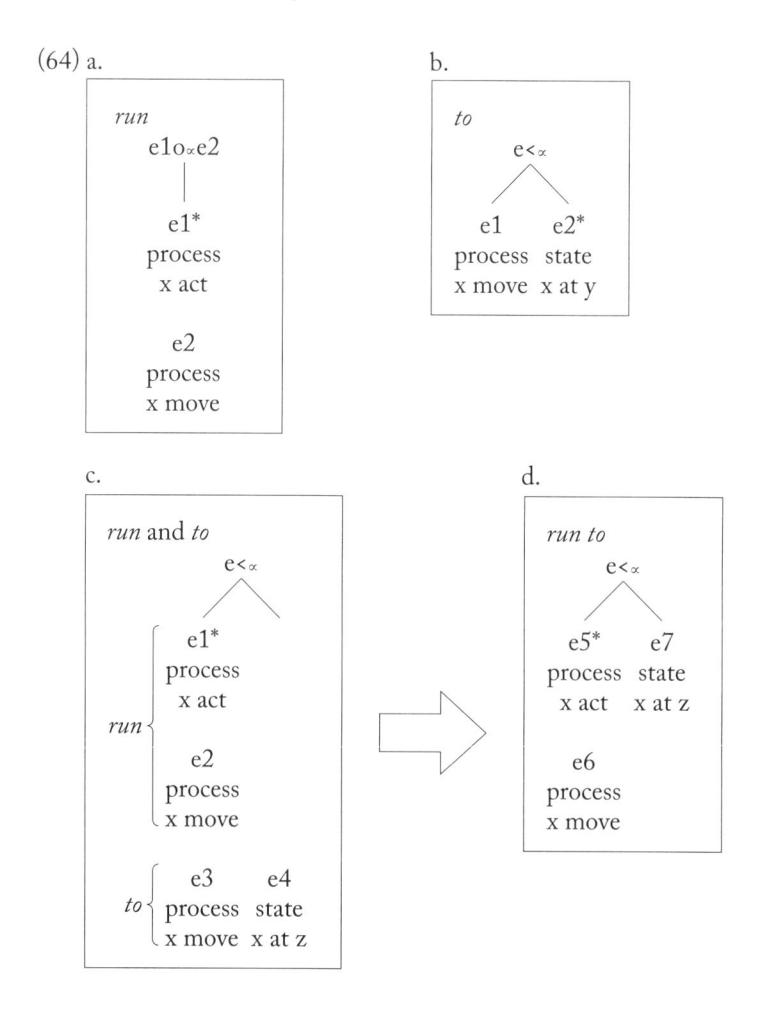

(64) a.

```
┌─────────────────┐
│ run             │
│    e1o∝e2       │
│      │          │
│     e1*         │
│    process      │
│    x act        │
│                 │
│     e2          │
│    process      │
│    x move       │
└─────────────────┘
```

b.

```
┌─────────────────────┐
│ to                  │
│      e<∝            │
│     ╱  ╲            │
│    e1   e2*         │
│  process state      │
│  x move  x at y     │
└─────────────────────┘
```

c.

```
┌─────────────────────────┐
│ run and to              │
│         e<∝             │
│        ╱  ╲             │
│     ┌ e1*               │
│     │ process           │
│     │ x act             │
│ run ┤                   │
│     │ e2                │
│     │ process           │
│     └ x move            │
│                         │
│     ┌ e3    e4          │
│  to ┤ process state     │
│     └ x move  x at z    │
└─────────────────────────┘
```

⇒

d.

```
┌─────────────────────┐
│ run to              │
│      e<∝            │
│     ╱  ╲            │
│    e5*    e7        │
│  process state      │
│  x act   x at z     │
│                     │
│    e6               │
│  process            │
│  x move             │
└─────────────────────┘
```

In event fusion, which we saw in the last subsection, the event structure of a verb and the event structure derived by the operation are the same type (See (55), (60) and (61).). This is because the verbs' event structure contains the state subevent by nature. On the other hand, in (64d) it seems that the resultant state subevent is "added" to the verb's original events.

As we mentioned above (52), the co-composition operation conforms to the notion of action chain: if an entity does some action and some entity moves by this action, it reaches some location. For example, the verb *run* expresses some entity's intentional activity (of moving legs) and the entity's movement as is shown in (64a), and by being paired with *to* this verb is provided with a resultant state. In this case, the whole event expressed by *run* and *to* forms an action chain. Since the event structures of *run* and *to* meet the condition stated in (50a), (that is, both contain subevents of movement), these event structures are combined through co-composition, as is schematically shown in (64c)–(64d). Thus, the derived representation in (64d) accords with the situation that an entity does some activity; the activity causes the entity itself to move and it reaches some location.

Following Kageyama (2003), we consider the co-composition operation in (50a), which seems to add a resultant state subevent, to be peculiar to Germanic languages. Kageyama (2003: 354-360) argues that Germanic languages such as English and German have prepositions expressing transition while Japanese and Korean do not and that the languages holding the transition prepositions have the operation of LCS composition. So, the latter two languages do not have the co-composition operation. See Table 2:

Table 2. Languages and Transition Prepositions and Postpositions

	DIRECTION	EXTENT	TRANSITION	LOCATION
English	*toward*	*up to*	*To*	*at*
German	*auf...zu*	*bis zu*	*Zu*	*an, zu*
Japanese	*e*	*made*	*(ni)*	*ni*
Korean	*eulo*	*ggaji*	*(ey)*	*eye*

Now, let us see an example where the co-composition operation does not operate. In (65) the co-composition operation does not work, because *laugh*'s representation does not have a subevent of movement or change; *laugh*'s lexical representation is shown in (66).

(65) *John laughed to the classroom.

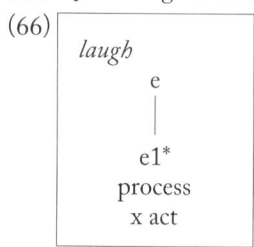

(66)
```
laugh
     e
     |
    e1*
  process
   x act
```

The event structure of *to* holds a subevent of movement and a state subevent. By (50a), in order for the co-composition operation to operate, *laugh*'s event structure must contain a subevent of movement; however, it does not. Thus, co-composition does not apply here and the *to*-phrase is not permitted to co-occur with *laugh*.

6.2.3 Residual Issues: Possibility of Extending the Co-composition Operation

We have three residual issues relating to the co-composition operation and its conditions in (50). In this subsection we discuss them one by one.

6.2.3.1 Verbs of Emission with Directional Phrases

As is often said, verbs of sound emission, which we discussed in the previous chapter, when co-occurring with directional or path phrases, are used as verbs of motion.[12] (cf. Levin (1993), Levin and Rappapport Hovav (1995) and Kageyama (2006) among others.)

(67) a. The cart <u>rumbled down</u> the street. (Levin (1993: 235))
 b. THOUSANDS of islanders fled in terror yesterday as 20ft walls of boiling mud and ash <u>roared down</u> the slopes of Mount Pinatubo in the Philippines. (BNC: HAF 338)
 c. As soon as his life raft <u>boomed into</u> the sea, Delaney pulled the quick release tag and dropped from his harness. (BNC: BPA 580)

As for verbs of light emission, these verbs express existence of light emitted by some entity.

(68) a. As the lights blinked in the overhead monitors we could see more and more buses were sold out. (BNC, G2W: 595)
 b. The high tower which held some lights blinked across the sky.

However, many light emission verbs can be used as verbs of motion, as is shown in (69). The lights placed on the Titanic are considered to move in (69f), and so, *blazing into* expresses movement of the lights.[13]

(69) a. The burning car blazed across the field.
 b. A shooting star flashed across the sky.
 c. The satellite blinked across the sky.
 d. An image flickered across the screen.
 e. Missiles blazed in every direction through the darkness, crossing paths in zigzags. (BNC, BNU: 1308)
 f. For at the very time he was sitting alone in the house, in the early hours of the morning of the funeral day, reading again his father's will, the most modern ship in the world, the SS Titanic, was going down stern first, with all its lights blazing into the icy waters of the North Atlantic. (BNC, ATE: 2244)
 g. When the house exploded, pieces of the balcony blazed across the sky.

We argue that this motion-verb usage of emission verbs is given through co-composition which is motivated by nonvolitionality of activity denoted by verbs. Following the discussion in section 5.3 and section 5.4.1, we consider that the lexical representation of the verb *blaze*, which is a verb of light emission, is the one in (70).

(70) *blaze*
event structure = $\begin{bmatrix} E1 = e1\text{: process} \\ S\text{-}E2 = e2\text{: state} \\ \qquad e2 = e3 \text{ or } e4 \\ \qquad \begin{bmatrix} e3\text{: state} \\ e4\text{: state} \end{bmatrix} \\ e1o_{\alpha}e2 \\ \text{head: underspecified} \end{bmatrix}$

$$\text{argument structure} = \begin{bmatrix} \text{ARG1} = x \\ \text{ARG2} = y \end{bmatrix}$$

$$\text{qualia structure} = \begin{bmatrix} \text{FORMAL} = \textbf{at}\,(e3,\,\text{BLAZE\&x},\,y) \\ \phantom{\text{FORMAL} =}\textbf{with}\,(e4,\,y,\,\text{BLAZE\&x}) \\ \text{AGENTIVE} = \textbf{act}\,(e1,\,z) \\ z = x \text{ or } y \end{bmatrix}$$

It has been pointed out that verbs which describe the expression of sounds by animals cannot be used as verbs of motion even if they co-occur with directional phrases, as is shown in (71).

(71) a. *The duck quacked down the path.　　　　(Levin (1993: 212))
　　　　　　　　　　　　　　　(Verbs of Sounds Made by Animals)
　　b. *He yelled down the street.　　　　　　　(Lupsa (2002))
　　　　　　　　　　　　　　　(Verbs of Manner of Speaking)

In contrast, verbs describing sound that necessarily occurs when some entity makes locomotion can be utilized as a verb of motion with directional phrases, as pointed out by Levin and Rappapport Hovav (1995), Kageyama and Yumoto (1997) and Ueno and Kageyama (2001) among others: this is the case of verbs of emission in (67). (However, see Kageyama (2006).) The verbs in (71) do not undergo locative inversion, which shows that their lexical representation does not contain **at** (e, x, y) in the qualia structure.

(72) a. *Outside barked the dog.　　(Verbs of Sounds Made by Animals)
　　b. *Outside cooed the pigeon.
(73) a. *In the room whispered a secret agent.　(Verbs of Manner of Speaking)
　　b. *Into Mary's ear hissed Julie.

Thus, we consider the verb *quack* to be an activity verb and propose its lexical representation as in (74).

(74)　*quack*
　　　event structure = $\begin{bmatrix} \text{E1} = e1\text{: process} \\ \text{head: } e1 \end{bmatrix}$

argument structure = [ARG1 = x]
qualia structure = $\begin{bmatrix} \text{AGENTIVE} = \textbf{act}(e1, x) \\ \text{TELIC} = \textbf{make}(e, x\text{'s throat}, \text{QUACK}) \\ \textbf{at}(e, \text{QUACK}, y) \end{bmatrix}$

The activity denoted in the lexical representation of *quack* is intentionally conducted to make quack sounds. Thus, there are no factors which cause movement of an entity which quacks, and there is no **move** (e, y) in (74). Since the lexical representation of *quack* does not satisfy the condition for the co-composition operation in (50), the co-composition operation does not work for the expression *quack across* in (75), and *quack* in this expression is not interpreted as a motion verb.

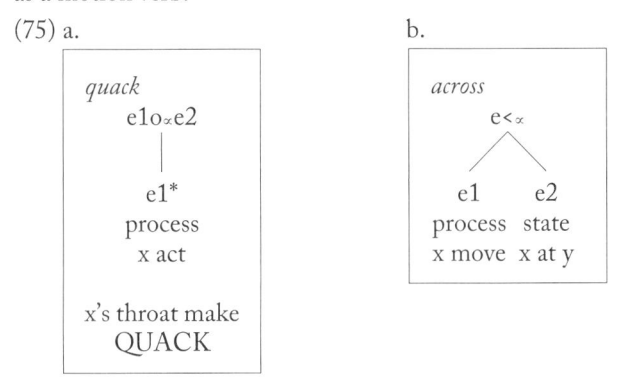

(75) a.

quack
$e1o_\alpha e2$

$e1^*$
process
x act

x's throat make
QUACK

b.

across
$e <_\alpha$

e1   e2
process state
x move x at y

The representation of *blaze*, which we have just proposed in (70), does not contain **move** (e, y). Thus, the co-composition operation seems not to operate on the expression *blaze across* at first glance. However, we should note the difference between *blaze* and *quack*. The activity represented in *quack*'s lexical representation in (74) is volitional; this activity is conducted in order to make quack sounds. In this respect, *quack*'s activity is semantically salient by having its own purpose, and this event serves as a head. In contrast, the activity in *blaze*'s representation is nonvolitional, as we mentioned concerning *sparkle* in (52) in the last chapter. The nonvolitional activity is conducted without any purpose. We consider nonvolitional activities without purposes expressed by emission verbs not to be semantically focused: therefore, in these verbs' lexical representations any subevent can become a head, which leads to their polysemy such as we examined from section 5.1 to section 5.4.

When *blaze* co-occurs with a directional PP which holds its own head subevent, the co-composition operation works in order to introduce, or determine, a head subevent in the entire event structure consisting of the verb and the PP. Through the co-composition the directional PP provides the subevent of movement. That is, the interpretation of movement, and no semantic contradiction arises because of the underspecificity of the verb's headedness. Although the lexical representations of the verb and the PP do not meet condition (50), the co-composition operation exceptionally works owing to this underspecificity of *blaze*'s head and the PP's headedness.

In contrast, *quack*'s lexical representation holds its own head since the activity denoted by this verb is volitional, so it is not necessary for the co-compositional operation, whose role in this case is to introduce a head event, to work. Besides, *quack*'s activity forms an action chain including the occurrence of quack sounds, and there may arise a semantic discrepancy between this action chain and the action chain brought by a directional PP which includes an entity's movement (and a goal of the movement).

The event structures and the qualia structures of the expression *blaze* and *across* in (69a) are schematically shown in (76). The representation in (76c) is the one for *blaze across*.

(69) a. The burning car blazed across the field.

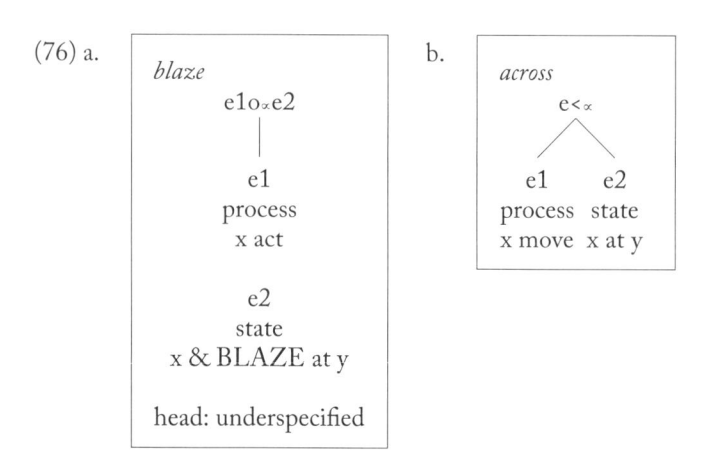

(76) a.

blaze

$e1o_\alpha e2$

$e1$
process
x act

$e2$
state
x & BLAZE at y

head: underspecified

b.

across

$e <_\alpha$

$e1 \quad e2$
process state
x move x at y

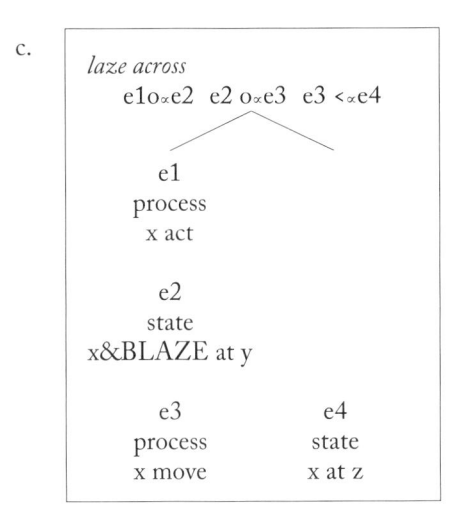

c.
```
laze across
    e1o∝e2  e2 o∝e3  e3 <∝e4

         e1
       process
        x act

         e2
        state
    x&BLAZE at y

      e3           e4
    process       state
    x move        x at z
```

We assume that *blaze*'s subevents and *across*'s subevent of movement overlap. Owing to this overlap, the interpretation that "the car moved across the field, blazing," where *blaze* seems to modify the car's movement, occurs. Levin and Rappaport Hovav (1992) suggest that in the interpretation of examples such as the one in (69a), the prepositional phrase *across the field* functions as if it were a predicate of this sentence and the verb *blaze* just expresses the manner of the motion. The preposition *across* has a head subevent in its lexical representation by nature, and thus, the meaning of this preposition is salient in the interpretation.

We can find some other verbs that behave as motion verbs together with directional PPs even though they express nonvolitional activities without any purpose. Those are in (77), and in (78) they act as motion verbs.

(77) a. A large flag fluttered over the fort.   (Levin (1993: 251))
     b. Helium balloons were joggling above the crowds.
(78) a. The leaves of a ginkgo tree fluttered to the ground.
     b. The carriage joggled down the street.

The verbs in these examples are classified in the verb class named "verbs of modes of being involving motion" in Levin (1993: 251), in which she explains that "[t]hese verbs describe states of existence of inanimate entities that involve types of motion typical of these entities. That is, a type of motion characterizes the existence of these entities." As Levin (1993) writes, these verbs take inanimate entities as their subjects and express their existence. These characteristics are similar to emission verbs' characteristics, and we consider the verbs in (77) to denote some entities' nonvolitional activities and their existence.

The verb *flutter* in (77a) and (78a) undergoes LI, as is shown in (79).

(79)   Over the fort fluttered a large flag.   (Levin (1993: 252))

We consider this verb's lexical representation to be the one in (80).

(80) *flutter*
event structure = $\begin{bmatrix} E1 = e1: \text{process} \\ E2 = e2: \text{state} \\ e1o_\alpha e2 \\ \text{head: underspecified} \end{bmatrix}$
argument structure = $\begin{bmatrix} ARG1 = x \\ ARG2 = y \end{bmatrix}$
qualia structure = $\begin{bmatrix} FORMAL = \mathbf{at}(e2, x, y) \\ AGENTIVE = \mathbf{act}(e1, x) \end{bmatrix}$

As we saw in (18) in the present chapter and in (34) in the previous chapter, LI verbs contain **at** (e2, x, y) in their representation and the result subevent is a head. Since this verb can be used in the progressive form as in (81), the process subevent can also function as a head, so in (80) a head event is underspecified.

(81)   The flag was fluttering aloft.

The function **act** in (80) denotes a nonvolitional activity and this activity itself is a light irregular or trembling motion, that is, a "fluttering" motion. When this verb co-occurs with a directional PP *to the ground*, the movement interpretation is given by the preposition, like verbs of light emission in (69). When the lexical representations of *flutter* and *to* are combined, *flutter*'s process subevent and *to*'s process subevent overlap each other. The former is related to **act** and the latter is related to **move**. Thus, the derived interpretation is that the leaves fell to the ground with fluttering motion.

The examples in (82) support our claim that the nonvolitionality of activities denoted by emission verbs is crucial to the co-composition operation which gives rise to these verbs' motion-verb usage. As Levin (1993: 236) notes, the verb *whistle* functions as a motion verb only when the sound expressed by this verb "is a necessary concomitant of the motion of some entity".

(82) a. *Shelly whistled down the street.
     b. The bullet whistled through the air.

The **act** function of *whistle* in (82a) denotes an activity to make a sound and the event related to this function makes into a head. The co-composition operation does not work in this case and *whistle* in (82a) does not behave as a motion verb. On the other hand, the activity denoted by *whistle* in (82b) is nonvolitional. This verb is combined with *through* and acts as a motion verb.

Summarizing so far, emission verbs in (67), (69) and (82) and verbs of modes of being involving motion in (78), co-occurring with directional PPs, act as motion verbs. This motion-verb interpretation is built on the co-composition operation, but this operation, in fact, violates the condition in (50) as these verbs' lexical representations do not contain the **move** function. However, since the **act** function denoted by these verbs is nonvolitional and the subevent related to this function is not a head, co-composition provides the verb lexical representations with directional PP head subevents that denote movement. Thus, we contend that the nature of nonvolitionality yields these verbs' verb-of-motion interpretations.

The representation of the verb *blaze* in (70) represents some activity of some entity emitting light and the existence of the emitted light but, by itself, does not express the motion of the entity or the light. We consider that this is a character common to verbs of light emission that function as verbs of motion, except for the verb *beam*. The verb *beam* expresses some entity's emitting light and, at the same time, the motion of the light, as is stated in (83). Note the examples in (84), which are shown in COBUILD.

(83) *beam* (COBUILD): If something such as the sun or a lamp beams down, it sends light to a place and shines on it.
(84) a. All you see of the outside world is the sunlight beaming through the cracks in the roof.
     b. A sharp white spot-light beamed down on a small stage...

The lexical representation of *beam* is the one in (85).

(85) *beam*
event structure = $\begin{bmatrix} E1 = e1: \text{process} \\ S\text{-}E2 = e2: \text{state} \\ \quad e2 = e3 \text{ or } e4 \\ \quad \begin{bmatrix} e3: \text{process} \\ e4: \text{state} \end{bmatrix} \\ e1o_\propto e2 \\ \text{head: underspecified} \end{bmatrix}$

argument structure = $\begin{bmatrix} ARG1 = x \\ ARG2 = y \end{bmatrix}$

qualia structure = $\begin{bmatrix} \text{FORMAL} = \textbf{with}(e4, y, \text{BEAM\&x}) \\ \text{AGENTIVE} = \textbf{act}(e1, z) \\ \quad z = x \text{ or } y \\ \quad \textbf{move}(e3, \text{BEAM}) \end{bmatrix}$

(e.g., (86a): x = the car, y = the tunnel)

The agentive role represents that the light itself moves. Thus, when this verb is used with a directional phrase, it expresses either the motion of the light itself or the motion of the entity which is emitting the light. In fact, the example in (86a) has the interpretation in (86b), in addition to expressing the car's motion into the tunnel.

(86) a. The car beamed into the tunnel.
 b. The car stopped in front of the tunnel and beamed its head lights into the tunnel.

In this subsection, we have shown that the representation for emission verbs we have proposed in section 5.4.1 and the interrelation between nonvolitionality and co-composition explain the verb-of-motion usage of light-emission verbs. This particular usage has not been discussed much to date in the literature. It is left for future research to determine how volitionality and the notion of action chain are represented in lexical and semantic representations in GL.

6.2.3.2 *In* and *On* as Directional Phrases

As we saw in subsection 6.1.4, the prepositions *in* and *on* are sometimes used as directional phrases, and in these usages these prepositions seem to be combined with verbs by the co-composition operation. One such example is in (87a). If the co-composition operation works in (87), it is problematic to our analysis, since this operation violates (50).

(87) a. A lot of children ran in the room.
  b.

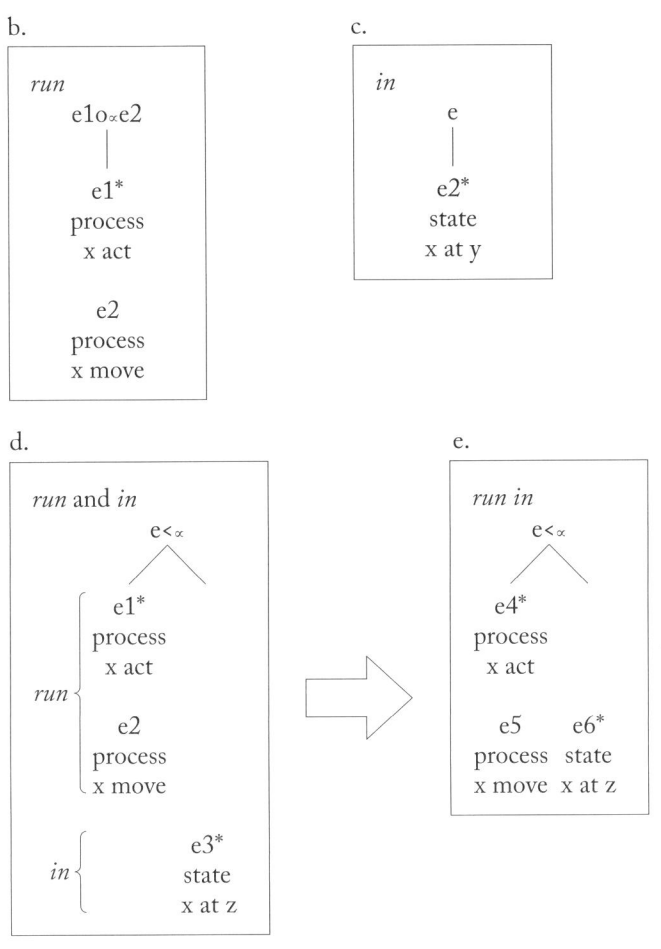

```
┌─────────────────┐
│ run             │
│    e1o∝e2       │
│      │          │
│     e1*         │
│    process      │
│    x act        │
│                 │
│     e2          │
│    process      │
│    x move       │
└─────────────────┘
```

  c.

```
┌─────────────────┐
│ in              │
│       e         │
│       │         │
│      e2*        │
│     state       │
│     x at y      │
└─────────────────┘
```

  d.

```
┌──────────────────────────┐
│ run and in               │
│           e<∝            │
│          /  \            │
│       ┌  e1*             │
│       │  process          │
│       │  x act            │
│  run ─┤                  │
│       │  e2              │
│       │  process          │
│       └  x move           │
│                          │
│       ┌  e3*             │
│  in ──┤  state            │
│       └  x at z           │
└──────────────────────────┘
```

  e.

```
┌─────────────────────┐
│ run in              │
│       e<∝           │
│      /  \           │
│    e4*              │
│   process           │
│   x act             │
│                     │
│    e5      e6*      │
│  process   state    │
│  x move    x at z   │
└─────────────────────┘
```

We schematized the event structure and the associated qualia of *run* and *in* in (87b)–(87c) and those of the expression *run in* in (87d)–(87e). The event structure of *in* lacks the process subevent which expresses movement or change in contrast to *to*, which we saw in (64b), and does not meet (50).

The preposition *in* implies the notion of boundary; this notion might help the co-composition work in (87). When we say "a lot of children ran in the room" in the meaning that a lot of children ran into the room, this sentence implies the children moved across the boundary of the room. The preposition *in* in (88) is used as a directional phrase, and here the movement into the boundary of the train or the water is suggested.

(88) He jumped in the train/water. (Lindstromberg (1997))

Crossing a boundary suggests movement of some entity, and this suggestion of movement may supplement the lack of the subevent of movement in *in*'s event structure in (87c), which requires some co-composition work in order to gain the expression *run in*.

In contrast to *in*, the preposition *at* only expresses some location without any mention of the relation between some entity and some location such as boundary. So, we predict that the operation working in (87d, e) does not operate in an example which contains *at*. This prediction is borne out:

(89) The dog ran at the boy in 5 minutes.

The example in (89) does not necessarily imply the dog reached the boy, and, in addition, the prepositional phrase *in 5 minutes* is interpreted as the length of time which was needed before the occurrence of the dog's action, which shows that the co-composition does not operate in (89).

6.2.3.3 Caused Motion Construction and Resultative Construction

The third residual issue is related to the caused motion construction (in Goldberg (1995)) and strong resultative construction sentences such as the ones in (90).

(90) a. Tom sneezed the handkerchief off the table.
    b. They laughed the poor guy out of the room.
    c. Sally hammered the metal flat.

The lexical representations of the verb *hammer* and the adjective *flat* in (90c) are given in (91). In strong resultative construction sentences, only non-gradable adjectives or closed-scale and maximal endpoint adjectives appear (cf. Wechsler (2005), Hay et al. (1999) and Mihara (2007) among others).

(91) a. *hammer*
   event structure = $\begin{bmatrix} \text{E1} = \text{e1: process} \\ \text{head: e1} \end{bmatrix}$

   qualia structure = $\begin{bmatrix} \text{AGENTIVE} = \textbf{act-on}(\text{e1}, x, y) \\ \text{TELIC} = \textbf{at}(e, y, \text{AFFECTED}) \end{bmatrix}$

   b. *flat*
   event structure = $\begin{bmatrix} \text{E1} = \text{e1: state} \\ \text{head: e1} \end{bmatrix}$

   qualia structure = $\begin{bmatrix} \text{FORMAL} = \textbf{at}(\text{e1}, y, \text{FLAT}) \\ \begin{bmatrix} \text{FORMAL: SCALE<FLAT>} \\ \text{Min..........Max*} \\ \text{AGENTIVE} = \textbf{move}\,(e, y) \end{bmatrix} \end{bmatrix}$

The event structure of *hammer* contains **at** (e, y, AFFECTED) as a telic role in its qualia structure although this role is not related to any event in the event structure. *Flat* is a closed-scale, maximal endpoint adjective. We tentatively suggest the lexical representation of *flat* in (90b). The formal role of *flat* has its own qualia structure which contains the closed scale of flatness and the agentive role, **move** (e, y), representing an entity's change of state on that scale. The relation of the event structure and the qualia structure of the expression *hammer NP flat* is schematized in (92). (In (92) the qualia in the rectangles are the ones which are not associated with any subevents in the event structure.)

(92)

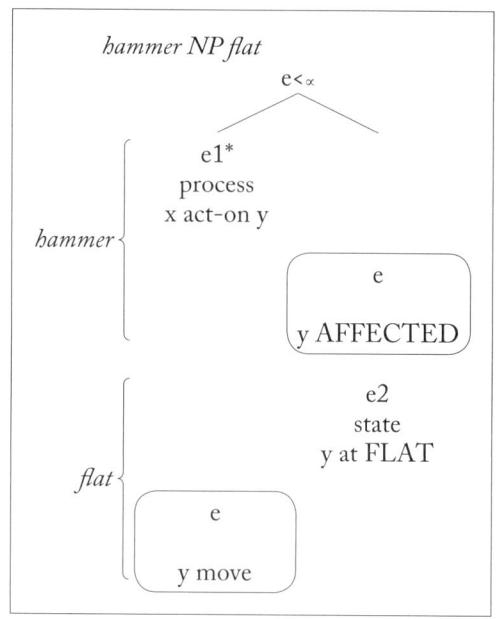

```
          hammer NP flat
                      e<α
                    ╱     ╲
              e1*
              process
              x act-on y
   hammer ⎰                      ┌─────────────┐
          ⎱                      │      e      │
                                 │  y AFFECTED │
                                 └─────────────┘

                                      e2
                                     state
                                    y at FLAT
        ⎰                        ┌─────────────┐
   flat ⎱                        │      e      │
                                 │   y move    │
                                 └─────────────┘
```

In (92) a complete action chain such as action, movement or change and resultant state is not formed, since the telic role of *hammer* and the agentive role of the scale of flatness of *flat* are not correlated to any subevents. However, co-occurrence of the verb *hammer* and the NP *metal* gives rise to the interpretation that the action of hammering the metal affects the metal and its form may change (into a flat form), and furthermore, the resultant state subevent of the adjective *flat* describes the final state of the metal. In this way, the combination of meanings of the verb, the internal argument NP and the adjective may help a complete action chain be formed.

The verb *sneeze* in (90a) contains **act** (e, x), which represents the action of sneezing, and may hold **move** (e, BREATH), which represents the motion of breath emitted by sneezing, in its qualia structure. Although the latter role is not associated with any subevents in the event structure, some operation may apply and give rise to the semantic representation of *sneeze the handkerchief off the table* in the same way as that of *hammer the metal flat*. The verb *laugh* in (90b) may contain only **act** (e, x), which represents the action of laughing, and not the one such as **move** (e, LAUGH); the event structure of *laugh* also does not meet (50).

An exceptional co-composition operation may apply here, too.

We consider that the semantic representations of emission verbs with directional PPs, verbal expressions containing *in*, caused motion construction sentences and strong resultative construction sentences are formed through the co-composition operation and that subevents and qualia, which are needed for the co-composition operation may be supplemented by nonvolitionality, action chains and some generative functions of the qualia structure such as we saw in (92).

6.3 Summary

In this chapter we have examined the relations between motion verbs and argument PPs and treated the event structure and the operation of co-composition. First, in section 6.1, being concerned with the operation of co-composition and locative inversion sentences, we proposed the representation of the preposition *to*, and made clear the nature of the co-composition operation and the relation between the co-composition operation and headedness. In section 6.2 we discussed the co-composition operation and its conditions. We showed that the co-composition operation has two functions. One is to make a verb's argument appear in syntax as an argument PP. This function corresponds to the argument fusion operation proposed in Jackendoff (1990), and we named this operation event fusion in section 6.2.1. The other function is to add a resultant subevent to verb event structures and to give a semantic representation of such a verbal expression as *run into*, as we saw in section 6.2.2. As residual issues we referred to three problems. First, the verb-of-motion usage of light emission verbs was accounted for by the characteristics of these verbs' lexical representation and the interrelation between nonvolitionality and co-composition. Second, *in*- and *on*-phrases which act as directional phrases and semantic representations of caused motion construction sentences. Third, strong resultative construction sentences may be dealt with by extending the co-composition operation and its conditions in (50).

Discussion in this chapter has revealed the nature of the co-composition operation, the event structure and the qualia structure and the way of determination of the head event in a co-composed event structure. In the next chapter we will consider relations between motion verbs and adjunct PPs and the composition operation which forms the semantic representation of VPs.

Endnotes

1 Moreover, the verbs belonging to the class of verbs of existence and appearance in their basic meanings are excluded when they are used in extended senses, as shown in (i). The verbs in (i) denote ascription of property rather than existence in spatial location, and they are unacceptable. This suggests that for a verb to occur in the locative inversion sentence, the semantic field of the verb needs to be spatial location.
 (i) a. *In effect remained a very old law.
   b. *Up stayed an old man.
2 Nakajima (2001) does not mention which role the function **at** (ei, x, y) belongs to in the qualia structure. From the meaning expressed by this function, we assume it is of the formal role.
3 Lexical representations, especially qualia structures, of prepositions may represent more detailed information. For example, the lexical representation of *in* we propose in (6) in chapter 7 holds the quale **at-the-inside-of** (e1, x, y). In this chapter, however, we would like to focus on headedness and event types in the event structure in order to grasp interaction among lexical representations and co-composition.
4 See (10) in chapter 7 for the Inheritance of Headedness (ii), which is the case of composition of adjunct PPs.
5 Verbs of emission are used as motion verbs when they co-occur with directional PPs.
 (i) a. The cart rumbled down the street.
   b. ?The burning car blazed across the field.
 The headedness of *across* affects the telicity of the verb *blaze* (or the verbal expression *blaze across*), and in addition, in (i) the headedness of the prepositions gives rise to motion sense. We should notice that (35) explains the interpretation of the examples in (i). See section 6.2.3, where we discuss this use of verbs of emission.
6 This example was pointed out to me by Takane Ito.
7 For the final version of the representation for *in*, see section 7.1.
8 As we saw in section 6.1.4, the *in*-phrase of *run in* in (46a) is interpreted as a directional phrase. We suggested that the co-composition operation exceptionally should operate on this example and that the *in*-phrase is re-interpreted as expressing a resultant state in order to satisfy condition (18) on verbal expressions appearing in locative inversion sentences.
9 In the event structure of some verbs, the temporal order of event 1 and event 2 is "overlap (e1 o$_\propto$ e2)".
10 A lot of verbs of existence (i.e. *exist*, *stay*, *remain* and so on) and some verbs of inherently directed motion such as *arrive* require a PP to denote a location where an entity or entities exist. In our GL, these verbs' argument z in their quale **at** (e, y, z) is introduced to syntax by a PP.
11 The final version of *in*'s representation is proposed in section 7.1.
12 The underlines are added by the author.
13 The examples in (69a-d) were pointed out to the author by James Postle and the one in (69g) by Christopher Tancredi (personal communication). Some of my informants judged the examples in (69) marginal. See Isono (2012) for further discussion.

Chapter 7

Adjuncts and Semantic Representation: The Japanese Particle *Made*

In this chapter we explore the relationship between the event structure of motion verbs and that of adjunct phrases, namely adverbial prepositional phrases in English and Japanese phrases containing the particle *made*. There are three types of relations between motion verbs and co-occurring PPs: in the first two types, PPs function as argument phrases of verbs, and in the third one PPs behave as adjuncts. In the previous chapter we examined phrases consisting of argument PPs and motion verbs, and we argued that the co-composition operation forms these phrases' semantic representation. We also proposed its conditions. In this chapter we study the third relation type mentioned above: that is, we deal with VPs containing adjunct PPs and motion verbs. This discussion will reveal the semantic representation of a VP which contains a motion verb and an adjunct phrase, and we will uncover the overall relation between motion verbs and PPs and their semantic representations.

In the course of our discussion, we will propose the composition operation in which subevents in the event structure of a verb's lexical representation are inserted into an argument position in the argument structure of an adjunct phrase which co-occurs with the verb. With this proposal, we will have accounted for two kinds of operations: the co-composition operation for argument-type PPs and the composition operation for adjunct PPs. We will also argue the way the head event and the event type of the derived event structure is determined and that the qualia structure contributes to the interpretation of sentences which contain an adjunct phrase. In frameworks mainly utilizing LCS, it has been suggested that an adjunct modifies the event template of a verb. As we saw in the last chapter, *in*-phrases function as argument phrases in some cases and as adjuncts in other cases. Japanese *made*-phrases also seem to have both argument usage and adjunct usage, as we will see in section 7.2. In the LCS approach, one LCS is assumed for each usage: *in* and *made* are given two LCSs. The GL approach assumes only one lexical representation for *in* or *made*, and semantic representations containing these phrases are composed through the co-composition or composition operations. We will show that the representation proposed in this chapter, especially the event structure and the qualia structure, appropriately represents the polysemy and behavior of adjunct phrases we consider in this chapter.

In section 7.1, we will deal with English *in*-phrases as in (1), and will propose that in the semantic representation of the VP, the event in the event structure of the verb *run* is substituted for an argument in the argument structure of the preposition *in*. (The interpretation of *run in* discussed here is different from the one in (46a) in section 6.1.4.)

(1)   The children ran in the park.   (*in the room*: a locational PP)

In section 7.2, we will show that the proposal in section 7.1 accounts for various usages of the Japanese particle *made*, which is also considered to form an adjunct. One example of a *made*-phrase is in (2).

(2)   Taroo-ga   kisi-made   30-pun-kan   oyoi-da.
        Taro-NOM   shore-as.far.as   thirty-minutes-long   swim-PAST
        'Taro kept swimming for thirty minutes and got to the shore.'

Furthermore, in section 7.3 we will discuss the semantic representation of the Japanese *naka-o* construction, an example of which is shown in (3).[1]

(3)   Kare-wa   ame-no-naka-o   soto-o   de-arui-ta.
        He-TOP   rain-GEN-inside-ACC   outside-ACC   out-walk-PAST
        'He walked around outside in the rain.'

We will suggest that we can obtain the correct semantic representation of a *naka-o* construction sentence by adopting our suggestion proposed in section 7.1 without employing the operation of conceptual cloning which was proposed in Kageyama (2002, 2003b). We will also show that the meanings and usages of *naka-de* as well as *naka-o* can be accounted for by the combination of the lexical representation of *naka* and the characteristics of the particle *de* and the accusative case marker *o*. In section 7.4 we will summarize the discussion.

7.1 Adjunct *In*-phrase and its Semantic Representation

The *in*-phrase in (1) is regarded as an adjunct phrase in the reading in which the activity of running was performed inside the park, since in this reading this sentence undergoes neither the locative inversion operation nor the pseudo-passive operation, as is shown in (5). (Example (1) is repeated below as (4)).

(4) The children ran in the park.
       'The children ran inside the park.'
(5) a. *The park was run in by the children.
      b. *In the park ran the children.

In order to deal with this *in*-phrase, we propose the lexical representation of *in* shown in (6).

(6) *in*
       event struture = $\begin{bmatrix} E1 = e1: \text{state} \\ \text{head: e1} \end{bmatrix}$
       argument structure = $\begin{bmatrix} ARG1 = x: \text{entity/event} \\ ARG2 = y \end{bmatrix}$
       qualia structure = [FORMAL = **at-the-inside-of**(e1, x, y)]

In the argument structure in (6) there are two arguments, x and y. We propose here that not only an entity but also an event which is expressed by a verb can serve as argument 1 of *in*.[2] We propose that the semantic representation of the VP *run in the park* in (4) is formed by the composition operation, which is shown in (7).

(7) Composition of Semantic Representations of Verbs and Adjunct PPs: Event Insertion
       When subevents of a verb are substituted for an argument in a lexical representation of a PP by a composition operation, the PP functions as

an adjunct.

The semantic representation for the VP *run in the park* in (4) is derived from the lexical representation of *in* and that of *run* in (8): the derived representation is shown in (9).

(8) *run*
event structure = $\begin{bmatrix} E1 = e1: \text{process} \\ E2 = e2: \text{process} \\ e1 <o_\alpha e2 \\ \text{head: } e1 \end{bmatrix}$
argument structure = $[\text{ARG1} = w]$
qualia structure = $[\text{AGENTIVE} = \textbf{act}(e1, w) \; \textbf{move}(e2, w)]$

(9) *the children ran in the park*
event structure = $[E1 = e1: \text{process}]$
argument structure = $\begin{bmatrix} \text{ARG1} = x: \text{event } [e2 \& e3)] \\ \text{ARG2} = y \end{bmatrix}$
qualia structure = $\begin{bmatrix} \text{FORMAL} = \textbf{at-the-inside-of}(e1, [\textbf{act}(e2, w) \& \\ \textbf{move}(e3, w)], y) \end{bmatrix}$

In (9) and the following representations, when more than one subevent is substituted for an argument position, we tentatively utilize square brackets and "&". For example, in (9), where the subevents e2 corresponding to e1 in (8) and e3 corresponding to e2 in (8) are substituted for argument *x* of *in*, we denote the argument as "x: event [e2 & e3]" in the argument structure and the quale as "**at-the-inside-of** (e1, [**act** (e2, w) & **move** (e3, w)], y)" in the qualia structure.

The composition operation which forms a representation such as the one in (9) is different from the co-composition operation we saw in chapter 6, since here subevents are substituted for an argument in (6). The qualia structure in (9) says that the subevents represented by the verb, e2 and e3, exist inside *y*, namely "the park". In this example, the phrase *in the park* sets a scene in which the running event occurs. In other words, *in the park* fixes the place of the process subevents, "the children ran".[3]

In *in*'s representation, e1 is the head, and in (9) the event structure consists of a process subevent. This subevent is associated with the formal role containing two functions, namely **act** and **move**, as its arguments. These two functions are originally denoted by *run* and thus, the event structure of the VP *run in the park* inherits the event type of *run*: in the event structure in (9) the head subevent of *run* functions as the head. We propose (10) as a way to account for the inheritance of event types and headedness in the composition operation of the event structure:[4]

(10) Composition and Headedness: The Inheritance of Headedness (ii)
 a. When subevents of a verb are substituted for an argument in another lexical representation, the head subevents among the substituted subevents behave as the head in the newly composed event. And
 b. the event type of the head subevents is carried over to the event containing the head subevent.

For example, in (9) the head subevent, event 2, of *run* functions as the head in the newly composed event 1 (as generalized in (10a)), and event 1, which contains the head subevent, inherits the event type of the head subevent and becomes a process event (as generalized in (10b)).

Our assumption in (10) is supported by the examples in (11)–(14). The telicity of the activity verb *bake* in (11) and of the creation verb *bake* in (12) is not changed even if these verbs are used with an adjunct phrase.

(11) a. John baked potatoes for/*in 5 minutes.
 b. John baked potatoes in the kitchen for/*in 5 minutes.
(12) a. John baked a cake *for/in 1 hour.
 b. John baked a cake in the kitchen *for/in 1 hour.

The consistency in telicity in (11) and (12) suggests that headedness and the event type of these verbs are not affected by the adjunct phrases. Similarly, the telicity of the verb of motion *run* is not affected by the co-occurring adjunct phrase in (13), and in (14b) the interpretation that Sally stayed in the old station for 10 minutes is maintained.

(13) a. Sally ran for/*in 10 minutes.
 b. Sally ran in the park for/*in 10 minutes.
(14) a. Sally ran into an old station for 10 minutes.
 b. In Tokyo Sally ran into an old station for 10 minutes.

These examples suggest that telicity of verbs or verbal expressions consisting of a verb and a preposition is not affected by adjunct phrases and is maintained at the VP level or the sentential level, and thus these examples support (10).

As for (10), we should mention the following. The event structure of *in* consists of a single head event and this event is the head, and so, all the subevents included in e1 in (9) are salient. If among these subevents there is a lexically determined head subevent, the subevent is more salient than the other. As a result, *run*'s inserted head subevent behaves as the head in the event structure of the VP in (9). However, we should note that if the event structure of some preposition or particle consists of complex subevents and one of the subevents is a head, the preposition's or the particle's head subevent also behaves as the head in a derived VP. One example of such particles is the Japanese *made*, the lexical representation of which we will discuss in the next section (See discussion about (43b)). There is a possibility that the semantic representations containing *made* hold more than one head subevent.

In this section we have proposed the lexical representation of the preposition *in* as (6). Also we have proposed the substitution of the event expressed by a verb for an argument in the argument structure of an adjunct *in*-phrase. We argued that this substitution should be conducted by a composition operation in (7). We have also generalized a mechanism that determines the inheritance of headedness, (10), in the composition operation of the semantic representation.

7.2   The Japanese Particle *Made*

In this section we will see that the two proposals discussed in section 7.1, namely (7) and (10), properly deal with the semantic representation of Japanese sentences with the particle *made*. This *made*-phrase is peculiar in that it can co-occur with both a durative adverbial such as *30 pun kan* 'for thirty minutes' and a frame adverbial such as *30 pun de* 'in thirty minutes' in its natural usage. Examples are shown below.

(15) a.   Taroo-ga   kisi-made   30-pun-kan   oyoi-da.
           Taro-NOM   shore-as.far.as   thirty-minutes-long   swim-PAST
           'Taro swam to the shore for thirty minutes.'
     b.   Taroo-ga   kisi-made   30-pun-de   oyoi-da.
           Taro- NOM   shore- as.far.as   thirty-minutes-in   swim-PAST

'Taro swam to the shore in thirty minutes.'

Before we advance our proposal, we review preceding studies by other researchers, namely Kageyama and Yumoto (1997), Kageyama (2003a), and Matsumoto (1997).

7.2.1   Kageyama and Yumoto (1997) and Kageyama (2003a)

Kageyama and Yumoto (1997) analyze the meanings of some Japanese particles (see (16)) and propose LCSs for some of them. (The LCSs are shown in (17).)

(16)   *o*: route (or path), *kara*: starting point, *e*: direction (of movement), *ni*: goal, *made*: range of movement

(17)   *ni*: [AT z],   *kara*: [NOT AT z],   *o*:[Path VIA z]

Kageyama and Yumoto (1997) argue that although the particles *ni* and *made* (and *e*) have been analyzed as expressing a goal, their meanings should be distinguished for two reasons. First, *made* can co-occur with a manner-of-motion verb such as *aruku* 'walk', with which *ni* cannot co-occur.

(18) a.   *Kanozyo-wa   eki-ni   arui-ta.
          She-TOP   station-LOC   walk-PAST
          'She walked to the station.'
     b.   Kanozyo-wa   eki-made   arui-ta.
          She-TOP   station-as.far.as   walk-PAST
          'She walked as far as the station.'

Second, *made* cannot be used with goal-oriented motion verbs such as *tuku* 'arrive' and *tyakuriku-suru* 'land', whereas *ni* can.

(19) a.   *Hikooki-ga   kuukoo-made   tyakuriku-si-ta.
          airplane-NOM   airport-as.far.as   land-do-PAST
          'An airplane landed at the airport.'
     b.   Hikooki-ga   kuukoo-ni   tyakuriku-si-ta.
          airplane-NOM   airport-LOC   land-do-PAST
          'An airplane landed at the airport.'

Since *ni* can co-occur with *tyakuriku-suru* 'land', which puts a semantic focus on the result subevent, Kageyama and Yumoto analyze *ni* as expressing a goal, and regard *made* as expressing a range of movement.

Kageyama (2003a)proposes the LCS of *made*. For *made* in (20) he gives the LCS in (21).

(20) Hutari-wa   Hakone-made   doraibu-si-ta.
      two people-TOP   Hakone-as.far.as   drive-do-PAST
      'The two people drove as far as Hakone.'
(21) [x MOVE ∀$_p$R(p)[$_{Path}$ VIA-[$_{Route}$ p$_0$, p$_1$, ..., p$_n$]]

In the LCS he utilizes the function ∀$_p$R(p) which links any arbitrary location to a location on the path along which the referent of a verb moves and argues that *made* expresses the last location of the motion, p$_n$. Furthermore, for the *made* in (22) he gives the function in (23).

(22) a. Taroo-wa   tookyoo-made   CD-o   kii-ta.
         Taro-TOP   Tokyo-as.far.as   CD-ACC   listen.to-PAST
         'Taro listened to a CD all the way to Tokyo.'
     b. Hanako-wa   Oosaka-made   soto-o   mite-ita.
         Hanakao-TOP   Osaka-as.far.as   outside-ACC see-ing.PAST
         'Hanako was looking outside all the way to Osaka.'
(23) ∀p∀t R(p→t)

He argues that this function links each event which occurs on the path of a motion to a point of time and that because of this function *made* can co-occur not only with motion verbs but also with state verbs and activity verbs.

In Kageyama's account, he utilizes ∀p∀t R(p→t) in (23) in order to link the event denoted by a verb, e.g. "listened to a CD" (*CD-o kii-ta*) in (22a), to temporal points. In GL, however, the temporal relation between events denoted by verbs is represented in the event structure. By utilizing the concept of temporal order relation among events we propose the lexical representation for *made*.[5]

7.2.2 Matsumoto (1997)

Matsumoto (1997) analyzes Japanese case markers *o* and *ni* and the particle *made*. He argues that *o* marking a path NP puts a semantic focus on a process of movement, and *ni* on a resultant subevent. His analyses are based on (24).

(24) a. Kare-wa   ima   sono-saka-o   nobot-teiru
        He-TOP   now   the-slope-ACC   go.up-ing.PRES
        'He is now going up the slope.'
     b. Kare-wa   ima   tyoozyoo-ni   nobot-teiru.
        He-TOP   now   top-LOC   go.up-PERF.PRES
        'He has gone up and is now on the top.'

In (24a) *te-iru* puts a focus on the progressive aspect, whereas in (24b) it makes the resultant state salient. So, Matsumoto (1997) regards *o* and *ni* as focusing the process of movement and the resultant state, respectively.

As for *made*, he maintains that a *made*-phrase behaves as an argument of the verb in some sentences and as an adjunct in others. A *made*-phrase can co-occur with both a durative PP *30-pun-kan* 'for thirty minutes' and a frame PP *30-pun-de* 'in thirty minutes', as already seen in (15). According to Matsumoto (1997), the *made*-phrase in (15a) is an adjunct since it expresses the temporal terminal point, so (15a) can be paraphrased as shown in (25).

(25) Taroo-wa   kisi-ni   tuku-made   30-pun-kan   oyoi-da.
     Taro-TOP   shore-LOC   arrive-until 30-minutes-long   swim-PAST
     'Taro swam for 30 minutes until he got to the shore.'

Furthermore, he suggests that this type of *made*-phrase can co-occur with activity or state predicates, as shown in the example in (26).

(26) Syuuten-made   odeguti-wa   migigawa-desu.
     terminus-up.to   exit-TOP   rightside-be
     'The exit is on the right hand side as far as the terminus.'

As for the *made*-phrase in (15b), he maintains that this phrase is an argument since it expresses the terminal point of movement.[6] His observation and claim are insightful for formalizing the lexical representation of *made*.

7.2.3 Analysis and Proposal
In this subsection we discuss some features of *made* and propose a semantic

representation for this particle.

7.2.3.1 Characteristics of *Made*

First of all, as we mentioned at the beginning of section 7.2, *made* can co-occur with both a durative adverbial and a frame adverbial. The relevant examples are repeated below as (27).

(27) a. Taroo-ga kisi-made 30-pun-kan oyoi-da.
 'Taro swam to the shore for thirty minutes.'
 b. Taroo-ga kisi-made 30-pun-de oyoi-da.
 'Taro swam to the shore in thirty minutes.'

(27a) is peculiar in view of the fact that a *made*-phrase implies an arrival at some place. For example, *Taroo-ga kisi-made oyoi-da* 'Taro swam up to the shore' in (27) implies Taro's reaching the shore. In English, as is shown in (28), when typical goal phrases such as a *to*-phrase or an *into*-phrase are used with verbs of motion like *swim* and *run*, derived verbal expressions become telic even though these verbs are inherently atelic.

(28) a. Sally ran {for/*in} ten minutes.
 b. Sally ran to the station {*for/in} ten minutes.

Second, a *made*-phrase semantically emphasizes activity subevents and motion subevents, as Kitahara (1998) suggests. We can confirm this by the possibility of co-occurrence with *itizitekini* 'temporarily'.[7] This adverbial phrase emphasizes that some state of being continues temporarily, and so this phrase is accepted when it is used with a verb whose result state subevent is a head. The relevant examples are in (29).

(29) a. Ziroo-ga   itizitekini   syuudan-kara   nuke-ta.
       Jiro-NOM   temporarily   group-from   withdraw-PAST
       'Jiro temporarily withdrew from the group.'
   b. *Ziroo-ga   itizitekini   hasit-ta.
       Jiro-NOM   temporarily   run-PAST
       'Jiro temporarily ran.'
   c. *Ziroo-ga   itizitekini   eki-ni   tui-ta.

Jiro-NOM temporarily station-LOC arrive-PAST
'Jiro temporarily arrived at the station.'

The example in (29a) is accepted because the head subevent of the verb *nukeru* 'withdraw' is a resultant state subevent, whereas (29b) is not accepted because the head subevent of *hasiru* 'run' is an activity subevent. The verb *tuku* 'arrive' in (29c) has a resultant state subevent just like *nukeru*; however, the head subevent of *tuku* is not the resultant subevent but the instantaneous process subevent which is the Binary opposition type, as it is for the English verb *arrive*. We can confirm this by the unacceptability of (30) below.

(30) Kaori-ga Tookyoo-ni {10-pun-de / *10-pun-kan}
 Kaori-NOM Tokyo-LOC {10-minutes-within/10-minutes-long}
 tui-ta.
 arrive-PAST
 'Karoi arrived at Tokyo {in ten minutes / for ten minutes}.'

The unacceptability of (30) shows that the instantaneous subevent is the head, as we will discuss below as (45) in this section. Thus, *tuku* cannot co-occur with the adverbial *itizitekini* in (29c), and our claim that this adverbial can be used with a verb whose head is the resultant subevent is is supported.[8]

Now, *itizitekini* can co-occur with a VP like *Oosaka-ni it-ta* 'went to Osaka', which demonstrates that in the event structure of this VP the resultant subevent is the head. See (31).

(31) a. Tomoko-ga Oosaka-ni it-ta.
 Tomoko-NOM Osaka-LOC go-PAST
 'Tomoko went to Osaka.'
 b. Tomoko-ga itizitekini Oosaka-ni it-ta.
 Tomoko-NOM temporarily Osaka-LOC go-PAST
 'Tomoko temporarily went to Osaka.'

In contrast to (31b), the acceptability of (32b), where a *made*-phrase takes place of the *ni*-phrase, becomes rather low.

(32) a. Tomoko-ga   Oosaka-made   it-ta.
       Tomoko-NOM   Osaka-as.far.as   go-PAST
       'Tomoko went as far as Osaka.'
   b. ??Tomoko-ga   itizitekini   Oosaka-made   it-ta.
       Tomoko-NOM   temporarily   Osaka-as.far.as   go-PAST
       'Tomoko temporarily went as far as Osaka.'

We argue that the low acceptability of (32b) is due to semantic conflict over head subevents: *itizitekini* 'temporarily' requires that the resultant state subevent be the head, whereas the *made*-phrase semantically emphasizes the motion subevent of the verb *iku* 'go'. That is, the subevent of the *made* phrase is the head.

In light of the characteristics of *made* discussed above, we would like to make three suggestions: 1) The event structure of *made* should contain a transition from a subevent to another subevent since a *made*-phrase can co-occur with a frame adverbial as we saw in (27b); 2) A *made*-phrase emphasizes activity or motion subevents of a verb; 3) *Made* should basically form an adjunct phrase although a *made*-phrase co-occurring with a verb of motion functions as if it were an argument phrase since this phrase co-occurs with various types of verbs (See (22) and (26)).

7.2.3.2 The Lexical Representation of *Made*

Taking these into consideration, we propose that the lexical representation of *made* should be as shown in (33).

(33) *made*

$$\text{event structure} = \begin{bmatrix} \text{E1} = \text{e1: state} \\ \text{D-E2} = \text{e2 : state} \\ \text{e1} <_\alpha \text{e2} \\ \text{head: e1} \end{bmatrix}$$

$$\text{argument structure} = \begin{bmatrix} \text{ARG1} = \text{x: event} \\ \text{D-ARG2} = z \\ \text{[qualia structure} = \text{FORMAL} = z \neq y] \\ \text{ARG3} = y \end{bmatrix}$$

$$\text{qualia structure} = \begin{bmatrix} \text{AGENTIVE} = \mathbf{at}(\text{e1}, x, z) \\ \text{FORMAL} = \mathbf{at}(\text{e2}, x, y) \end{bmatrix}$$

Event 1 of *made* is the head subevent, that is, this subevent is foregrounded semantically. Furthermore, event 1 is followed by a default event, event 2, with no subevent intervening between them and denotes an event which leads to a resultant state. So, by definition the quale related to event 1 is in the agentive role and the quale related to event 2 is in the formal role. In the argument structure of *made* an event expressed by a verb is inserted into argument 1 (x) in the same way as the English preposition *in*. We should keep in mind that in examples containing *in* such as (4), the composed expression *the children run in the park* inherits its event type from the verb *run*. A process event contains duration by definition, and so, the event structure in the semantic representation of (4) expresses the duration of the children's running. Recall the way of event type/headedness inheritance in the composition operation of the event structure proposed in (10), which is repeated as (34):

(34) Composition and Headedness: The Inheritance of Headedness (ii)
   a. When subevents of a verb are substituted for an argument in another lexical representation, the head subevents among the substituted subevents behave as the head in the newly composed event. And
   b. the event type of the head subevents is carried over to the event containing the head subevent.

The same applies to the case of *made*. If *made* is used with the verb *hasiru* 'run', event 1 in (33) inherits the event type from *hasiru* and expresses the duration of running. In this respect, event 1 does not represent just an initial state (or the beginning of the event denoted by a verb), but an entire event denoted by a verb. So, (33) represents the following. In the preceding subevent e1, an event expressed by a verb exists at z and does not exist at y since z and y denote different locations. This event continues until the beginning of the following subevent e2, in which the verb's event exists at y. There is no intervening subevent between e1 and e2.[9]

The representation of *made* is different from that of *in* in the organization of event structure. While an event expressed by *in* is a simple event, an event expressed by *made* is a complex event which consists of two subevents and event 2 is a default event. We assume that a default event is inactive in interpreting a sentence. That is, default event e2 in (33) does not contribute to the interpretation of a sentence which contains it and does not appear in the syntax. So, the transition from e1 to e2 in (33) is also inactive in interpretation.

As for the example containing a *made*-phrase such as (22a), which is repeated below as (35a), the relevant semantic representation is shown in (35b).

(35) a. Taroo-wa   Tookyoo-made   CD-o   kii-ta.
         Taro-TOP   Tokyo-as.far.as   CD-ACC   listen.to-PAST
         'Taro listened to a CD all the way to Tokyo.'

  b. *Taroo-wa Tookyoo made CD-o kiku*

  event structure = $\begin{bmatrix} E1 = e1: \text{process} \\ D\text{-}E2 = e2 : \text{process} \\ e1 <_\propto e2 \\ \text{head: } e1 \end{bmatrix}$

  argument structure = $\begin{bmatrix} ARG1 = \text{event } [e3] \\ D\text{-}ARG2 = z \\ [\text{qualia structure} = \text{FORMAL} = z \neq \text{Tokyo}] \\ ARG3 = \text{Tokyo} \end{bmatrix}$

  qualia structure = $\begin{bmatrix} \text{AGENTIVE} = \textbf{at}(e1, \textbf{listen.to}(e3, \text{Taro, CD}), z) \\ \text{FORMAL} = \textbf{at}(e2, \textbf{listen.to}(e3, \text{Taro, CD}), \text{Tokyo}) \end{bmatrix}$

In (35b) the event represented by the verb *kiku* 'listen' is substituted for *x* of *made*. By (10a) the subevents of *made*, namely e1 and e2, inherit the verb's headedness, and by (10b) their event type changes into a process. The representation in (35b) represents the following: in subevent e1, the process event of Taro's listening to a CD exists at a location other than Tokyo and this event continues until the beginning of subevent e2 (as we argued below (33)); in subevent e2, the event of Taro's listening exists at Tokyo. The default argument 2 (*z*) is dependent on argument 3 (*Tokyo*), and argument 3 appears in the syntax instead of argument 2. Even if the event of *kiku* is substituted for x of *made*, default event e2 and the transition of *made* are still inactive, because *kiku*'s event structure and *made*'s do not have any subevents of the same type and the co-composition operation is not working in this case. Thus, the aspect of example (35a) is atelic (See (50) in chapter 6.).[10]

Now, we argue that there is a case in which default subevent e2 of *made* is activated owing to interaction among event structures and qualia structures of *made* and of co-occurring verbs. If a default event undergoes semantic operations such as co-composition, the event can be activated and play a role in the interpretation of a sentence.

In section 6.2.3.3 we suggested that subevents which are contained in lexical representations and are not associated with event structures get activated through interaction among two words' event structures and qualia structures, contribute to the co-composition operation and form the semantic representation of a resultative sentence. A relevant example and its schematized event structure and qualia structure are shown in (36) and (37).

(36) Sally hammered the metal flat. (= (90c) in section 6.2.3.3)

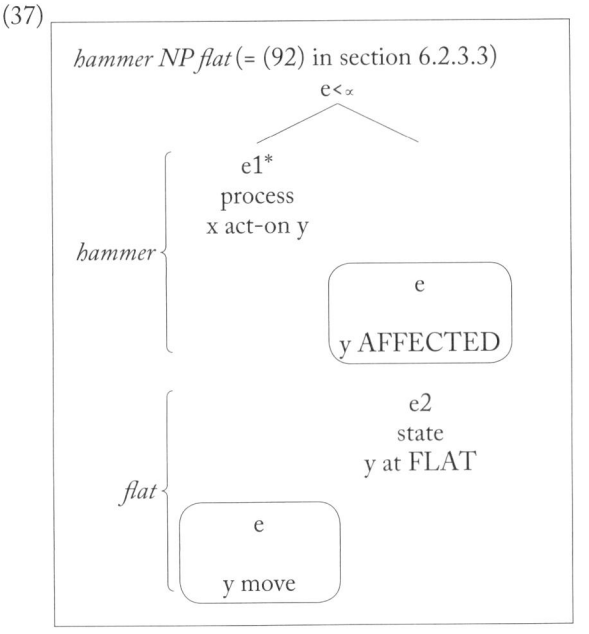

(37)
hammer NP flat (= (92) in section 6.2.3.3)

$$e <_\alpha$$

hammer {
  e1*
  process
  x act-on y

  e
  y AFFECTED
}

flat {
  e2
  state
  y at FLAT

  e
  y move
}

The action of hammering the metal affects the metal and its form may change; the adjective *flat* can express the metal's resultant state. This causes the agentive role, **move** (e, y), contained in *flat*'s qualia structure to become activated, and the subevent of change is provided and the co-composition operation applies to the lexical representations here.

We propose that event 2 of *made* is activated if the qualia structure of a verb occurring with *made* contains a function of movement such as **move** (e, w) and the event of the verb is inserted into argument 1 of *made*. The relevant part of the semantic representaion is shown in (38). The representation in (38) is composed from the lexical representation of a motion verb such as *ugo-ku* 'move' and that of *made* by composition.

(38) verbs of motion + *made* (e.g. *made ugo-ku* 'move all the way to')
event structure = $\begin{bmatrix} E1 = e1\text{: process} \\ E2 = e2\text{: process} \\ e1 <_\alpha e2 \\ \text{head: e1} \end{bmatrix}$
qualia structure = $\begin{bmatrix} \text{AGENTIVE} = \textbf{at}(e1, \textbf{move}(e3, w), z) \\ \text{FORMAL} = \textbf{at}(e2, \textbf{move}(e3, w), y) \end{bmatrix}$

When the event of the verb is inserted into argument 1 (x) of *made*, the event structure and the related qualia of *made* represent that the event denoted by the verb exists at z in subevent e1 and at y in subevent e2. In this case, subevent e1 represents the existence of w's movement at a location other than y, namely at z, and so, e1 implies that the referent of w exists at z. In the same way, subevent e2 implies that the referent of w exists at y. So, the movement function of the verb, namely **move** (e3, w), and the agentive role of *made*, **at** (e1, x, y), cooperatively represent a path of w's movement to y and w's resultant location. Thus, the *made* phrase behaves as if it were a goal phrase. Owing to this cooperative work of qualia, *made*'s subevent e2 is activated and, as a result, the transition from e1 to e2 is activated.[11, 12] Thus, we assume that when an event of movement is given by a verb *made*'s event 2 and, as a consequence, the transition is activated.

Furthermore, the temporal relation between subevents is relevant to the formation of a semantic representation. We assume that if the event types of a verb and a particle (or a postposition) are both complex, the temporally preceding subevents of the verb are inserted into a preceding subevent of the particle. Additionally, the temporally following subevents of the verb are inserted into subsequent ones. For example, when the subevents e1 and e2 of a verb in (39a) are substituted for argument x in a particle in (39b), the temporally preceding subevent e1 is inserted into x in the quale **move** (e3, x) which is associated with the temporally preceding subevent e3. Likewise, subevent e2 is inserted into x in the quale **at** (e4, x, y) associated with the temporally following subevent e4.

(39) a. a verb

$$\text{event structure} = \begin{bmatrix} E1 = e1: \text{process} \\ E2 = e2: \text{state} \\ e1 <_\alpha e2 \end{bmatrix}$$

b. a particle (or a postposition)

$$\text{event structure} = \begin{bmatrix} E3 = e3: \text{process} \\ E4 = e4: \text{state} \\ e3 <_\alpha e4 \end{bmatrix}$$

$$\text{argument structure} = \begin{bmatrix} \text{ARG1} = x \\ \text{ARG2} = y \end{bmatrix}$$

$$\text{qualia structure} = \begin{bmatrix} \text{AGENTIVE} = \mathbf{move}(e3, x) \\ \text{FORMAL} = \mathbf{at}(e4, x, y) \end{bmatrix}$$

We can observe the salience of temporal relationality between subevents also in the co-composition operation. When the subevents of the verb *run* and those of the preposition *to* are combined, the temporally preceding subevents of *run* and *to* are combined with each other. As we saw in the last chapter, *to*'s subevent e1 in (40b) is combined with *run*'s subevent e2 in (40a) and forms the event structure in (40d).[13]

(40) a.

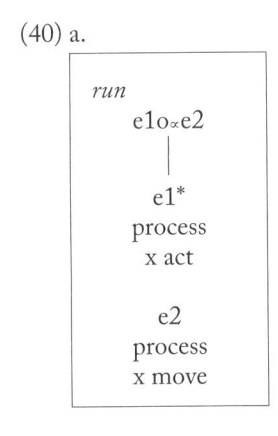

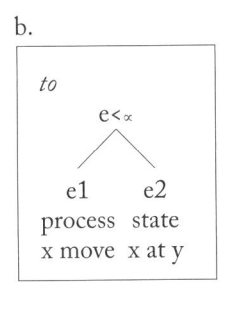

```
run
   e1o_αe2
   |
   e1*
   process
   x act

   e2
   process
   x move
```

b.

```
to
       e<_α
      /    \
    e1      e2
  process  state
  x move   x at y
```

c.

```
run and to
        e<α
       /  \
run { e1*
      process
      x act
      e2
      process
      x move }
to  { e3   e4
      process state
      x move x at z }
```

d.

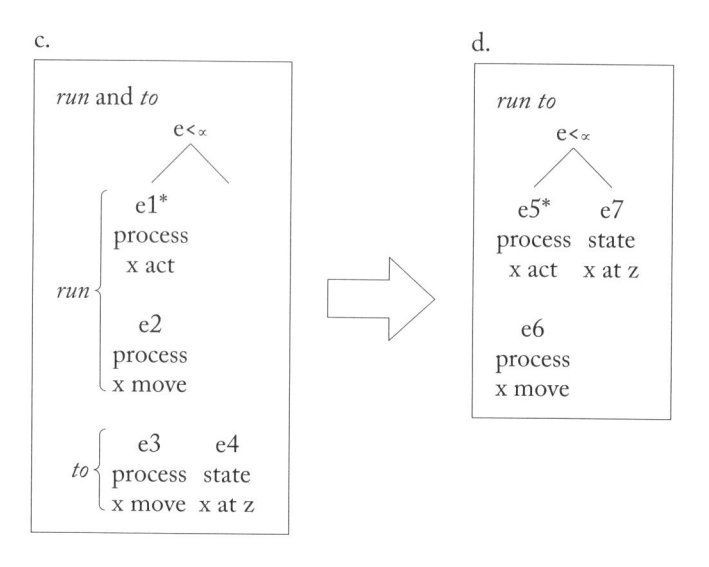

```
run to
    e<α
   /  \
e5*      e7
process  state
x act    x at z
e6
process
x move
```

7.2.3.3 *Made* and Various types of Verbs

Now, let us see how our proposal (33) and the assumptions discussed above account for the unique behavior of *made* which we saw in (15), repeated as (41a, b) below.

(41) a. Taroo-ga   kisi-made   30-pun-kan   oyoi-da.
        Taro-NOM   shore-as.far.as   thirty-minutes-long swim-PAST
        'Taro swam to the shore for thirty minutes.'

   b. Taroo-ga   kisi-made   30-pun-de   oyoi-da.
       Taro- NOM   shore-as.far.as   thirty-minutes-in   swim-PAST
       'Taro swam to the shore in thirty minutes.'

   c. *Hanako-ga   ie-made   1-jikan   it-ta.
       Hanako-NOM   home- as.far.as   one-hour-long   go-PAST
       'Hanako went home for an hour.'

   d. Hanako-ga   ie-made   1-jikan-de   it-ta.
       Hanako-NOM   home- as.far.as   one-hour-in   go-PAST
       'Hanako got home in an hour.'

First, let us see the examples such as (41a, b) in which an atelic verb of motion is used. As we have already seen in (28), *made*-phrases are unlike *to*-phrases in that the sentences containing *made*-phrases and atelic motion verbs can co-occur with durative adverbials. The lexical representation of *oyogu* is shown in (42a). We suggest that the composed semantic representation of the expression *made oyogu* 'swim to' should be the one in (42b).

(42) a. *oyogu*
event structure = $\begin{bmatrix} E1 = e3: \text{process} \\ E2 = e4: \text{process} \\ e3 \circ_\alpha e4 \\ \text{head: } e3 \end{bmatrix}$
argument structure = [ARG1 = x]
qualia structure = [AGENTIVE = **act**(e3, x) **move**(e4, x)]

b. *made oyogu*
event structure = $\begin{bmatrix} E1 = e1: \text{process} \\ E2 = e2: \text{process} \\ e1 <_\alpha e2 \\ \text{head: } e1 \end{bmatrix}$

argument structure = $\begin{bmatrix} \text{ARG1 = x: event [e3 \& e4]} \\ \quad \text{qualia structure = [FORMAL = event [e3\&e4]]} \\ \quad \text{qualia structure = } \begin{bmatrix} \text{AGENTIVE = } \textbf{act}(e3, w) \\ \textbf{move}(e4, w) \end{bmatrix} \\ \text{D-ARG2 = z} \\ \quad \text{qualia structure = [FORMAL = z} \neq \text{y]} \\ \text{ARG3 = y} \end{bmatrix}$

qualia structure = $\begin{bmatrix} \text{AGENTIVE = } \textbf{at}(e1, [\textbf{act}(e3, w)\&\textbf{move}(e4, w)], z) \\ \text{FORMAL = } \textbf{at}(e2, [\textbf{act}(e3, w)\&\textbf{move}(e4, w)], y) \end{bmatrix}$

The activity subevent and the motion subevent of *oyogu* 'swim' are substituted for argument x of *made* in (42b). In the argument structure the qualia structure of the inserted events contains the agentive role holding the **act** function and the **move** function. In the qualia structure the activity subevent and the motion subevent of *oyogu* are inserted into argument x of *made*, and by (10a) e3 of *oyogu* is a head in e1 and e2 and, furthermore, e1 itself also serves as the head due to the nature of *made*, as we suggested below (14). Thus, although both e1 and e2 contain the head subevent e3, e1 is more salient than e2 as a head since e1 itself is a head. By (10b) e1 and e2 inherit the event type of the head subevent e3, and therefore, e1 and e2 become process subevents. The qualia related to e4 has "**move**", and due to the operation in the qualia structure we have suggested in (38), e2 of *made oyogu* is activated and the transition occurs. As Pustejovsky (1995: 72–75) points out, a durative adverbial such as *30 pun kan* 'for thirty minutes' can co-occur with a process head subevent or a stative head subevent, thus, (41a) is accepted. Furthermore, since the event structure in (42b) contains the transition from e1 to e2 and a frame adverbial can be used if the event structure of a verb or a VP contains a transition, (41b) is judged acceptable.

Next, let us go on to examples (41c, d) in which a telic verb of motion *iku* 'go to' is used. As (41c) shows, *made iku* cannot co-occur with a durative adverbial. We suggest that the semantic representation of the expression *made iku* should be (43b). (The lexical representation of the verb *iku* is in (43a).[14])

(43) a. *iku*

event structure = $\begin{bmatrix} E1 = e1: \text{process} \\ E2 = e2: \text{process} \\ E3 = e3: \text{state} \\ e1 \circ_\alpha e2 \quad e2 <_\alpha e3 \\ \text{head: } e3 \end{bmatrix}$

argument structure = $\begin{bmatrix} \text{ARG1} = x \\ \text{D-ARG2} = y \end{bmatrix}$

qualia structure = $\begin{bmatrix} \text{AGENTIVE} = \textbf{act}(e1, x) \; \textbf{move}(e2, x) \\ \text{FORMAL} = \textbf{at}(e3, x, y) \end{bmatrix}$

b. *made iku*

event structure = $\begin{bmatrix} E1 = e1: \text{process} \\ E2 = e2: \text{state} \\ e1 <_\alpha e2 \\ \text{head: } e1 \; e2 \end{bmatrix}$

argument structure = $\begin{bmatrix} \text{ARG1} = x: \text{event } [e3 \& e4 \& e5] \\ \text{D-ARG2} = z \\ \quad \text{qualia structure} = [\text{FORMAL} = z \neq y] \\ \text{ARG3} = y \end{bmatrix}$

qualia structure = $\begin{bmatrix} \text{AGENTIVE} = \textbf{at}(e1, [\textbf{act}(e3, v) \& \textbf{move}(e4, v)], z) \\ \text{FORMAL} = \textbf{at}(e2, [\textbf{at}(e5, v, w)], y) \end{bmatrix}$

In composition of the semantic representation of *made* and that of *iku*, the temporal order of subevents is relevant, because both are complex events. The subevents in the event structure of *iku* are inserted into the temporally corresponding subevents in the event structure of *made*. So, the activity subevent and the motion subevent of *iku* are inserted into e1 of *made* and the result subevent of *iku* into e2. Since the role related to e2 of *iku* has **move**, e2 of *made iku* is activated. Furthermore, both e1 and e2 of *made iku* are heads, because e1 of *made* is a head by nature and e2 inherits the headedness from the result subevent of the verb by (10a). This double-headedness of the composed semantic representation of *made iku* accounts for the incompatibility of a *made*-phrase and the durative adverbial 1 *zikan* 'for an hour' in a sentence containing a telic verb, e.g., (41c). The durative adverbial modifies the head subevent, but since in the event structure of *made iku* both e1 and e2 are heads, it is not clear which event the durative adverbial modifies. This leads to an ambiguity in the interpretation of (41c). The example (41c) seems to be unacceptable because of this ambiguity; however, indeed it is acceptable. In fact, if e1 or e2 in (43b) is emphasized by modifying expressions, the acceptability of (41c) is improved. *Kokudoo-2-Goosen-o* 'along Route 2' in (41c') expresses a path along which Hanako moves and emphasizes the subevent of movement, that is, e1. The purpose phrase *sooko-o-katazukeru-tameni* 'in order to clear up the warehouse' in (41c") focuses on Hanako's activity at the warehouse and so, we take this phrase to emphasize the resultant subevent, namely e2. The acceptability of (41c') and (41c") is better than that of (41c).[15]

(41) c'. ?Hanako-wa   Kokudoo-2Goosen-o   ie-made
        Hanako-TOP   national.road-2-ACC   home-as.far.as
        1-zi-kan   it-ta.
        one-hour-long   go-PAST
        'Hanako went home along Route 2 for an hour.'
     c". ?Hanako-wa   sooko-o-katazukeru-tameni
        Hanako-TOP   warehouse-ACC-clear.up-in.order.to
        kaisya-made   1-zi-kan   it-ta.
        office- as.far.as one-hour-long   go-PAST
        'Hanako went to the office for an hour in order to clear up the warehouse.'

As for the frame adverbial *1 zikan-de* 'in an hour', since the event structure of *made iku* contains a transition from e1 to e2, (41d) is acceptable.

Furthermore, a *made*-phrase is incompatible with achievement verbs such as *tuku* 'arrive', which is shown in (44b). Judging from (30), which is repeated as (44a), the verb has a transition in its event structure and an instantaneous subevent as head. Following the discussion about the English verb *arrive* in section 4.2.1, we assume the lexical representation of *tuku* as the one in (45).

(44) a. Kaori-ga   Tookyoo-ni   {10-pun-de / *10-pun-kan}
       Kaori-NOM   Tokyo-LOC   {10-minutes-within/10-minutes-long}
       tui-ta.   (= (30))
       arrive-PAST
       'Kaori arrived at Tokyo {in ten minutes / for ten minutes}.'
   b. *Kaori-ga   Tookyoo-made   tui-ta.
       Kaori-NOM   Tokyo-as.far.as   arrive-PAST
       'Kaori arrived at Tokyo.'

(45) *tuku*
     event structure = $\begin{bmatrix} E1 = e1: \text{process} \\ E2 = e2: \text{state} \\ e1 <_\alpha e2 \\ \text{head: } e1 \end{bmatrix}$
     argument structure = $\begin{bmatrix} ARG1 = x \\ ARG2 = y \end{bmatrix}$
     qualia structure = $\begin{bmatrix} \text{AGENTIVE} = \textbf{move}(e1, x) \\ \qquad\qquad\qquad [\text{CONST} = p_0 <_\alpha p_1] \\ \text{FORMAL} = \textbf{at}(e2, x, y) \end{bmatrix}$

The agentive role of *tuku* denotes the shift from x not being at the location denoted by *made* to x's existence at the location. Also, the corresponding subevent e1 is a Binary opposition and lacks an in-between path (or change). Since e1 of *made* is a head and needs semantic content to receive a semantic focus, the instantaneous subevent e1 of *tuku* does not work well. Thus, the interpretation of the sentence containing *made tuku* becomes anomalous and (44b) is unacceptable.

If subevent 1 of *tuku* gives some in-between path, it can contribute to the interpretation and the sentence will be acceptable. One such example is a sentence containing V-V compounds, where the second V is *tuku* 'arrive' and the first V denotes the manner of "arriving", like *tadori-tuku* 'proceed and arrive', *oyogi-tuku* 'swim and arrive' and *nagare-tuku* 'drift and arrive'. The sentence, which has *made tadori-tuku*, is fully acceptable, as is shown in (46a). Subevent 1 of *tadori-tuku* is related to the **move** function in the qualia structure and provides information for the derived *made-tadori-tuku* phrase.[16, 17]

(46) a. Kaori-ga   Tookyoo-made   tadori-tui-ta.
         Kaori-NOM   Tokyo-as.far.as   proceed-arrive-PAST
         'Kaori proceeded and arrived at Tokyo.'

   b. *tadori-tuku*
      event structure = $\begin{bmatrix} E1 = e1: \text{process} \\ E2 = e2: \text{process} \\ E3 = e3: \text{state} \\ e1 <_\alpha e2 \quad e2 <_\alpha e3 \\ \text{head: e2} \end{bmatrix}$

      argument structure = $\begin{bmatrix} ARG1 = x \\ ARG2 = y \end{bmatrix}$

      qualia structure = $\begin{bmatrix} \text{AGENTIVE} = \textbf{move}(e1, x) \\ \qquad\qquad\quad \textbf{move}(e2, x) \, [\text{CONST} = p_0 <_\alpha p_1] \\ \text{FORMAL} = \textbf{at}(e3, x, y) \end{bmatrix}$

In this section we have suggested that the Japanese particle *made* should form an adjunct phrase and we also proposed its lexical representation. We have also contended that events expressed by a verb are inserted into argument positions in *made*'s argument structure and showed that our proposal concerning composition and headedness in (10) appropriately gives rise to semantic representations of VPs containing *made*.

7.3 Japanese *Naka-o* Construction

In this section we discuss the semantic representation of Japanese *naka-o* construction. An example of this construction is shown in (47), which is cited from Kageyama (2002: 4).

(47) Kare-wa   ame-no-naka-o   soto-o
     he-TOP   rain-GEN-inside-ACC   outside-ACC
     de-arui-ta.
     out-walk-PAST

'He walked around outside in the rain.'

The basic meaning of *naka* 'inside' in (47) is the space surrounded by fixed boundary lines, and when it follows an NP, a genitive case marker *no* is inserted between the NP and *naka*, as in *heya-no-naka* 'inside the room'. Furthermore, when following some kinds of noun or clause, *naka* also expresses "during some event", as in *ame-no-naka* ('in the rain' or 'during the rain'). In (47) *naka* is combined with *o*, an accusative case marker, and makes a *naka-o*-phrase. In section 7.1 above, we proposed the operation wherein events expressed by a verb are inserted into the argument position in the event structure of an adjunct phrase. We claim that this operation plays an important role in composing the semantic representation of *naka-o* construction sentences. In addition, we argue that we can explain the behavior of the Japanese phrases, *naka-de* and *naka-o* without recourse to the process of "conceptual cloning" proposed by Kageyama (2002, 2003b). We accomplish this by combining the semantic representation of *naka* and the characteristics of the particle *de* or of the accusative case marker *o*.

7.3.1 *Naka-o* Construction and Proposals by Kageyama (2002, 2003b)

Kageyama (2002) points out four characteristics of *naka-o* phrases. First, this phrase describes the circumstances surrounding a path along which some entity or person moves. Second, as the acceptability of (47) shows, this phrase is free from the double-*o*-constraint, which rules out a sentence in which two *o*-phrases appear. Third, this phrase can be used with verbs which do not subcategorize an *o*-phrase as their complements, as is shown in (48b):

(48) a. Hikooki-wa   Kansai-Kuukoo-ni/*o   tyakurikusi-ta.
        airplane-TOP   Kansai-Airport-LOC/-ACC   land-PAST
        'The airplane landed at Kansai Airport in the storm.'
    b. Hikooki-wa   arasi-no-naka-o
        airplane-TOP   storm-GEN-inside-ACC
        Kansai-Kuukoo-ni   tyakurikusi-ta.
        Kansai-Airport-LOC   land-PAST
        'The airplane landed at Kansai Airport in the storm.'

Lastly, *naka-o*-phrases cannot be used with verbs which do not contain ACT in their LCS. See the example in (49a). Kageyama (2002) maintains that the LCS of the verb *korogaru* 'roll' does not contain ACT in it, as is shown in (49b).[18]

(49) a. *Dosyaburi-no-naka-o   iwa-ga   korogat-ta.
     hard.rain-GEN-inside-ACC   rock-NOM   roll-PAST
     'In the hard rain a rock rolled.'
   b. *korogaru*: [x MOVE [PATH   ]]

Taking the first three characteristics into consideration, Kageyama (2002, 2003b) suggests that a *naka-o* phrase should be an adjunct. Furthermore, from the fourth characteristic he maintains that verbs which occur in the *naka-o* construction contain ACT as well as MOVE and PATH in their LCS. In order to explain the correlation between verbs' LCS and this construction, he proposes the operation of conceptual cloning.

According to Kageyama (2002, 2003b), a *naka-o* phrase picks out the relevant semantic components of a verb and sets them up in a higher position. (50a) is the conceptual structure of a VP. The *naka-o* phrase copies this and attaches it on top of the original structure. Thus, the conceptual structure of the *naka-o* construction takes the form of (50b).

(50) a. Kare-wa   soto-o   de-arui-ta
      'He walked around outside.'

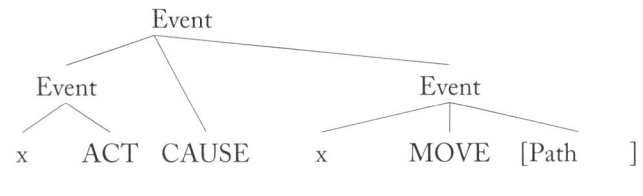

```
                         Event
              ┌────────────┴────────────┐
           Event                      Event
          ┌──┴──┐                   ┌───┴───┐
         x   ACT  CAUSE            x   MOVE  [Path  ]

         he                        walk-around  outside
```

   b. Kare-wa ame-no-naka-o soto-o de-arui-ta
      'He walked around outside in the rain.'

```
                          Event
                ┌───────────┴──────────┐
             Event                    Event
           ┌───┴───┐              ┌─────┴─────────────────┐
           x   ACT  CAUSE        MOVE  [Path situational path]

           he                                    in the rain
                            Event
                     ┌────────┴────────┐
                   Event             Event
                 ┌──┴──┐         ┌─────┴─────┐
                 x  ACT CAUSE    x  MOVE  [Path    ]

                                walk-around    outside
```

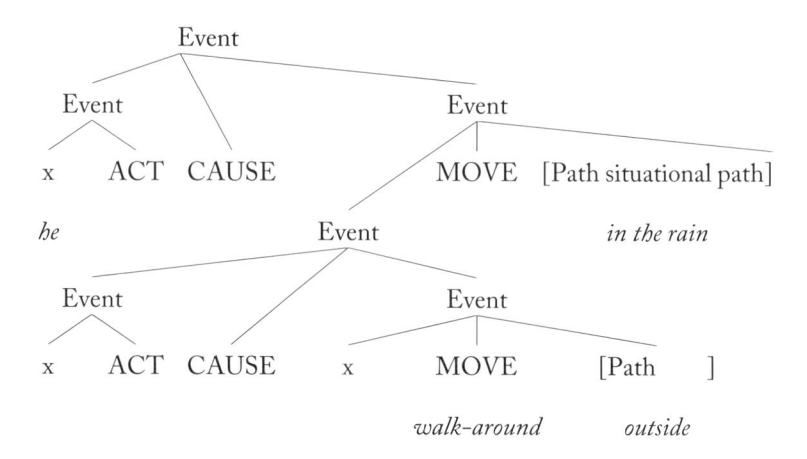

The operation of conceptual cloning forms the same type of conceptual structure as the one of the VP and places it at a higher position than the original one in order to make a position for a path (phrase) in the conceptual structure. In (50b) the newly formed conceptual structure, which contains a slot for the situational path, is added on top of the original one which contains an argument path. Kageyama (2002, 2003b) argues that sentences including a *naka-o*-phrase form one class of construction in the grammar, and that this construction has the conceptual structure as in (50b).

In the following subsection, we will argue that we can compose the semantic representation of sentences containing a *naka-o*-phrase without recourse to the operation of conceptual cloning.

7.3.2 Analysis

In this subsection, by way of the composition operation (which inserts a subevent into an argument position), we propose the semantic representation of sentences which include a *naka-o*-phrase. *Naka* 'inside' forms adverbials without the accusative case marker *o*, and in addition, *naka-de* also makes adverbials, as exemplified in (51) and (52), respectively. (*De* in the expression *naka-de* is a particle expressing a location where an event occurs.)

(51) a. ??Ame-no-naka   bokinbako-ga
        rain-GEN-inside   collection.box-NOM
        kyookai-no-mae-ni   at-ta.
        church-GEN-in.front.of-LOC   exist-PAST

'In the rain a collection box was in front of the church.'

(a state verb, verb of existence)

b. Arasi-no-naka   kootuu-ziko-ga   sono-koosaten-de
storm-GEN-inside traffic-accident-NOM the-intersection-LOC
at-ta.
occur-PAST

'A traffic accident occurred at the intersection in the storm.'

(an achievement verb, verb of occurrence)

c. Ame-no-naka   otosiyori-ga   kaidan-de
rain-GEN-inside   elderly.person-NOM   stairs-LOC
koron-da.
fall.down-PAST

'In the rain an elderly person fell down the stairs.'

(an achievement verb)

d. Mina-ga   mimamotteiru-naka   Yamada-kun-hitori-ga
everyone-NOM   watching-inside   Yamada-Mr.-alone-NOM
syabet-ta.
talk-PAST

'Only Yamada talked in front of everyone who was just watching.'

(an activity verb, verb of speaking)

(52) a. *Ame-no-naka-de   bokinbako-ga
rain-GEN-inside-LOC   collection.box-NOM
kyookai-no-mae-ni   at-ta.
church-GEN-in.front.of-LOC   exist-PAST

'In the rain a collection box was in front of the church.'

(a state verb, verb of existence)

b. ?Arasi-no-naka-de   kootuu-ziko-ga
storm-GEN-inside-LOC   traffic-accident-NOM
sono-koosaten-de   at-ta.
the-intersection-LOC   occur-PAST

'A traffic accident occurred at the intersection in the storm.'

(an achievement verb, verb of occurrence)

c. Ame-no-naka-de   otosiyori-ga   kaidan-de
rain-GEN-inside-LOC   elderly.person-NOM   stairs-LOC
koron-da.
fall.down-PAST

'In the rain an elderly person fell down the stairs.'

(an achievement verb)

d. Mina-ga   mimamotteiru-naka-de
   everyone-NOM   watching-inside-LOC
   Yamada-kun-hitori-ga   syabe-tta.
   Yamada-Mr.-alone-NOM   talk-PAST
   'Only Yamada talked in front of everyone who was just watching.'

(an activity verb, verb of speaking)

We argue that a *naka-o*-phrase should basically share the same semantic representation with *naka* 'inside' and that it is restricted by the semantic character of the accusative case marker *o*. This analysis will appropriately account for the characteristics of the *naka-o* construction which we saw in the last subsection. By taking this approach, we can deal with the semantic representations of sentences which include a *naka*-phrase, a *naka-de*-phrase or a *naka-o*-phrase.

In (51) and (52), various types of verbs are used, and as (51) shows, a *naka*-phrase is compatible with these verbs. We assume that an adjunct phrase does not select the class of verbs it occurs with, and take the *naka*-phrase to function as an adjunct. We also assume that some operator such as a zero suffix enables the noun *naka* to form an adverbial phrase such as the one in (51) and places the formed adverbial in an adjunct position in the syntax. The semantic representation of the adverbial *naka* with the operator is the same as that of *in*, as is shown in (53).

(53) *naka*
    event structure = [E1 = e1: state]
    argument structure = $\begin{bmatrix} \text{ARG1} = x: \text{entity/event} \\ \text{ARG2} = y \end{bmatrix}$
    qualia structure = [FORMAL = **at-the-inside-of**(e1, x, y)]

The event expressed by a verb is inserted into argument 1 in (53). The semantic representation of the sentence in (54a), which contains a *naka*-phrase, is shown in (54b). (In (54b) we show only a part of the semantic representation which is relevant to the discussion here.)

(54) a. Dosyaburi-no-ame-no-naka   Hanako-ga   de-aruku.
       hard-GEN-rain-GEN-inside   Hanako-NOM   out-walk

'Hanako walks around in heavy rain.'

b. *Dosyaburi-no-ame-no-naka*   *Hanako-ga*   *de-aruku*

$$\text{event structure} = \begin{bmatrix} E1 = e1: \text{process} \\ \text{head: } e1 \end{bmatrix}$$

$$\text{argument structure} = \begin{bmatrix} ARG1 = x: \text{event } [e2\&e3] \\ ARG2 = y \end{bmatrix}$$

$$\text{qualia structure} = \begin{bmatrix} FORMAL = \textbf{at-the-inside-of}(e1, \\ [\textbf{act}(e2, w)\&\textbf{move.along}(e3, w, v)], y) \end{bmatrix}$$

(cf. w: Hanako, y: dosyaburi-no-ame, v: a path (optional))

(54b) is almost the same as (9), which represents the semantic representation of (the VP of) *The children ran in the park*. In the argument structure in (54b) the process events expressed by the verb *dearuku* 'walk around' are inserted into argument 1. Thus, the formal role in the qualia structure represents the situation in which Hanako walks around existing in the heavy rain. Since the event structure inherits the event type of the head event of the verb in the same way as the English adjunct *in*-phrase, the event type of the whole sentence is a process. The representation of *naka* in (53) may permit any event type of a verb to be inserted into argument 1 in its argument structure.

Next, let us consider the semantic representation of *naka-de* and sentences including this phrase in (52). Although this phrase can co-occur with various classes of verbs, the acceptability of (52a), which expresses a stative event, is lower than that of (51a) containing a *naka*-phrase. Furthermore, the classes of verbs with which a *naka-de*-phrase can co-occur coincide with those with which a *de*-phrase can co-occur, which is shown in (52) and (55).

(55) a. *Kyookai-no-mae-de   bokinbako-ga
       church-GEN-in.front.of-LOC   collection.box-NOM
       at-ta.
       exist-PAST
       'A collection box was in front of the church.'
                                           (a state verb, verb of existence)

b. Sono   kooen-de   ziko-ga   at-ta.
       that   park-LOC   accident-NOM   occur-PAST
       'An accident occurred in the park.'
                                 (an achievement verb, verb of appearance)

c. Sono kaidan-de otosiyori-ga koron-da.
   that stairs-LOC elderly.person-NOM fall.down-PAST
   'An elderly person fell down the stairs.' (an achievement verb)
d. Kaigi-de Yamada-kun-hitori-ga syabet-ta.
   meeting-LOC Yamada-Mr.-alone-NOM talk-PAST
   'In the meeting only Yamada talked.'
   (an activity verb, verb of speaking)

A *de*-phrase is an adjunct expressing the location where an event happens, and so, it cannot be used to indicate a location of an entity, which lacks an event, as is shown in (55a).[19] In (52a) the subject *bokinbako* 'collection box' denotes an entity, in contrast to the subject *kootuu-ziko* 'traffic accident' which denotes an event in (52b). We consider (55a) as corresponding to (52a) in this respect. The expression *bokinbako-ga at-ta* 'a collection box exists' in (52a) is a stative event, so this expression cannot be substituted for an argument of *naka* and (52a) is unacceptable. Thus, a *naka-de*-phrase is similar to a *naka*-phrase on the one hand, and it resembles a *de*-phrase on the other hand. We assume that the lexical representation of *de* is the one in (56).

(56) *de*

event structure = [E1 = e1: state]

argument structure = $\begin{bmatrix} \text{ARG1} = \text{x: event} \\ \quad \text{qualia structure} = \text{FORMAL} = \text{x is eventive} \\ \text{ARG2} = \text{y} \end{bmatrix}$

qualia structure = [FORMAL = **at**(e1, x, y)]

In (56) the qualia structure in the argument structure specifies argument 1's qualia structure. That is, the event which is inserted into argument 1 must be eventive. As for *naka-de*, e1 of *naka* and e1 of *de* are temporally overlapping, and if argument 1 of *naka* is a stative event like (52a), the argument cannot become argument 1 of *de*.

Lastly, we discuss the semantic representation of a *naka-o*-phrase. In almost the same way as that of a *naka-de*-phrase, the semantic representation of a *naka-o*-phrase is made by the combination of the semantic representation of *naka* and the semantic feature of the accusative case marker *o*. In Japanese, the accusative case *o* marks a complement which expresses a path of some locomotion or a patient of some activity. In the representation of a verb, a path is represented as y in [**act**(e1, x), **move-along**(e2, x, y)] or [**move-along**(e1, x, y)] in the qualia structure, as is shown in (57).

(57) a. *aruku*
event structure = $\begin{bmatrix} E1 = e1: \text{process} \\ E2 = e2: \text{process} \\ e1 \circ_\alpha e2 \\ \text{head: e1} \end{bmatrix}$

qualia structure = [AGENTIVE = **act**(e1, x) **move-along**(e2, x, y)]

b. *nagareru*
event structure = $\begin{bmatrix} E1 = e1 \\ \text{head: e1} \end{bmatrix}$

qualia structure = [AGENTIVE = **move-along**(e1, x, y)]

The qualia structures of *aruku* 'walk' and *nagareru* 'flow' hold the function **move-along** since these verbs take expressions denoting path as their objects (or give an accusative case marker *o* to expressions denoting path) (cf. the lexical representation for the English verb *run* in (8)). So, we argue that a *naka-o*-phrase can basically co-occur with verbs which contain the functions **act** and **move-along** or the function **move-along** in their lexical representation because the pair of **act** and **move-along** or the sole **move-along** license the accusative case marker *o* to attach to *naka*, which already has the ability to form adverbial phrases by itself.

The lexical representation of *dearuku* 'walk around' is given in (58b) and the relevant part of the semantic representation of (47) is shown in (58c).

(58) a. Kare-wa   ame-no-naka-o   soto-o
       he-TOP   rain-GEN-inside-ACC   outside-ACC
       de-arui-ta.   (=(47))
       out-walk-PAST
       'In the heavy rain he walked around outside.'

b. *dearuku* 'walk around'
  event structure = $\begin{bmatrix} E1 = e1: \text{process} \\ E2 = e2: \text{process} \\ e1 \text{ o}_\alpha \text{ e2} \\ \text{head: e1} \end{bmatrix}$
  argument structure = $\begin{bmatrix} \text{ARG1} = w \\ \text{D-ARG2} = v \end{bmatrix}$
  qualia structure = [AGENTIVE = **act**(e1, w) **move-along**(e2, w, v)]

c. *Kare-wa   ame-no-naka-o   soto-o   de-aruku*
  event structure = $\begin{bmatrix} E1 = e1: \text{process} \\ \text{head: e1} \end{bmatrix}$
  argument structure = $\begin{bmatrix} \text{ARG1} = x: \text{event [e2\&e3]} \\ \text{ARG2} = y \end{bmatrix}$
  qualia structure = $\begin{bmatrix} \text{FORMAL} = \textbf{at-the-inside-of}(e1, \\ \qquad [\textbf{act}(e2, w)\&\textbf{move-along}(e3, w, v)], y) \end{bmatrix}$
  (cf. w: kare, v: soto, y: ame)

In (58c) the events of *dearuku* are inserted into argument 1. The representation in (58c) is the same as the one in (54b), which is the representation of (54a) containing a *naka*-phrase. Because in (58c) the qualia structure contains **move-along**(e3, w, v), the accusative case marker *o* can be attached to y, which represents *ame* 'rain'.

Kageyama (2002) argues that verbs containing ACT and MOVE in their LCS can appear in *naka-o* construction sentences. As we mentioned above, the case marker *o* is also attached to an argument functioning as a patient. A patient role is represented in an **act** function like "**act-on**" in the qualia structure. (Furthermore, unergative verbs of motion contain the **act** function in their qualia structure in addition to the **move-along** function.) So if a *naka-o* construction sentence contains **act**(e, x) in its qualia structure, that sentence may sound more natural to a hearer than a sentence which does not have **act**(e, x) in its qualia structure. Now, we can explain the full acceptability of (58a), whose qualia structure contains **act**(e2, w) as well as **move-along**. In contrast to (58a), some people find (49a) is only marginally acceptable. We can ascribe this to the lack of **act** in the verb's lexical representation.[20]

In this subsection, we have proposed the semantic representation of *naka* which forms adverbials. We have shown that the event insertion we proposed in

(7) works also in this case: one of the two arguments which *naka* takes, namely argument 1, is replaced by an event expressed by a verb. Assuming this lexical representation for *naka*, we can account for the semantic characteristics of a *naka-o*-phrase as well as those of a *naka-de*-phrase.

7.4 Another Approach

As we surveyed in chapter 2, Davidson (1967) and Parsons (1990) among others utilize the notion of "event" in logical forms to represent meanings of sentences. Parsons (1990: 217) proposes the logical form of the sentence in (59a), which contains a locative PP as well as a temporal adverbial, as the one in (59b).

(59) a. Yesterday in Rome Brutus stabbed Caesar.
  b. $(\exists\ I)[I<\text{now}\ \&\ I\subset\text{Yesterday}\ \&\ I\subset\text{Rome}\ \&\ (\exists e)(\exists t)[t\in I\ \&\ \text{Stabbing}(e)\ \&\ \text{Agent}(e, \text{Brutus})\ \&\ \text{Theme}(e, \text{Caesar})\ \&\ \text{Cul}(e, t)]]$

In (59b) the I denotes a spatiotemporal region and the t a spatiotemporal point. That is, roughly, (59b) says that the event of Brutus stabbing Caesar existed somewhere in Rome at some point in time preceding the present. The Davidsonian approach and our proposal of event insertion resemble each other in treating event as an argument in the semantic representation. However, the two approaches are different in this point. In the Davidsonian approach, an event and a location where the event occurs are considered to be in the relation of conjunction. Because of its unique behavior concerning co-occurrence with durative-frame adverbials or verbs, the particle *made* would be analyzed differently from other locational adjunct phrases such as *in*. On the other hand, in our approach a location is predicated of an event. Adjunct phrases have their lexical representation, and their meanings are denoted through interaction of the three structures as other lexical items' meanings are. Our GL can deal with adverbials including *in* or *made* uniformly with the proposed machinery properly.

7.5 Summary

In this chapter, we have discussed adjunct phrases, the third type of PPs we saw in section 3.2.3 in English and Japanese, in order to understand the semantic representation of VPs containing motion verbs and PPs. We proposed the composition operation (7) which substitutes events of a verb for an argument in the argument structure of an adjunct. Assuming this operation and the lexical representation of *in* in (6) and *made* in (33), the semantic representations of sentences including these adjunct phrases were correctly composed. Together with the operation, we have discussed how the event type and the head event of a composed event structure are determined. We have also argued that the qualia structure plays an important role in relating the meaning of a verb to that of an adverbial phrase. Owing to this operation in the qualia structure, a *made*-phrase sometimes seems to function as a goal phrase. In addition to this crosslinguistic adequacy, our proposal explains the characteristics of the three Japanese phrases, *naka*, *naka-de* and *naka-o*.

Through the research in the previous chapter and this chapter, we have understood the relations between the lexical representation of motion verbs and that of PPs, composed semantic representations of phrases containing the verbs and the PPs, and the operations of co-composition and composition.

Endnotes

1. This construction was named by Kageyama (2002).
2. The representation in (6) is different from the one we showed in (47) or (54) in chapter 6, where argument x denotes only some entity. The representation in (6) is the final version.
3. As for the event type of *in*, we might assume another type which represents the characteristics of this preposition: *in* specifies the situation of the subevents denoted by a verb.
4. See chapter 6 for the Inheritance of Headedness (i), which is the case for the co-composition operation. In order to understand the determination process of headedness and event types of VPs which include adjunct PPs, we need to explore semantic fields other than spatial relations. See also the previous note.
5. Furthermore, Kageyama (2004) makes use of qualia structure and an operation similar to type coercion for the conceptual structure of the English expression *all the way* corresponding to the Japanese *made* in its meaning and usage.
6. Ueno (2000) also makes a proposal similar to Matsumoto's (1997).
7. This test using the adverbial *itizitekini* is utilized in Imaizumi and Gunji (2002).
8. See the discussion about *arrive* in section 4.2.1.
9. It might be that in (33) we should assume another type of an event other than state for E1 in the event structure and a function other than **at** for e1 in the qualia structure. We would like to leave this question for future research.
10. As we suggested below (33), subevent e1 in (35b) does not specify the beginning of the event denoted by the verb *kiku*. In contrast, the particle *kara* specifies the beginning of the event denoted by a verb. The representation for the phrase *Tookyoo kara Oosaka made* 'from

Tokyo to Osaka' will be formed by the composition of the lexical representation of *kara* and that of *made*.

11 This operation of compulsory interpretation in the qualia structure accounts for the ambiguity of PPs in English, such as the one in (i) below.
(i) A bottle floated under the bridge.
We consider that this operation is optional in contrast to the co-composition operation, which makes the verbal expression *run to* telic obligatorily. This optionality yields the ambiguous interpretations of (i).

12 We argued in the last chapter that a similar operation should work in the qualia structure when a kind of co-composition operation does. This co-composition operates to form semantic representations of caused motion construction and resultative construction sentences. (See the discussion in section 6.2.3.)

13 In the co-composition operation, types of function in the qualia structure as well as the temporal relation in the event structure are relevant. So, although subevent e1 in (40a) is temporally overlapping with e1 in (40b), these subevents are not combined.

14 In (43a) subevent e1 represents the intention of the referent of x. We would like to leave open the questions over whether *iku* contains this subevent in its representation and whether a function other than **act** should be used.

15 Although the possibility that the durative adverbial modifies either e1 or e2 should permit two readings of (41c), this example seems to be judged unacceptable. This may be due to the event type of the verb *iku*, which contains a transition in its event structure. The event structure of *iku* as well as that of *made* contains a transition, which may prevent the durative adverbial from appearing in this sentence. We would like to leave this matter open.

16 Tomohiro Miyake pointed out the example in (46a) to the author.

17 The operation which derives the semantic representation of *tadori-tuku* should be made clear; however, we would like to leave this matter for future research.

18 (48b) and (49a) are cited from Kageyama (2002: 39).

19 The difference between *naka-de* and *de* lies in that although *naka-de* can follow a clause as well as a nominal, *de* can only follow a nominal.

20 (49a) is not unacceptable but marginal to some of my informants and me although Kageyama (2002) suggests it is unacceptable. The verb *korogaru* does not have **act** in its conceptual structure.

Chapter 8

Conclusion

The aim of this book is to account for word polysemy, reveal how polysemy and compositionality are related to each other and establish the linguistic theory which holds the minimum lexicon and the co-compositional and compositional operations. In order to attain our goal, we have mainly focused on verbs of motion, sometimes paying attention to verbs of existence or appearance and verbs of change of state in the framework of The Generative Lexicon.

Verbs of motion express unbounded events in some cases and bounded events in others (when co-occurring with PPs), while a broad range of verb classes are used as motion verbs when they are accompanied by PPs. Verbs of motion and verbs which express verb-of-motion sense show variable behaviors in the forms of verbal expressions that consist of a verb and a PP or in the forms of VPs. The notion of compositionality as well as the semantic representations of verbs, PPs, verbal expressions and VPs is crucial to understanding the variable behaviors of verbs. Through the discussions in this book, the polysemy of motion verbs has been explained according to the interaction among the event structure, the qualia structure and the co-composition and composition operations. Furthermore, these two types of operations have turned out to manage semantic and syntactic relations between verbs and PPs.

In chapter 3 we posed the four issues concerning GL proposed in Pustejovsky (1995). They are shown in (1).

(1) i) The number of event types of subevents
   ii) Headedness
   iii) The rule of the co-composition operation

iv) Functions of the qualia structure

Conditions for the co-composition operation are not made so clear in Pustejovsky (1995). The notion of headedness, whose characteristics are also not so clear in Pustejovsky (1995), is closely related to the event structure and the qualia structure. In chapter 6 we found that headedness is concerned with the co-composition operation. In order to attain our aim, we devoted chapters 4 through chapter 7 to finding answers to the four issues above by taking up motion verbs and related linguistic phenomena.

In order to find answers to the issues in (1), we have discussed and elaborated our own Generative Lexicon theory. Our discussions began with the lexical representation itself, moved on to relations between verbs and their prepositional arguments and ended up with VPs that include locational adjunct PPs.

As for the issue in (1i), we proposed the subevent which represents movement or change in chapter 4. We also proposed the functions which are associated with these subevents, as is shown in (2).

(2) The functions which are associated with the subevent of movement or change
   a.   **move** (e, x): the referent of x autonomously changes or moves.
   b.   **cause-move** (e, x, y): the referent of x changes or moves that of y.

The subevent of movement or change is crucial to the conditions for the co-composition operation proposed in chapter 6. Assuming the notion of the causal chain, we argued that the event structure could contain at most three subevents, namely two process subevents and one state subevent. In the event structure, the contained subevents are arranged in a temporal order. From the assumed types of subevents, we can conclude that the possible event types of the event structure should be the ones in (3).

(3) The Possible Event Types of the Event Structure
   a.   a process event - a process event - a state event
   b.   a process event - a process event
   c.   a process event - a sate event
   d.   a process event
   e.   a state event

The event structure of verbal expressions and VPs which are derived through the co-composition operation need to correspond to one of the five types offered in (3).

For the issue in (1ii) we claimed in chapter 5 that in some lexical representations any subevent could be a head. Examples discussed in the chapter were verbs of emission. In addition, we argued for the relationship between headedness and the co-composition operation or the composition operation in chapters 6 and 7. Specifically, in chapter 6 we were concerned with the relationships between verbs and their prepositional arguments in the semantic representation, and in chapter 7 we discussed how the semantic representation of a VP is formed. Each proposal is repeated below:

(4) Co-composition and Headedness
   The head of a PP becomes the head of a derived verbal expression when a verb and a PP form a verbal expression. When the head of the PP is underspecified, the head of the derived verbal expression is carried over from the verb contained in the expression.

(5) Composition and Headedness
   a. When subevents of a verb are substituted for an argument in another lexical representation, the head subevents among the substituted subevents behave as the head in the newly composed event. And
   b. the event type of the head subevents is carried over to the event containing the head subevent.

Related to the issue in (1iii), in chapter 6 we discussed operations at the event structure level which combine the lexical representations of a verb and its prepositional arguments into one semantic representation. We proposed the conditions on these operations at the level of event structure as (6).

(6) Co-composition Operation and its Conditions
   a. If the event structure of a preposition contains a subevent of movement or change, and if the event structure of a verb contains the same type of subevent and the qualia associated with the two subevents are the same type, the two subevents must be combined. In this case, if the event structures of the two lexical items have state subevents, the two subevents are also combined. Or

b. if the event structure of a preposition consists of only a state subevent, and if the event structure of a verb contains the same type of subevent and the qualia associated with the two subevents are the same type, the two subevents must be combined.

The co-composition operation we saw has two functions: one is to introduce a prepositional argument such as *in Japan* in (7a), and the other is to add an event to a verb's event structure and derive a verbal expressions like *run to NP* in (7b). We called the former function, event fusion.

(7) a. This kind of dog exists only in Japan.
    b. John ran to the station.

In the condition in (6a) the subevent of movement or change (or the quale associated with this subevent, namely **move** (e, x)), which we proposed in chapter 4, plays a crucial role.

The qualia structure plays an important role in the co-composition operation. Therefore, the set of conditions in (6) is a partial answer to the issue in (1iv). In chapter 5 we also argued that the qualia structure of subject NPs should play a significant role in omission of *with*-phrases in locative alternation sentences. The generative characteristics as a whole of the qualia structure, however, are left for future research.

After confirming the semantic representations of verbs and verbal expressions which are derived by the combination of verbs and their prepositional arguments, in chapter 7 we discussed how the semantic representation of a VP is formed. We argued that a composition operation should serve to combine semantic representations of verbs and locational PPs. Our proposal is in (8).

(8) Composition of Semantic Representations of Verbs and Adjunct PPs: Event Insertion
    When subevents of a verb are substituted for an argument in a lexical representation of a PP by a composition operation, the PP functions as an adjunct.

The English preposition *in* and the Japanese particle *made* express not only spatial relations between events but also temporal relations. We can extend the discussion in chapter 7 to the semantic representation of adverbials expressing temporal relations. In this way, we investigated and cleared up the four issues concerning Pustejovsky (1995) in (1). Our GL, which has been elaborated by the proposals we have just surveyed, now accounts for polysemy of motion verbs and their behavior in phrases and sentences.

Verb polysemy derives from both a verb's lexical representation itself and the interaction between lexical representations of verbs and prepositions. In GL a verb's behavior is determined by qualia structure which is related to a head subevent, that is a semantically salient subevent. We argued that the qualia structure of some verbs contains various functions and that any subevent denoted by the verb can behave as the head. This is the crux of a verb's polysemy. Verbs of emission which we analyzed in chapter 5 are this case.

Verb polysemy also derives from the interrelation among event structure, qualia structure and the co-composition and composition operations. We showed that this interrelation is managed by the co-composition and composition operations. Thus, these operations are concerned with the overall relationship between verbs and spatial PPs. There are three types of spatial PPs which co-occur with verbs. Two of them function as argument phrases: we called one operation "event fusion" and the other "event addition." In both, the lexical representation of the PPs are combined with the verb's representation through co-composition operations. The third type of PPs, which are combined with verbs by composition, behave as adjunct phrases. We maintained that in these operations, especially subevents of movement or change (introduced in chapter 4), play a crucial role. By co-composition these types of subevents are composed and consequently a state subevent following the subevent of movement or change enters into the event structure of verbal expressions. A subevent of movement or change also provides a path of movement for VPs which are combined by the composition operation. Our proposals concerning these operations are important for comprehending general properties of the semantic structure and the relationship between semantic structure and syntactic structure.

We have mainly examined verbs and prepositions concerning spatial relation in the notion of semantic field. Adopting the localist approach maintained by Gruber (1976) and Jackendoff (1990) among others, some of what we proposed in this book will also be extended to temporal relations and property identification. In addition, co-composition operations act on grammatical categories other than PPs which co-occur with verbs, an example of which is *bake a cake* which

Pustejovsky (1995) discussed. The mechanism and conditions we proposed will be the basis for research of these cases. Exploration of these issues is our next task of research.

Bibliography

Abbott, Barbara (1997) "Definiteness and Existentials," *Language 73* (1), 103–108.
Ackema, Peter and Maaike Shoorlemmer (1994) "The Middle Construction and the Syntax-Semantics Interface," *Lingua 93*, 59–90.
Alsina, Alex (1999) "On the Representation of Event Structure," *Grammatical Semantics: Evidence for Structure in Meaning*, ed. by Tara Mohana and Lionel Wee, 77–122, CSLI Publications, Stanford.
Asher, Nicholas and Pierre Sablayrolles (1996) "A Typology and Discourse Semantics for Motion Verbs and Spatial PPs in French," *Lexical Semantics: the Problem of Polysemy*, ed. by James Pustejovsky and Branimir Boguraev, Oxford University Press, Oxford.
Baker, Mark C. (1989) "Object Sharing and Projection in Serial Verb Constructions," *Linguistic Inquiry 20*, 513–553.
Baron, Irene and Herslund, Michael (2001) "Semantics of the verb HAVE," *Dimensions of Possession*, ed. by Irene Baron et al., 85–98, Benjamins, Amsterdam.
Birner, Betty J. (1994) "Information Status and Word Order: an Analysis of English Inversion," *Language 70* (2), 233–259.
Bolinger, Dwight. (1977) *Meaning and Form*, Longman, London.
Bouillon, Pierrette and Federica Busa (2001) "Qualia and the Structuring of Verb Meaning," *The Language of Word Meaning*, ed. by Pierrette Bouillon and Federica Busa, Cambridge University Press, Cambridge.
Bresnan, Joan (1994) "Locative Inversion and the Architecture of Universal Grammar," *Language 70* (1), 72–131.
Brisson, Christine (1994) "The Licensing of Unexpressed Objects in English Verbs," *Papers from the 30th Regional Meeting of the Chicago Linguistic Society 1: The Main Session*, 90–102, Chicago Linguistic Society, University of Chicago.
Collins, Chris (1997) *Local Economy*, MIT Press, Cambridge, MA.
Coopmans, Peter (1989) "Where Stylistic and Syntactic Processes Meet: Locative Inversion in English," *Language 65*, 728–751.
Culicover, Peter (1991) "Topicalization, Inversion, and Comprementizers in English," Unpublished manuscript. Ohio State University, Columbus, Ohio.
Den Dikken, Marcel and Naess, Alma (1993) "Case dependencies: The case of Predicate Inversion," *The Linguistic Review 10*, 303–336.
Dowty, David (1979) *Word Meaning and Montague Grammar*, Kluwer, Dordrecht.
Dowty, David (1991) "Thematic Proto-Roles and Argument Selection," *Language 67* (3), 547–619.
Dowty, David (2000) "'The Garden Swarms with Bees' and the Fallacy of 'Argument Alternation'," *Polysemy: Theoretical and Computational Approaches*, ed. by Ravin, Yael and Claudia Leacock, 111–128, Oxford University Press, Oxford.
Drijkoningen, Frank (1999) "Two Types of Ergativity," *Lexical Specification and Insertion*, ed. by Peter Coopmans, Martin Everaert and Jane Grimshaw, John Benjamins, Amsterdam.

Folli, Raffaellia and Heidi Harley (2005) "Flavors of v: Comsuming Results in Italian & English," *Aspectual inquiries*, ed. by Paula Marie Kempchinsky and Roumyana Slabakova, 95–120, Springer, Dordrecht.

Folli, Raffaella and Heidi Harley (2008) "Teleology and Animacy in External Arguments," *Lingua 118* (2), 190–202.

Fujita, Koji (1994) "Middle, Ergative and Passive in English: A Minimalist Perspective," *The Morphology-Syntax Connection, MIT Working Papers in Linguistics 22*, 71–90.

Fujita, Koji (1996) "Double Objects, Causatives, and Derivational Economy," *Linguistic Inquiry 27*, 146–173.

Fukui, Naoki, Shigeru Miyazawa and Carol Tenny (1985) "Verb Classes in English and Japanese: A Case Study in the Interaction of Syntax, Morphology and Semantics," *Lexicon Project Working Papers 3*, MIT, Cambridge, MA.

Grimshaw, Jane (1990) *Argument Structure*, MIT Press, Cambridge, MA.

Grimshaw, Jane (1993) "Semantic Structure and Semantic Content in Lexical Representation," Unpublished manuscript, Rutgers University, New Brunswick, N.J.

Grimshaw, Jane and Sten Vikner (1993) "Obligatory Adjuncts and the Structure of Events," *Knowledge and Language II: Lexical and Conceptual Structure*, ed. by Eric Reuland and Werner Abraham, 143–155, Kluwer, Dordrecht, The Netherlands.

Gruber, Jefferey S. (1976) *Lexical Structures in Syntax and Semantics*, North-Holland, Amsterdam.

Hasegawa, Yoko (1996) *A Study of Japanese Clause Linkage: The Connective TE in Japanese*, CSLI publication, Stanford.

Hatori, Yuriko (1997) "On the Lexical Conceptual Structure of Psych-Verbs," Verb Semantics and Syntactic Structure, ed. by Taro Kageyama, 15–44, Kurosio Publisher, Tokyo.

Hay, Jennifer, Christopher Kennedy, and Beth Levin (1999) "Scalar Structure Underlies Telicity in 'Degree Achievements'." *Proceedings of SALT 9*, 127–144.

Hoekstra, Teun and Rene Mulder (1990) "Unergatives as Copular Verbs; Locational and Existential Predication," *The Linguistic Review 7*, 1–79.

Imaizumi, Shinako (2001) "The Role of AFFECTED in Lexical Causative Alternations in Japanese," *Journal of Japanese Linguistics 17*, 1–28.

Imaizumi, Shinako and Takao Gunji (2002) "Goiteki-Hukugo-ni okeru Hukugo Zisho: *dasu*, *deru*-ni mirareru Sieki-to Zyudo-no Yakuwari [Complex Events in Lexical Compounds: Causative and Passive Relations in the Japanese Verbs *dasu* and *deru*]," *Rekisikon-to Togoron-no Setten* [The Interface of Lexicon and Syntax], ed. by Takane Ito, 33–59, The University of Tokyo Press.

Isono, Tatsuya (1998) "Locative Inversion and Lexical Conceptual Structure," *Proceedings of TACL Summer Institute of Linguistics*, 37–48.

Isono, Tatsuya (2001) "Meanings of Prepositions and Inversion in English," *English Linguistics 18*, 460–481.

Isono, Tatsuya (2003) "Jidoshigata Bashokaku Kotai [Intransitive Locative Alternation: Meanings of Verbs, Event Structure, Headedness]," *Gengo Joho Kagaku* [Language and Information Science] *1*, 17–33, The University of Tokyo.

Isono, Tatsuya (2004) "Ido-doshi-to Zenchishi-ku Kochishi-ku-no Gainen-kozo [Conceptual Structure of Motion Verbs, Prepositions and Postpositions]," *JELS: Papers from the Twenty-second National Conference of the English Linguistic Society of Japan 22*, 11–20.

Isono, Tatsuya (2006a) "Semantic Representations of Verbs of Motion, English Prepositions and Japanese Particles," *Rekishikon Foramu* [Lexicon Forum] *2*, ed. by Taro Kageyama, 145–177, Hituzi Syobo, Tokyo.

Isono, Tatsuya (2006b) "Jisho-no Kyogosei-to Kuoria Kozo-no Yakuwari [Co-composition of Events and Function of Qualia Structure]," *Gengo Kagaku-no Shinzui-wo Motomete* [In Search of the Essence of Language Science: Festschrift for Professor Heizo Nakajima], ed. by Yubun Suzuki, Keizo Mizuno and Kenichi Takami, 251–270, Hituzi Syobo, Tokyo.

Isono, Tatsuya (2006c) "Eigo-no Doshi-ga Arawasu Dekigoto: Henka-to Idono-no Jisho [The Event Structure of English Verbs: Subevents of Change and Movement]," *Kurashiki Sakuyo Daigaku Kenkyu Kiyo* [Bulletin of Kurashiki Sakuyo University] *39* (1), 185–202.

Isono, Tatsuya (2007) "Polysemy and Lexical Representation: Verbs of Emission and Its Qualia Structure," *Kurashiki Sakuyo Daigaku Kenkyu Kiyo* [Bulletin of Kurashiki Sakuyo University] *40* (2), 43–61.

Isono, Tatsuya (2010) "Lexical Aspect and Event Structure of Verbs: Punctuality and Scale Structure," *Kurashiki Sakuyo Daigaku Kenkyu Kiyo* [Bulletin of Kurashiki Sakuyo University] *43* (1), 73–84.

Isono, Tatsuya (2012) "Verbs of Emission as Motion Verbs," *Ryotokuji Daigaku Kenkyu Kiyo* [The Bulletin of Ryotokuji University] *6*, 51–61.

Iwamoto, Enoku (2000) "Kukan Kankei-wo Arawasu *wo*-to Koro-no Chumitsusei-nitsuite [On the Relation Between *wo* Representing Spatial Relation and Density of Path]," Unpublished manuscript, Kanda University of International Studies, Chiba, Japan.

Iwata, Seiji (1998) *A Lexical Network Approach to Verbal Semantics*, Kaitakusha, Tokyo.

Jackendoff, Ray (1983) *Semantics and Cognition*, MIT Press, Cambridge, MA.

Jackendoff, Ray (1990) *Semantic Structures*, MIT Press, Cambridge, MA.

Jackendoff, Ray (1993) "Parts and Boundaries," *Lexical and Conceptual Semantics*, ed. by Beth Levin and Steven Pinker, 9–45, Blackwell, Cambridge, MA.

Jackendoff, Ray (1996a) "The Proper Treatment of Measuring Out, Telicity, and Perhaps Even Quantification in English," *NLLT 14*, 305–354.

Jackendoff, Ray (1996b) "Conceptual Semantics and Cognitive Linguistics," *Cognitive Linguistics 7*, 93–129.

Jackendoff, Ray (1997) "Twistin' the night away" *Language 73* (3), 534–559.

Kaga, Nobuhiro (2001) "Imiyakuwari-to Eigo-no Kobun [Thematic Roles and Constructions in English]," *Go-no Imi-to Imiyakuwari* [Meanings of Words and Thematic Roles], ed. by Shosuke Haraguchi, Heizo Nakajima, Masaru Nakamura and Seisaku Kawakami, Kenkyusha, Tokyo.

Kageyama, Taro (1980) "The Role of Thematic Relations in the *Spray Paint* Hypallage," *Papers in Japanese Linguistics 7*, 35–64.

Kageyama, Taro (1993) *Bunpo-to Gokeisei* [Grammar and Word Formation], Hituzi Syobo, Tokyo.

Kageyama, Taro (1996a) "Nichi-eigo no Ido-doshi [Verbs of Motion in Japanese and English]," *Ei-bei Bungaku* [Literature of U.K. and America] *40*, Kuwansei Gakuin Daigaku, Hyogo, Japan.

Kageyama, Taro (1996b) *Doshi Imiron: Gengo-to Ninchi-no Setten* [Verb Semantics: the Interface of Language and Cognition], Kurosio, Tokyo

Kageyama, Taro (1997a) "Denominal Verbs and Relative Salience in Lexical Conceptual

Structure," *Verb Semantics and Syntactic Structure*, ed. by Taro Kageyama, 45–96, Kurosio, Tokyo.

Kageyama, Taro (1997b) "The Syntax and Semantics of *Spray/Load* Verbs" *Verb Semantics and Syntactic Structure*, ed. by Taro Kageyama, 97–114, Kurosio, Tokyo.

Kageyama, Taro (1999) *Keitairon-to Imi* [Morphology and Meaning], Kurosio, Tokyo.

Kageyama, Taro (2000) "Jita-kotai-no Imiteki Mekanizumu [Semantic Mechanism of Causative-inchoative Alternation]," *Nichi-eigo-no Ji-ta-kotai* [Causative-inchoative Alternation in Japanese and English], ed. by Tadao Maruta and Kazuyoshi Suga, 33–70, Hituzi Syobo, Tokyo.

Kageyama, Taro (2001) "Kekka Kobun [Resultative Construction]," *Doshi-no Imi-to Kobun* [Meanings of Verbs and Constructions], ed. by Taro Kageyama, Kenkyusha, Tokyo.

Kageyama, Taro (2002a) "Gainen-kozo-no Kakuju-patan-to yukaisei [Boundedness and the Patterns of Conceptual Structure Expansion]," *Journal of Japanese Grammar 2* (2), 29–45.

Kageyama, Taro (2002b) "Hitaikaku Kozo no Tadoshi [Transitives in Unaccusative Structure]," *Bunpoo Riron: Rekishikon to Togo* [Grammatical Theory: The lexicon and Syntax] ed. by Takane Ito, 119–145, University of Tokyo Press, Tokyo.

Kageyama, Taro (2003a) "'Tokyo-made Zutto Neteita' to-iu Kobun-no Gainen Kozo [The Conceptual Structure of the Construction 'I slept all the way to Tokyo']," *Japanese Literature* [Kokubungaku] *48* (4), 37–44. Gakutosha, Tokyo.

Kageyama, Taro (2003b) "Conceptual Cloning: The Semantic Licensing of Adjuncts and Nonselected Arguments," *Japanese/Korean Linguistics 12*, ed. by Hajime Hoji, 20–33.

Kageyama, Taro (2003c) "Why English motion verbs are special," *Korean Journal of English Language and Linguistics 3* (3), 341–373.

Kageyama, Taro (2004) "*All the way* adjuncts and the syntax-conceptual interface," *English Linguistics 21*, 265–293.

Kageyama, Taro (2005) "Jishoteki Chishiki to Goyoronteki Chishiki: Goi Gainen Kozo-to Kuoria Kozo-no Yugo-ni Mukete [Lexical Knowledge and Pragmatic Knowledge: Toward the Integration of Lexical Conceptual Structure and Qualia Structure]," *Lekishikon Foramu* [Lexicon Forum] *1*, ed. by Taro Kageyama, 65–101, Hituzi Syobo, Tokyo.

Kageyama, Taro (2006) "Oto-hoshutsu-doshi-wo Tomonau Ido-kobun-to Kekka-kobun [Motion Construction and Resultative Construction Including Verbs of Sound Emission]," *Eibei Bungaku* [English and American Literature] *50* (2), 57–73, Kwansei Gakuin University, Hyogo, Japan.

Kageyama, Taro (2007a) "Eigo Kekka Jutsugo no Imi Bunrui to Togo Kozo [The Semantic Classes and Syntactic Structure of English Resultative Predicates]," *Kekka Kobun Kenkyu no Shin Shiten* [New Perspectives on Resultative Constructions], ed. by Naoyuki Ono, 33–65, Hituzi Syobo, Tokyo.

Kageyama, Taro (2007b) "Jisho Joho to Kekka Jutsugo no Gan'i-teki Fuhen-sei [Lexical Information and Implicational Universals of Resultative Predicates]," *Lexicon Forum 3*, ed. by Taro Kageyama, 145–177, Hituzi Syobo, Tokyo.

Kageyama, Taro (2008) "Goi Ginen Kozo (LCS) Nyumon [Introduction to Lexical Conceptual Structure]," *Lexicon Forum 4*, ed. by Taro Kageyama, 239–264, Hituzi Syobo, Tokyo.

Kageyama, Taro and Yoko Yumoto (1997) *Go-keisei-to Gainen-kozo* [Word Formation and Conceptual Structure], Kenkyusha, Tokyo.

Kallulli, Dalina (2006) "Argument Demotion as Feature Suppression," *Demoting the Agent: Passive, Middle and Other Voice Phenomena*, ed. by Benjamin Lyngfelt and Torgrim Solstad, 143–166, Benjamins, Amsterdam.
Kaneko, Yoshiaki and Yoshio Endo (2001) *Kino-hanchu* [Functional Category], ed. by Shosuke Haraguchi, Heizo Nakajima, Masaru Nakamura and Seisaku Kawakami, Kenkyusha, Tokyo.
Kearns, Kate (2007) "Telic Senses of Deadjectival Verbs," *Linga 117* (1), 26–66.
Kennedy, Christopher and Louise McNally (2005) "Scale Structure, Degree Modification, and the Semantics of Gradable Predicates," *Language, 81* (2), 345–81.
Kishimoto, Hideki (2001) "Kabe-nuri Kobun [Wall-painting Construction]," *Doshi-no Imi-to Kobun* [Meanings of Verbs and Constructions], ed. by Taro Kageyama, Kenkyusha, Tokyo.
Kitahara, Hiroo (1998) "Ido-doshi-to Kyoki-suru *Ni*-kakuku-to *Made*-kakuku [On *Ni*-phrases and *Made*-phrases Co-occurring with Verbs of Motion]," *Kokugo-gaku* [Japanese Linguistics], 195, 84–98.
Langacker, Ronald W. (1993) "Reference-point Constructions," *Cognitive Linguistics 4* (1), 1–38.
Langendonck, Willy Van (1993) "Towards a Cognitive Dependency Grammar," *Cognitive Linguistics 4* (3), 311–329.
Larson, Richard (1995) "Semantics," *An Invitation to Cognitive Science 1*, ed. by Lila R. Gleitman and Mark Liberman, MIT Press, Cambridge, MA.
Levin, Beth (1993a) *English Verb Classes and Alternations: A Preliminary Investigation*, Chicago University Press, Chicago.
Levin, Beth (1993b) "Building a Lexicon: The Contribution of Linguistic Theory," *Challenges in Natural Language Processing*, ed. by M. Bates and R. Weischedel, 76–98, Cambridge University Press, Cambridge.
Levin, Beth and Steven Pinker (1992a) *Lexical and Conceptual Semantics*, Blackwell, Cambridge, MA.
Levin, Beth and Steven Pinker (1992b) "The Lexical Semantics of Verbs of Motion: the Perspective from Unaccusativity," *Thematic Structure: Its Role in Grammar*, ed. by Iggy M. Roca, 247–269, Foris, Berlin.
Levin, Beth and Malka Rappaport Hovav (1986) "The Formation of Adjectival Passives," *Linguistic Inquiry 17*, 623–661.
Levin, Beth, and Malka Rappaport Hovav (1992) "The Lexical Semantics of Verbs of Motion: The Perspective From Unaccusativity," *Thematic Structure: Its Role in Grammar*, ed. by Iggy M. Roca, 247–269, Foris, Berlin.
Levin, Beth and Malka Rappaport Hovav (1995) *Unaccusativity: At the Syntax-Lexical Semantics Interface*, MIT Press, Cambridge, MA.
Levin, Beth and Tova R. Rapoport (1988) "Lexical Subordination," *CLS 24*, 275–289.
Lieber, Rochelle (1998) "The Suffix *-ize* in English: Implications for Morphology," *Morphology and its Relation to Phonology and Syntax*, ed. by Steven G. Lapointe, Diane K. Brentari and Patrick M. Farrell, 12–33, CSLI, Stanford.
Lindstromberg, Seth (1998) *English Prepositions Explained*, John Benjamins, Amsterdam.
Lupsa, Daniela (2002) "The Unergativity of Verbs of Motion," *Explorations in English Linguistics 17*, 1–30, Tohoku University, Miyagi, Japan.
Maruta, Tadao (1997) "The Syntax and Semantics of *Spray-load* Verbs," *Verb Semantics and*

Syntactic Structure, ed. by Taro Kageyama, 97–114, Kurosio, Tokyo.

Maruta, Tadao (1998) *Shieki-doshi-no Anatomi: Goi-teki Shieki-doshi-no Goi-gainen-kozo* [The Anatomy of Causative Verbs: Lexical Conceptual Structure of Lexical Causative Verbs], Shohakusha, Tokyo.

Maruta, Tadao (2000) "Basho-kaku-kotai-doshi-no LCS-to Shieki-kotai [LCS of Locative Alternation Verbs and Causative-inchoative Alternation]," *Nichi-eigo-no Ji-ta-kotai* [Causative-inchoative Alternation in Japanese and English], ed. by Tadao Maruta and Kazuyoshi Suga, 241–257, Hituzi Syobo, Tokyo.

Maruta, Tadao (2001) "Basho-kaku-kotai-doshi [Locative Alternation Verbs]," *Eigo Kobun Jiten* [Dicitonary of English Construction], ed. by Heizo Nakajima, 647–661, Kenkyusha, Tokyo.

Masukawa, Mikio (1997) *On Restriction on the Verb in There-Sentences*, a thesis for B.A., University of Tokyo.

Matsumoto, Yo (1996) *Complex Predicates in Japanese*, CSLI publication, Stanford.

Matsumoto, Yo (1997) "Kukan-ido-no Gengo-hyogen-to Sono Kakucho [Linguistic Expressions of Motion in Space and its Extension]," *Kukan-to Ido-no Hyogen* [Expressions of Space and Motion], ed. by Minoru Nakau, 125–230, Kenkyusha, Tokyo.

Mihara, Kenichi (2007) "Resultatives: Direction and Existence," Paper Presented at The 79th General Meeting of The English Literary Society of Japan.

Mihara, Kenichi (2004) *Asupekuto Kaishaku-to Togo Gensho* [Aspectual Interpretations and Syntactic Phenomena], Shohakusha, Tokyo.

Miyake, Tomohiro (1996) "Nihongo-no Ido-doshi-no Taikaku-hyoji-ni-tsuite [On Accusative Case Marking by Japanese Movement Verbs]," *Gengo Kenkyu* [Language Studies] *110*, 169–176.

Morikawa, Fumihiro (2001) "Filled to Overflowing: A Study of Locative Alternation," *JELS: Papers from the Eighteenth National Conference of the English Linguistic Society of Japan 18*, 151–160.

Morita, Nobuko (1992) "A Note on *There*'s Status as an LF Affix," *Linguistic Research 12*, 85–101, University of Tokyo.

Morita, Nobuko (1994a) "The Structure of the Locative Inversion Construction: A Paradox Concerning the Subject," *Linguistic Research 12*, 91–121, University of Tokyo.

Morita, Nobuko (1994b) "Extraction out of the Locative Inversion Construction: A Functional Approach," *Linguistic Research 12*, 123–128, University of Tokyo.

Nakajima, Heizo (2001a) "Verbs in Locative Constructions and the Generative Lexicon," *The Linguistic Review 18*, 43–67.

Nakajima, Heizo (2001b) "Semantic Conditions for Verbs in Locative Inversion Constructions," *Researching and Verifying an Advanced Theory of Human Language (Report 4)*, ed. by Kazuko Inoue, Kanda University of International Studies, Chiba, Japan.

Nakamura, Masaru (1997) "Middle Construction and Semantic Passivization," *Verb Semantics and Syntactic Structure*, ed. by Taro Kageyama, 45–96, Kurosio, Tokyo.

Nakamura, Yoshihisa (1999) "Ninchi-bunpo-kara Mita Goi-to Kobun: Ji-ta-kotai-to Judotai-no Bunpo-ka [Words and Constructions from the Viewpoint of Cognitive Grammar: Grammaticalization of Causative-inchoative Alternation and Passive]," Paper Presented at the Second Cognitive Linguistics Forum, Kyoto.

Nakatani, Kentaro (2007) "Opposition Structure is not Event Structure: A Study of Cancellable

Transition in Japanese V-*teiru*," *The Fourth International Workshop on Generative Approaches to the Lexicon*.

Nakatani, Kentaro (2008) "Te kuru/Te iku no Doshi Kyoki Seigen no Hasei [Deriving the Collocational Constraints in the V-*te kuru/iku* Constructions in Japanese]," *Lexicon Forum 4*, ed. by Taro Kageyama, 64–90, Hituzi Syobo, Tokyo.

Nerbonne, John (1996) "Computational Semantics: Linguistics and Processing," *The Handbook of Contemporary Semantic Theory*, ed. by Shalom Lappin, 461–484, Blackwell, Cambridge, MA.

Nishihara, Toshiaki (1999) "On Locative Inversion and *There*-Construction," *English Linguistics 16* (2), 381–404.

Okunobo, Mitsuko (2001) "*Cram*-no Imi-kozo-to Togo-kozo [Conceptual Structure and Syntactic Structure of *Cram*]," *Imi-to Katachi-no Intafeisu* [Interface between Meanings and Forms: A Festschrift for Minoru Nakau], 105–117, Kurosio, Tokyo.

Ono, Naoyuki (2000) "Doshi Kurasu Moderu-to Ji-ta-kotai [Models of Verb Classes and Causative-inchoative Alternation], *Nichi-eigo-no Ji-ta-kotai* [Causative-inchoative Alternation in Japanese and English], ed. by Tadao Maruta and Kazuyoshi Suga, 1–32, Hituzi Syobo, Tokyo.

Ono, Naoyuki (2005) *Seisei Goi Imi-ron* [Generative Lexical Semantics], Kurosio, Tokyo.

Oya, Toshiaki (2008) *Doitsugo Saiki Kobun no Taisho Gengogaku-teki Kenkyu* [The Contrastive Linguistic Study of the Reflexive Constructions in German], Hituzi Syobo, Tokyo.

Pan, Haihua (1996) "Imperfective Aspect *zhe*, Agent Deletion, and Locative Inversion in Manadarin Chinese," *NLLT 14*, 409–432.

Pesetsky, David (1995) *Zero Syntax. Experiencers and Cascades*, MIT Press, Cambridge, MA.

Pinker, Steven (1989) *Learnability and Cognition: the Acquisition of Argument Structure*, MIT Press, Cambridge, MA.

Plag, Ingo (1997) "The Polysemy of -*ize* Derivatives: on the Role of Semantics in Word Formation," *Year book of Morphology*, 219–242, Kluwer, Dordrecht, The Netherlands.

Pustejovsky, James (1993) "The Syntax of Event Structure," *Lexical and Conceptual Semantics*, ed. by Beth Levin and Steven Pinker, 47–82, Blackwell, Cambridge MA.

Pustejovsky, James (1995) *The Generative Lexicon*, MIT Press, Cambridge, MA.

Pustejovsky, James (2000) "Events and the Semantics of Opposition," *Events as Grammatical Objects*, ed. by Carol Tenny and James Pustejovsky, 445–482, CSLI, California.

Rapoport, Toba R. (1999) "Structure, Aspect, and the Predicate," *Language* 75, 653–678.

Rappaport Hovav, Malka and Beth Levin (1998) "Building Verb Meanings," *The Projection of Arguments*, ed. by Miriam Butt and Wilhelm Geuder, 97–134, CSLI, Stanford.

Rappaport Hovav, Malka and Beth Levin. (2000) "Classifying Single Argument Verbs," *Lexical Specification and Insertion*, ed. by Peter Coopmans, Martin Everart and Jane Grimshaw, 269–304, John Benjamins, Amsterdam.

Rappaport Hovav, Malka and Beth Levin (2001) "An Event Structure Account of English Resultatives," *Language* 77, 766–797.

Rochemont, Michael S. and Peter W. Culicover (1990) *English Focus Constructions and the Theory of Grammar*, Cambridge University Press, Cambridge.

Rothstein, Susan (2004) *Structuring Events*, Blackwell, Oxford.

Salkoff, Morris (1983) "Bees Are Swarming in the Garden: A Systematic Synchronic Study of Productivity," *Language* 59 (2), 288–346.

Smith, Carlota S. (1991) *The Parameter of Aspect*, Kluwer, Dordrecht, The Netherlands.
Stroik, Thomas (1999) "Middles and Reflexivity," *Linguistic Inquiry 30*, 119–131.
Talmy, Leonard (1985) "Lexicalization Patterns: Semantic Structure in Lexical Forms," *Language Typology and Syntactic Description 3: Grammatical Categories and the Lexicon*, ed. by Timothy Shopen, 57–149, Cambridge University Press, Cambridge.
Tanaka, Kosuke (1997) "Locative Inversion-ni-tsuite [On Locative Inversion]", *JELS: Papers from the Fourteenth National Conference of the English Linguistic Society of Japan 14*, 201–210.
Taniguchi, Kazumi (1998) "Hitaikaku-sei Saiko: Sono Gainen-teki-kiban-to Bunpo-kobun-tono Kakawari (Reconsideration of Unaccusativity: Its Conceptual Basis and Relations with Constructions in Grammar]," *JELS: Papers from the Fifteenth National Conference of the English Linguistic Society of Japan 15*, 231–240.
Tenny, Carol L. (1994) *Aspectual Roles and the Syntax-Semantics Interface*, Kluwer, Dordrecht, The Netherlands.
Tenny, Carol L. (2000) "Core Events and Adverbial Modification," *Events as Grammatical Objects*, ed. by Tenny Carol and James Pustejovsky, 285–334, CSLI, Stanford.
Teramura, Hideo (1982) *Nihongo-no Shintakusu-to Imi 1* [Syntax and Meanings of Japanese 1], Kurosio, Tokyo.
Teramura, Hideo (1993) *Teramura Hideo Ronbun-shu 1: Nihongo Bunpo Hen* [Collected Papers by Hideo Teramura 1], Kurosio, Tokyo.
Tuschinsky, Joachim (2000) "The Lexical-Conceptual Structure of English Verbs of Possession," *Verbal Projections*, ed. by Hero Janssen, 123–140, Narr Verlag, Tuebingen.
Ueno, Seiji (2000) "Nihongo-no *Made*-ku-to Ido-doshi-no Imi Bunseki [Semantics of M*ade*-phrases and Verbs of Motion in Japanese]," *Nihon Ninchi Kagaku Kai Dai 17 Kai Happyo Ronbun Shu* [Papers from the 17th Annual Meeting of the Japanese Cognitive Science Society], 220–221.
Ueno, Seiji (2007) *Nihongo-ni-okeru Kukan-hyogen-to Ido-hyogen-no Gainen-imiteki Kenkyu* [Conceptual-Semantic Study of Spatial Expressions and Motion Expressions in Japanese], Hituzi Syobo, Tokyo.
Ueno, Seiji and Taro Kageyama (2001) "Ido-to Keiro-no Hyogen [Expressions of Movement and Path]," *Doshi-no Imi-to Kobun* [Meanings of Verbs and Constructions], ed. by Taro Kageyama, Kenkyusha, Tokyo.
Van Valin, Robert D. Jr. (1993) "A Synopsis of Role and Reference Grammar," *Advances in Role and Reference Grammar*, ed. by Robert D. Van Valin, Jr., John Benjamins, Amsterdam.
Van Valin, Robert D. Jr. and Randy J. LaPolla (1997) *Syntax: Structure, Meaning, and Function*, Cambridge University Press, Cambridge.
Vendler, Zeno (1967) *Linguistics in Philosophy*, Cornell University Press, Ithaca and New York.
Verkuyl, Henk J. (1993) *A Theory of Aspectuality*, Cambridge University Press, Cambridge.
Ward, Gregory and Betty Birner (1995) "Definiteness and the English Existential," *Language 71* (4), 722–742.
Ward, Gregory and Betty Birner (1997) "Response to Abbott," *Language 73* (1), 109–112.
Watanabe, Akira (1994) "Locative Inversion and Minimality," Kanda University of International Studies, Chiba, Japan.
Wechsler, Stephen (2005) "Resultatives Under the 'Event-Argument Homomorphism' Model of Telicity," *The Syntax of Aspect*, ed. by Nomi Erteschik-Shir and Tova Rapoport,

255–273, Oxford University Press.

Yoneyama, Mitsuaki (2001) "Go-no Imiron [Semantics of Words]," *Go-no Imi-to Imi-Yakuwari* [*Meanings of Words and Thematic Roles*], ed. by Shosuke Haraguchi, Heizo Nakajima, Masaru Nakamura and Seisaku Kawakami, Kenkyusha, Tokyo.

Source of Data

British National Corpus. (BNC)

Collins COBUILD for Advanced Learner's English Dictionary (New digital ed.). (COBUILD)

Oxford English Dictionary (2nd ed.). (OED)

Shinpen Eiwa Katsuyo Dai Jiten [The Kenkyusha Dictionary of English Collocations], ed. by Shigejiro Ichikawa et al. (1995), Kenkyusha, Tokyo. (KDEC)

Index

a
accomplishment   20, 22, 23
achievement   20, 22
action chain   105, 111
addition of events   104, 109
adjunct   27, 28, 101, 129, 131, 135, 151, 154, 159
agentive   11
agentive role   12, 15, 21
Aktionsart   18
appear   100, 101
approach   41, 42
argument structure   7, 8, 10, 18, 20, 21, 22, 23, 45, 79
arrive   22, 40, 41, 42
autonomous   47
autonomous event   45, 46

b
binary opposition   43, 148
build   14, 23, 35, 37

c
carry   35, 36, 37, 39, 43
causal chain   40
causative-inchoative alternation   18, 33, 34, 44, 45, 46, 47, 48, 52, 53
caused motion construction   122
co-composition   2, 3, 14, 16, 17, 19, 25, 26, 27, 28, 49, 51, 52, 55, 85, 92, 95, 96, 97, 98, 99, 103, 104, 105, 109, 110, 130, 165, 166
come   91, 92, 93, 95, 96, 99, 107, 108
composition   27, 28, 101, 127, 129, 130, 131, 139, 146, 152, 165, 166
composition operation   27
constitutive   11

d
Davidson   19
de-phrase   156
default argument   7, 8, 14
directional phrase   112, 114, 120
double goal phrase   40
double-*o*-constraint   150
Dowty   18, 20
durative   135
durative adverbial   28, 43, 132, 136, 147

e
emission verbs   62
event fusion   104, 105, 111, 166
event insertion   28, 129, 159
event of movement or change   27, 44
event structure   3, 8, 9, 10, 14, 17, 20, 21, 22, 23, 26, 27, 28, 29, 43, 79, 95, 98, 103, 106, 108
exist   106

f
for-phrase   10, 25, 29, 35, 43, 92, 93, 94
formal   11
formal role   12, 13, 15, 26
frame   135
frame adverbial   29, 132, 136, 147
from   88, 100
function   21, 22, 26, 27, 31, 37, 76, 130

g
generative lexicon (GL)   1, 2, 3, 7, 19, 25, 61, 79
generativity   79
grow   34, 35, 37, 38

h
hammer   122, 123
head subevent   9, 17, 26, 27, 61, 137, 139
headedness   9, 13, 26, 27, 28, 61, 62, 92, 95, 97, 108, 131, 139, 140, 147, 165
holistic interpretation   64, 77

i
iku   137, 138, 146
in   101, 102, 106, 120, 129, 130
in-phrase   25, 29, 30, 35
induced action alternation   54
inheritance of headedness   27, 131, 139
into   86, 87, 88, 92, 93, 95, 96, 97, 99, 100, 107, 108

k

Kageyama 18, 54, 70, 111, 114, 133, 134, 160
Kageyama and Yumoto 26, 87, 91, 110, 114, 133

l

laugh 111, 112
Levin and Rappaport Hovav 54, 114
lexical conceptual structure (LCS) 2, 3, 18, 19, 151
load 48, 50, 52
localist approach 38
location-type 63, 64, 67, 71, 72, 75, 76, 77
locative alternation (LA) 19, 48, 50, 53, 62, 63, 64, 65, 66, 68, 69, 70, 71, 73, 74, 75, 77, 84, 166
locative inversion (LI) 65, 66, 68, 74, 75, 77, 84, 86, 87, 88, 95, 99, 114, 129

m

made 132, 133, 134, 135, 136, 137, 138, 139, 140, 141, 142, 144, 145, 146, 147, 148, 160
manner-of-motion verb 133
mapping 12
march 54, 55, 56, 57
Maruta 54, 74, 84
Matsumoto 134
motion verb 27, 40, 61, 133

n

naka-de 155
naka-de-phrase 156
naka-o 149, 150
naka-o-phrase 152, 154, 156, 157
Nakajima 74, 84, 89

o

on 120
Ono 26, 32, 44
out of 88, 100

p

Parsons 19
polar opposition 43
prepositional argument 104, 166
pseudo-passive 129
pull 35, 37

q

qualia saturation 13
qualia structure 3, 10, 11, 12, 15, 17, 20, 21, 22, 23, 26, 27, 28, 45, 61, 76, 79, 103, 108, 166

r

Rappaport Hovav and Levin 18, 26, 110
reach 40, 41
resultant subevent 12, 91, 137
resultative construction 122
run 90, 91, 95, 96, 99, 102, 110, 130

s

Salkoff 64, 72
scale 43
selective binding 14, 17
shadow argument 8, 14, 31
shadow event 80
sparkle 63, 70, 75, 76, 77, 78, 79, 80
spray 48, 49, 50, 52
subevent 8, 9, 10, 17, 20, 21, 22, 23, 26, 27, 28, 29, 30, 37, 43, 45, 76
subevent of movement or change 33, 37, 38, 40, 46, 47, 48, 53, 54, 95
swarm verbs 66, 80, 81

t

-teiru 73
telic 11
telicity 18, 26, 28, 106, 131
there construction 68
through 98
to 42, 86, 87, 88, 92, 93, 94, 95, 97, 99, 100, 107, 108, 110, 112
to-phrase 41, 48, 50, 53, 96
true adjunct 8
true argument 8, 7, 13
tuku 133, 136, 137, 148
type coercion 14

u

underspecification 27
underspecified 63, 77, 94, 98, 100

V

Vendler   18, 20
verb of existence   77
verbs of change of state   38, 44, 46
verbs of emission   61, 112
verbs of light emission   66
verbs of manner of motion   54, 55
verbs of modes of being involving motion   66, 117
verbs of motion   38, 112, 113, 142
verbs of smell emission   66
verbs of sound emission   66
verbs of substance emission   66

W

with-phrase   80, 81, 82
with-type   63, 64, 71, 72, 73, 75, 76, 77, 79, 82

【著者紹介】

磯野達也（いその たつや）

1964年東京都生まれ。東京都立大学人文学部英文学科卒業。東京大学大学院総合文化研究科言語情報科学専攻修士課程、博士課程修了。博士（学術）。東京都立高等学校、くらしき作陽大学音楽学部を経て、現在、了德寺大学教養教育センター教授。

〈主な著書・論文〉

『英語の〈仕組み〉の探り方』ばる出版（共著）(2011)、「アスペクト概念と動詞の事象構造―瞬時性とスケール構造」『くらしき作陽大学・作陽音楽短期大学研究紀要』43(1)、73–84 (2010)、"Semantic Representations of Verbs of Motion, English Prepositions and Japanese Particles" 影山太郎（編）『レキシコンフォーラム』No.2、ひつじ書房、145–177(2006)。

Hituzi Linguistics in English No.17

Polysemy and Compositionality
Deriving Variable Behaviors of Motion Verbs and Prepositions

発行	2013年12月24日　初版1刷
定価	12000円＋税
著者	ⓒ 磯野達也
発行者	松本 功
印刷・製本所	株式会社シナノ
発行所	株式会社 ひつじ書房
	〒112-0011 東京都文京区千石2-1-2 大和ビル2F
	Tel.03-5319-4916　Fax.03-5319-4917
	郵便振替 00120-8-142852
	toiawase@hituzi.co.jp　http://www.hituzi.co.jp/

ISBN978-4-89476-545-0　C3080

造本には充分注意しておりますが、落丁・乱丁などがございましたら、小社かお買上げ書店にておとりかえいたします。ご意見、ご感想など、小社までお寄せ下されば幸いです。

刊行のご案内

Hituzi Linguistics in English No.18
fMRI Study of Japanese Phrasal Segmentation: Neuropsychological Approach to Sentence Comprehension
大嶋秀樹 著　定価15,000円+税

Hituzi Linguistics in English No.19
Typological Studies on Languages in Thailand and Japan
宮本正夫・小野尚之・Kingkarn Thepkanjana・上原聡 編　定価9,000円+税